Effectiveness of Habitation based Planning in Tamil Nadu

About the Author

Prof.G. Palanithurai is an academic activist served in Annamalai University and the Gandhigram Rural Institute for about 34 years in teaching, research and outreach activities integrally. He held several managerial positions form the Head of the Department to in-charge Vice-Chancellor. He has to his credit 73 books, 22 edited volumes, 95 monographs, 42 chapters in edited volumes, 136 research articles in refereed journals and 394 popular articles in newspapers and magazines in English and Tamil in his area of specialization local democracy and development. He has prepared 42 research reports for international and national research agencies and both the governments. He has evolved innovative training modules to build the capacity of the elected representatives of the people in rural local bodies. He has trained 8000 gram panchayat presidents and of them 5000 are women and dalits. He was the Professor in Rajiv Gandhi chair for Panchayati Raj studies in the Gandhigram Rural Institute. His research and action research activities are supported by various bilateral and multilateral institutions along with the Centre and state governments. He operated projects to the tune of Rs 5.47 crores. He closely worked with state and centre planning commissions for preparation of research reports in the field of rural development and Panchayati Raj. He was a visiting professor in cologne university Germany for a semester. He introduced two innovative master programme M.A. development administration and M.A. governance and development.

He was awarded fellowships by Shastri Indo Canadian Institute, World Academy of Art and Science USA, the Toolkit Foundation, Netherland to visit abroad to conduct studies and to write books. He has visited Canada, USA, Germany, Singapore, Malaysia, Srilanka, Senegal on academic assignments. He organized and participated innumerable workshops, seminars, conference at regional, national and global level. He received awards including Ram Reddy Award, V.R. Krishna Aiyar Award and Seven Generation Award for the outstanding activities done in the field of Panchayati Raj. Currently he is the Director of Rural Development Division (SARVAM) of Sri Aurobuido Society, Puducherry. To contact G.Palanithurai, Email: gpalanithunui@gnail.com, Mobile: 9159099809.

Effectiveness of Habitation based Planning in Tamil Nadu

An Evaluation

G. Palanithurai

CONCEPT PUBLISHING COMPANY PVT. LTD.
NEW DELHI-110059

ISBN: 978-93-5439-061-6

First Published 2022

Published and Printed by

Concept Publishing Company Pvt. Ltd.
A/15-16, Commercial Block, Mohan Garden,
New Delhi-110059 (INDIA)
T : 91 11 41101460, 91 11 25351460, 91 11 25351794
E : publishing@conceptpub.com; *W* : www.conceptpub.com

Cataloging in Publication Data--Courtesy: D.K. Agencies (P) Ltd. <docinfo@dkagencies.com>

Palanithurai, G., author.
Effectiveness of habitation based planning in Tamil Nadu : an valuation / G. Palanithurai.
pages cm
Study conducted in Dindigul, Pudukottai and Villupuram districts of Tamil Nadu, India.
Includes index.
ISBN 9789354390616

1. Tamil Nadu Village Habitations Improvement Scheme.--Evaluation. 2. Basic needs--India--Tamil Nadu. 3. Infrastructure (Economics)--India--Tamil Nadu. 4. Rural development--Government policy--India--Dindigul Anna (District) 5. Rural development--Government policy--India--Pudukkottai (District) 6. Rural development--Government policy--India--Viḻuppuram Irāmacāmip Paṭaiyātciyār Māvaṭṭam (District) I. Title.

LCC HN690.Z9C6 2022 | DDC 307.1412095482 23

To
THE DIVINE MOTHER

Preface

Tamil Nadu is known for its pro-poor policies, programmes and schemes and it is also known for its inclusiveness in every aspect of development schemes. It is a model for other states. The Tamil Nadu Village Habitations Improvement (THAI) scheme introduced in Tamil Nadu is unique in many respects as it enabled the hitherto excluded to access the basic resources and infrastructure facilities to lead a decent human life on par with other segments of the society. The scheme is aiming to provide needed basic infrastructure facilities to the habitations level by preparing a development plan with the active involvement of the key stakeholders. By implementing this scheme in the rural areas it declares that no one or no segment of the rural communities is deprived of basic infrastructure facilities which are necessary for the communities to lead a decent dignified life. This scheme will offset the trend and behaviour of the rural communities to capture the programme. Having said that it is necessary to see and evaluate to what extent this scheme has achieved intended results and where are the gaps in the programme. To do the job, Gandhigram Rural Institute has been asked to undertake this study. Hence, an attempt is made to evaluate the process of planning and implementation of the scheme in the rural areas and to assess the impact of the scheme in the life and livelihood of the people. It is an empirical study and hence it has adopted a combination of social science research methods to collect data from the field and analyze the data.

The study has brought out the significance of the scheme contextually and its planning and implementation process of the scheme. Further, it brings to light the impact it has achieved in the rural areas. It has also indicated, what are the bottlenecks? in the scheme while planning and implementing the scheme. While analysing the basic objectives of this scheme in the backdrop of the schemes implemented in the past, it is inferred that it has got its own creativity and innovation to make the scheme "inclusive" and to reach the unreached. From the analysis it has been noticed that it worked for the poorest of the poor that too the SC and ST. It produced several unintended positive consequences in the community. It has raised hope among the hopeless that this scheme will bring answer to many of the basic demands pertinent to infrastructure building and utility. Unless the bottlenecks in the scheme are cleared, the massive transformation the scheme achieved will not be sustained. Hence, the result conclude that the scheme has to continue further to satisfy the demands mentioned in the plan documents of the respective panchayats.

Acknowledgements

For any research, be it small or big, it requires money. In the same tenor it requires commitment. No doubt research will bring new knowledge or confirm the old knowledge but it has to help the humanity. The present study is being given to us by the State Planning Commission to evaluate a scheme "THAI" for the purpose of understanding the real utility of the scheme and to know the bottlenecks if any for course correction in the scheme for the better utility. Since it is an innovative inclusive scheme meant for the poorest and neglected segment of the village society, it gains significance and it needs in-depth study. It is an empirical study conducted in Tamil Nadu. First I must thank the vice-chairperson for her visionary guidance and approval for this study. In equal measure I have to thank the member secretary, State Planning Commission for his administrative support to complete this project. There are a few officials in the State Planning Commission and the District Rural Development agencies of the select districts who helped us in data collection and organizing focus group discussions in the villages. They deserve our complements and appreciation. A few rural development officials from the Block Development office and District Rural Development Agency of the selected district have helped the team of researchers in the process of data collection and for which I profusely express my thanks to them. I have to thank the panchayat leaders, SHG women and other opinion makers in the villages who have helped us to complete the data collection without much difficulty. I must thank them profusely for allotting their time generously for our data collection work. Finally, I must thank our university authorities and other officials for their support in completing this project. It is not fair on my part if I am not thanking my colleagues in the department without whose support I would not have completed this work. I thank Dr. M.A. Thirunavukkarasu and K. Tamilarasan, Research Associates for their hard work in collecting the needed data for this project.

Executive Summary

Since independence, India has implemented more than 2000 rural development schemes (as per the estimate of the World Bank) from Community Development Programme to the recent one Community Driven Development (CDD) approach evolved and advocated by the World Bank for poverty reduction. Among them provision of basic minimum facilities and infrastructure in the rural area is viewed as very important. Development experts argued that in the process of development, the traditional communities with its in-built authoritative characteristics always resist changes in the power structure to retain their interests and positions to get major shares in development. One could witness the backwardness in rural areas in spite of implementing slew of welfare schemes and programmes by the governments. In course of time especially after the formation of State Planning Commission, there have been many positive developments. There have been changes in the intensity and the extent of poverty and backwardness in the rural areas among the four South Indian states. Tamil Nadu being the first state who established its State Planning Commission to address the issues of poverty. Villages in Tamil Nadu are far better than many other states in terms of the infrastructure facilities besides service delivery. Yet there are constraints in providing basic amenities and infrastructure facilities evenly to all the habitations of the village panchayats in Tamil Nadu as programmes capture has been witnessed due to the power dynamics at the community level. Considering the frequent demands made by village communities for building infrastructure facilities, the state government responded properly the demands of the people. It is found out that the villages are equipped with basic facilities but the facilities provided are not evenly distributed and/or all have not been allowed to use the facilities created in the villages. In order to address the above issue, the Government of Tamil Nadu has chalked out an innovative rural development scheme called 'THAI' (Tamil Nadu Village Habitation Improvement). So far village panchayat is considered as the basic unit for planning and implementation of rural development schemes. But in this scheme 'THAI' Tamil Nadu has moved further and habitation has been considered as basic unit for planning.

THAI scheme was designed to cover all village panchayats within the five-year period of local bodies from 2011-2012 to 2015-16. It is fully state funded scheme. To cover 79,394 habitations in 12,524 village panchayats they are grouped into four categories (at the range of habitations) from a minimum grant of Rs. 20 lakhs to a maximum grant of Rs. 50 lakhs were allotted depending on the range of habitations. To ensure efficiency and effectiveness, the principle of participatory micro planning through local governance was undertaken. Creating awareness among the people, community mobilization, forming survey team, training the survey team, organizing Gram Sabha for prioritization of works have to be undertaken in this scheme, supervision and monitoring mechanisms and online reporting were in built activities incorporated in this scheme. It involved Panchayati Raj Institutions for planning and implementation. Further officials are involved along with elected representatives of local bodies to implement the scheme. The line departments are also involved in implementation of this scheme by contributing from their schemes the resources. While evaluating the impact of the scheme, it is found out that the schemes has created an everlasting impact in the minds of the marginalised communities as this scheme realized their long felt needs.

The major causes for the success of the scheme are many and of which the sincerity and commitment of government officials from the bottom to higher level, the guidelines and the periodical and flexible approach available under guidelines for effective planning and implementation. The roles and responsibilities entrusted to local government institutions have been discharged very effectively as they are fully sensitized on their functioning. People from the marginalised communities have been mobilized to participate in the decision making process. This scheme has contributed substantially to the marginalised communities and more particularly the women of the marginalised communities.

By implementing this scheme in the rural areas, it has enabled the communities' life in peace without quarrelling with each other on the issues of using the commons. At a cursory level this scheme gives a sense of construction and road works. But while looking at the scheme from the perspective of the poor and the marginalised, it is a creative scheme which has enabled the marginalized to keep their dignity intact.

By using a well-developed survey instrument, huge data have been collected for preparing a perspective development plan. Decisions have been taken in the Gram Sabha by convincing every one through a deliberative process. Hitherto unmet needs are being met through this scheme.

THAI-SWOT ANALYSIS

Strength

Habitation is the basic unit for planning covering all village panchayats in the state within 5 years.

- Participatory micro level.
- Capacity building to the key stakeholders for the successful planning.
- Rational fund allocation.
- Dovetailing.
- Delimit the basic facilities—priority basic—no deviation.
- Well structured survey format.
- Conducive environment for working together of key stakeholders.
- Availability of clear-cut instructions and guidelines for better understanding among the stakeholders regarding the roles and responsibilities.
- Minimum basic infrastructure facilities at each habitation is determined moreover priority among these facilities also in order so as within the allotted budget could be spent for water supply, street light, roads, culvert/bridge and other buildings

(burial/funeral ground).

- The planning process helped the community to work close with the official of RD department. It served as an information empowerment, exposure-cum-practical to them.
- A sincere attempt to reduce the gap in minimum basic facilities at habitations level.
- A new environment was down in the mindset of officials at all level that involving people from planning to evaluation is a factor for successful planning.

Weakness

- Considering the status of basic facilities existed at habitation of many village Panchayats, the duration of 5 years and the allotted budget based on the range of habitation numbers is not adequate.
- Survey work during its initial period, i.e. 2011/12 was serious and properly monitored by the higher officials. In course of further years, it was a little better than the initial period. It is learnt from the status of sample villages, many important details (might be taken) is not reported in the survey format as demanded (es. Water supply-scarcity level at each habitation).
- Dovetailing to fulfil the gap is not happened at expected level.
- Fund source available at various levels could be pooled provided its allocation to fill the gap under THAI must be ensured along with budget part of THAI.
- Role of the district administration of development sectors, i.e. water supply, street light, road and small bridges, minor ponds and tanks, other buildings like burial/funeral ground have to be involved at least during the planning stage. It will enable for effective planning so as encroachment could be removed, extension of space for drainage, road, passway etc. could be attempted before finalizing the work. It is noted during our field observation that some works finalized for implementation could not be done due to issue of ownership, encroachments, non-availability of spaces/area etc.

- Regarding role of Village Panchayats in implementation is not officially informed to them. Even the tender finalization/ works order copy was not given to them. Hence, the details of work/standard specified etc. were not known to the Panchayat administration. By providing due role to the Village Panchayat, it could be better delivery work.
- There was an expectation that THAI phase II would be declared to fill the major gaps of habitations of larger Panchayats which have more than 15 habitations. Of course, THAI phase II was declared but it focuses only on minor-medium irrigation tanks.
- Involvement of public in taking care and vigil over the maintenance of various structures created under THAI (e.g. Mini power pump/sintex/taps) is missed. Users' association could be attempted as in Kerala.

Opportunity

- A vision is built regarding the minimum needed basic facilities at habitation level. Moreover, the importance of minimum water requirement per head per days is realized by all villagers. Further at public facility like burial ground what type of basic facilities should be available is learnt by all. Actually, it is a felt need. Earlier days public just felt/adjust the one-day affairs at burial/funeral ground with limited facilities. Now as said earlier a vision is created. Compound wall, approach road, cement pathway, platform, water supply and electricity have to be existed at each burial ground become a norm. It is a progressive way of life; a decent way of life, the villagers acknowledged. In the same way, other facilities to ensure a decent life has to be planned and planning has to be done on the same way along with fund allocation to that planned work as in THAI. Just declaration of development works for popularity/compulsion based should be given away. In planning phase by phase for overall development is now realized by public. They would wait if it is a systematic planning and fund allocation in each five-year tenure becomes the policy and plan of the state.

- THAI phase II for strengthening the minor/medium irrigation tanks is a new more and really a correct step in ensuring the role of department of RD and PR towards decentralization and delegation of 3Fs—Finance, Functions and Functionaries. Under the 11th Schedule there are other development subjects listed out. The government makes it as a policy to take these development subjects one by one with clear cut schemes like THAI along with planning and fund allocation during the five-year tenure, GoI would show the way to other states in India.
- As it now GoI used THAI frame in finalizing development works under the 14th Finance Commission of GoI, it may negotiate with GoI to spare fund for other subjects listed under 11th Schedule.

Challenges

- Irrespective of change of government developmental planning and fund allocation has to be in system.
- Planning from grass-root level has to be the policy of the government.
- Allocation of area development fund to higher level representatives like MLA and MP could be channelized by district level planning. Otherwise they choice for on their own interest individuals become the rule though it is within the permitted works. Priority/felt needs finalized by the Gram Sabha are not properly considered by the higher-level representatives.
- More number of structures and facilities have been created at habitations in each Village Panchayat through various schemes. But maintenance and proper utility have to be verified and needed intervention for better usage could be ensured. A separate administrative wing has to be entrusted with this responsibility.

Contents

Preface vii
Acknowledgements ix
Executive Summary xi
List of Tables xix
Abbreviations xxi

1. Introduction **1**

1.1. Salient Features of THAI 2
1.2. Rationale for the Study 4
1.3. Objectives of the Study 5
1.4. Methodology 5
1.5. Chapterization 7
1.6. Status of Basic Facilities in Sample Villages (along with works implemented under THAI) 7

2. Planning and Implementation Process **84**

2.1. Introduction 84
2.2. Process Analysis in Sample Villages 85
2.3. District-wise Analysis 107
2.4. Role of Local Bodies 113
2.5. Conclusion 114

3. Benefits Acquired by the People **116**

4. Integrated Analysis **133**

4.1. Introduction 133

4.2. Achievements 153
4.3. Conclusion 156

5. Major Findings and Conclusion 159

5.1 Major Findings 159
5.2 Overall Impact 162
5.3 Suggestions 164
5.4 Conclusion 166
5.5 Constraints 169
Annexture 1: Case Studies 170
Annexture 2: Tables 179
Index 215

List of Tables

1.1: Details of the fund allocation per Panchayat 3
1.2: Details of the major categories of works 3
1.3: Details of the sample Village Panchayats 7
1.4: Population details of sample Village Panchayats 8

2.1: No. of works completed in sample Village Panchayats in Dindigul District 107
2.2: No. of works completed in sample Village Panchayats in Pudukottai District 109
2.3: No. of works completed in sample Village Panchayats in Villupuram District 112

3.1: No. of works completed under water supply in sample Village Panchayats 117
3.2: No. of works completed under street light in sample Village Panchayats 122
3.3: No. of works completed under Road works in sample Village Panchayats 124
3.4: No. of works completed under Building works in sample Village Panchayats 127

4.1: General Particulars of the Participants of FGD 158

Abbreviations

AD	Adi Dravidar
AD	Assistant Director
BT	Block Thar
CC	Cement Concrete
CM	Chief Minister
DRDA	District Rural Development Agency
EB	Electricity Board
FGD	Focused Group Discussion
GLR	Ground Level Reservoir
IAY	Indira Awas Yojana
MLA	Member of Legislative Assembly
MP	Member of Parliament
OHT	Over Head Tank
PDS	Public Distribution System
PQLI	Physical Quality of Life Index
RCC	Reinforced Cement Concrete
SC & ST	Scheduled Caste & Scheduled Tribe
SHG	Self Help Group
VWSC	Village Water and Sanitation Committee
WBM	With Blue Metal

1
Introduction

Tamil Nadu is known for its pro poor policies, programmes and schemes which are path breaking and models to other states. Equally its efforts to empower the poor, marginalized and more particularly the women are laudable. For all the achievements in delivering goods and services to the people, the commitment of the bureaucracy for service is yet another feature of Tamil Nadu Government and Administration. Creations of Panchayat Raj, reserving 50 per cent of the seats for women and reserving two terms consecutively, the positions for women and Dalits in the Panchayati Raj are the indicators of the progressive nature of the state government.

From community development programme initiated at the dawn of independence to last Annaithu Grama Anna Marumalarchi Thittam (AGAMT) series of development programmes had been launched and implemented in Tamil Nadu to fulfil the basic infrastructure facilities to the rural areas. While comparing with other states in terms of the infrastructural facilities, Tamil Nadu is far better than them. Yet there are certain areas excluded and the people who are in the excluded areas could not get such facilities. Since programme capture is the phenomenon in Indian rural areas many of the hamlets which have been left out in providing basic facilities and they continue to demand the same. They are mostly voiceless. They make feeble noise whenever they get opportunity to make noise. But the Government of Tamil Nadu is unequivocally committed to listen and redress the grievances of the poorest segment and by which it wants to address the equity issue. In order to fulfil the gap in infrastructure facilities in the remote villages a new scheme has been evolved innovatively and the scheme is called "Tamil Nadu Village Habitations Improvement" Scheme—THAI. It was implemented for a period of five years. At the fag-end of the period, it is decided to assess to what extent the scheme has fulfilled its objectives. Hence, this study has been proposed.

Tamil Nadu is a pioneering state in introducing many path breaking fully funded schemes for rural transformation. Every Gram Panchayat has got several habitations (human settlements). Gram Panchayat is an administrative unit, which has to plan and carry out development activities to enable the people living in all habitations to lead a decent dignified human life. Achieving equity at the grassroots is an issue in governance at the grassroots. Indian villages are having distinct socio-cultural characteristics. Achieving equity is an issue. Equally taking decision democratically in the hierarchical village society is a difficult task. Yet the responsibility of the state is to look at the issue through the newly created Panchayati Raj system. Hence, this new scheme is evolved to provide basic infrastructure to all habitations and same may be implemented through the panchayats. The panchayats have to prepare a perspective plan by involving the people of the habitations. It is reaching the unreached and the whole process has to be done through a democratic process in the established governance institution—the Gram Panchayats.

There are 79,394 habitations in 12,524 village panchayats in Tamil Nadu. On an average a single village panchayat has got seven habitations. The Nilgiri district has 37 habitations and Villupuram district has three such habitations. So allocating equal amount of fund to the village panchayats will not solve the problems of all the habitations. Hence, this new THAI scheme has been introduced. The new scheme has:

i. to reduce the disparities in providing infrastructure among the habitations in a village panchayat.
ii. to ensure minimum basic infrastructure facilities to all habitations which will enable them to improve the quality and standard of life.

1.1. Salient Features of THAI

- It is a flagship programme fully funded by the state government. It has been designed to implement in five phases from 2011-2012 to 2015-2016. It will provide basic minimum infrastructure facilities to all the habitations over a period of five years. Tamil Nadu is the only state focusing on

'Habitation' as the unit of planning and no other State in the Country is operating such an innovative scheme.

- Under this scheme, considering the varying size of the population of a Village Panchayat and the number of habitations within it, to determine the fund requirement for Village Panchayat matrix has been followed. Accordingly, funds have been allocated. It is shown in Table 1.1.

Table 1.1: Details of the fund allocation per Panchayat

Sl. No.	*Habitation Range*	*Allocation per Panchayat (Rs. in lakhs)*		
		Minimum Basic Grant	*Additional Funds*	*Total Funds*
1.	Below 5	20	0	20
2.	6-15	20	10	30
3.	16-25	20	20	40
4.	Above 25	20	30	50

Source: Computed.

Funds have to be spent under three major categories of works. They are:

(i) Minimum basic requirements,
(ii) Additional requirements, and
(iii) Other works.

They are shown in Table 1.2.

Table 1.2: Details of the major categories of works

Sl. No.	*Minimum Basic Requirements*	*Additional Requirements*	*Other Works*
1.	Water Supply	Anganwadi Centres	Any other permitted works
2.	Street Lights	Public Distribution System Shops	
3.	Roads	SHG Buildings	
4.	Burial Grounds	Threshing Floor	
5.	Pathway to Burial Grounds	Play Ground	

Sources: Computed.

- In order to ascertain the present status at each habitation on the availability of all minimum basic needs and to assess the habitation-wise requirements of all minimum basic infrastructure facilities, a detailed survey has been administered by a survey team involving the informed people in the panchayats.

- The members of the survey team have been selected considering the role they have to play in such a massive micro planning exercise. Hence, the team members have undergone an orientation programme on administering survey and doing follow-up activities. Following are the members of the survey team undergone the orientation programme:
  - Deputy Block Development Officer (V. Pt.)
  - Union Overseer
  - Panchayat Secretary
  - Panchayat President
- Survey being a massive exercise, to ensure proper collection of data and filling of data, the duly filled format has to be checked by a nodal officer. Further it will be verified by the district level team consisting of AEE (RD), EE (RD) and PD (DRDA). All are officials with rich experience.
- Only after the clearance of the district level technical team, the online data-base is created for public consumption and for planning.
- In respect of selection of works, scrutiny and administrative sanction and role and responsibility of the local bodies, clear cut guidelines have been published by the Department of Rural Development and Panchayati Raj. Accordingly, planning was done at panchayat level and the works have been carried out.

1.2. Rationale for the Study

Being a flagship programme, focusing habitation based planning with public participation to ensure minimum basic requirements in all habitation, first time in the country a detailed and comprehensive survey was undertaken in respect of assessing the present status on the availability of minimum basic needs and the need for future in each habitation. This exercise was done through a tool (questionnaire) developed by the experts at the state level through the State Planning Commission. Through the combined efforts of the officials and the elected representatives of local bodies the planning exercise at micro-level with the input of technical team at the district level have been done. The aim is to address the bottlenecks in distribution of resources to provide minimum basic requirements at all 79,394 habitations equitably over a period of five years. Hence, a study is an imperative need to assess the impact of the scheme in the community. Thus, this study has been undertaken. The study has got certain objectives.

1.3. Objectives of the Study

- To study the basic objectives of the THAI scheme;
- To study the planning process;
- To study the process of implementation;
- To assess the utility of the scheme;
- To assess the achievements of the scheme;
- To assess the gaps in the implementation process of the scheme;
- To assess and evaluate the role of the local bodies in planning and implementing the scheme.

1.4. Methodology

THAI scheme is a new initiative aiming to ensure minimum basic facilities in all habitation in each Village Panchayat. It is a step further from the existing practice of keeping Village Panchayat as a functional unit of planning to habitation as the basic unit for planning, financing and implementation of the scheme. It paves the way to reduce the centre and periphery divide in the villages in terms of infrastructure facilities. Basically it is an empirical study employing a combination of social science research methods. Apart from one to one interview with the officials, it followed the focus group discussion method to collect data. It consults records pertinent to planning and implementation of the scheme from the offices. The focus group discussions were with elected representatives, beneficiaries, SHG members, youth groups, opinion makers, PLF members to collect data to evaluate the utility of the scheme. Field physical verification was done through participant observation. Apart from the above, case studies have been conducted.

Sampling

In order to capture variations in all the regions, sampling of villages have been undertaken by keeping the following factors:

1. Village panchayats have been selected based on geographical zones namely hills, coastal and plain areas to capture the distinct nature of the facilities needed to their regions.
2. Since the numbers of habitations vary from 7 to 37, in order to capture the intensity of demands for infrastructure due to the number of habitations, village panchayats have been selected from different ranges of the number of habitations. Village panchayats have been selected from the ranges by categorizing the villages from 1 to 5, 6 to 15, and 16 to 25 and above 26.
3. In order to capture the effectiveness of the local bodies, village panchayats have been selected based on the category of leadership—General, SC, SC women and women.

By keeping all the above factors, the following districts have been selected for this study: Dindigul, Pudukottai and Villupuram.

Within the district selected for the study, four Village Panchayats from four Panchayat Unions were selected. In each panchayat union based on the guidelines of the study one village panchayat is selected in each category of habitation range namely below five, six to fifteen, sixteen to twenty-five and more than twenty-five. Totally 12 Village Panchayats have been selected for this study from the three districts. This is shown in Table 1.3.

In order to show the strength of beneficiaries, the population details of the village panchayats are given in Table 1.4.

Tools Constructed for the Study

Being an empirical study, the following tools have been constructed for data collection:

(i) Check-list for interaction with the key stakeholders—using a check-list.
(ii) Check-list for verification of document—at Village Panchayat level, Panchayat Union level and District Rural Development Agency.
(iii) Check-list for Focus Group Discussion with beneficiaries—in the villages.
(iv) Check-list for Physical verification of facilities created.

Table 1.3: Details of the sample Village Panchayats

Sl. No.	Sample District	Sample Union	Sample Village Panchayat	Habitation Range	Reservation category
1.	Dindigul	Athoor	Ambathurai	6-15	General
		Natham	Senthurai	16-25	Women (Gen.)
		Reddiyachatiram	Kasavanampatti	6-15	Women (Gen.)
		Kodaikkanal	Villpatti*	26 & above	SC (Gen.)
2.	Pudukottai	Pudukottai	Vagavasal	6-15	General
		Thirumayam	Thulaiyanur	26 & above	General
		Viralimalai	Viralur	6-15	Women (SC)
		Avudayarkovil	Mimisal**	6-15	Women (Gen.)
3.	Villupuram	Marakkanam	Singanur	0-5	Women (Gen.)
		Koliyanur	Thennamadevi	0-5	Women (SC)
		Kalrayan Hills	Vellimalai*	26 & above	ST (Gen.)
		Vanur	Bommaiyarpalayam**	0-5	Women (Gen.)

Note: * Hilly Village Panchayat, ** Coastal Village Panchayat.
Source: Computed.

1.5. Chapterization

The report consists of five chapters. First chapter deals with the basic framework of the scheme along with general introduction specifying the methodological nuances adopted to collect data. Second chapter deals with the planning process and the implementation process and the role of the local bodies in this respect. Third chapter brings to light the benefits acquired by the people. Fourth chapter forms integrated analysis which brings inferences and final chapter forms conclusion and recommendation.

1.6. Status of Basic Facilities in Sample Villages (along with works implemented under THAI)

DINDIGUL DISTRICT

1. Ambathurai Village Panchayat

It is a multicaste village panchayat, Population of this village panchayat is 10,642. It has 13 hamlets and the total number of houses are 2780 (Huts 156; Tiles1627; CC 747; Mixed 250). Regarding the community of the villagers, BC 5600; SC 2786; MBC 2256, regarding availability of household latrine 571.

Table 1.4: Population details of sample Village Panchayats

Sl. No.	Name of the Village Panchayat	Population			Scheduled Castes			Scheduled Tribes		
		Total	Males	Females	Total	Males	Females	Total	Males	Females
1.	Ambathurai	9,166	4,560	4,606	2,154	1,078	1,076	-	-	-
2.	Kasavanampatti	4,597	2,331	2,266	759	376	383	-	-	-
3.	Sendurai	15,055	7,635	7,420	1,871	924	947	-	-	-
4.	Vilpatti	15,820	7,924	7,896	4,028	2,046	1,982	221	114	107
5.	Vagavasal	3,852	1,956	1,896	790	400	390	4	2	2
6.	Thulaiyanur	5,685	2,845	2,840	1,165	575	590	2	-	2
7.	Viralur	4,090	1,987	2,103	951	471	480	1	-	1
8.	Mimisal	5,482	2,765	2,717	653	314	319	-	-	-
9.	Tennamadevi	2,842	1,446	1,396	1,104	537	567	19	11	8
10.	Singanur	3,255	1,572	1,683	2,496	1,199	1,297	-	-	-
11.	Bommayapalayam	8,266	4,095	4,171	614	295	319	4	2	2
12.	Vellimalai	6,603	3,278	3,325	14	6	8	6,363	3,167	3,196

Source: 2011 census.

Status of Water Supply

There are 129 public taps and 320 house service connections in this village panchayat. Highest HSC is at Perumalkovilpatti and the next is Ambathurai. There are 23 mini power pumps. Water from 9 mini pumps is not fit for drinking. Regarding hand pumps in the panchayat area are 23. Of which 17 are functioning and water from 12 hand pumps is not fit for drinking. Among the 13 hamlets, water supply is adequate in 4 hamlets. In the remaining hamlets, water supply is not adequate (30 liters per person per day). (*see* Table on p. 10).

Improvement through THAI

Water supply through OHT is distributed daily in all hamlets. Only at Ambathurai, the distribution is above 100 litters per day per person. There are 23 mini power pumps in the panchayat but water from 9 mini power pumps is not fit for drinking purpose. Regarding hand pumps there are 23 functioning in the panchayat and of which only 6 HP water is fit to drinking. Apart from the above water sources, under comprehensive water supply of TWAD scheme is also in operation. In spite of this arrangement during summer, there is scarcity of water at big hamlets like Ambathurai, Perumalkovilpatti and Muruganpatti. As ground water level is going down, many bore wells are dysfunctional. The village panchayat administration of Ambathurai sends a special proposal with a big budget for enhancing water supply to the district administration. Hence under THAI scheme, no water supply work is being carried out.

Status of Street Lights

There are 362 street lights in the panchayat areas. (Tube lights 264; CFL 84; Mercury 14). Highest number of lights are at Ambathurai (84) and the least is at Velampatti (2) where the distance of the streets is 562 meters. (*see* Table on p. 11).

Sl. No.	Name of the Village	Total Household	Total Population	Public Tap	House connection	Status of Drinking Water															
						Mini Power Pump					THAI		Hand Pump					THAI	OHT	Conditions	
						Total	Fit for Drinking	Not Fit for Drinking	Not working	Conditions	New Bore Well	New MPP	Total	Fit for Drinking	Not Fit for Drinking	Not working	Conditions		No. of OHT	Partially damage	Totally damaged
1	RAMANATHAPURAM	281	1047	-	1027	5	4	1	1	bore dry			0	1					1	1	
2	NADUPATTI	129	486	-	486	0							0	1					3	1	
3	KURUMBAPATTI	130	476	-	476	2		2	1	bore dry			1		1	0			3		
4	AMBATHURAI	601	2103	-	2103	5	1	4	4	bore dry			11		10	2	1 repair 1 dry		6	1	
5	RENGASAMINAGAR	107	422	-	422	0							0						2		
6	AMALINAGAR	111	476	-	507	1	1						0						1		
7	INDIRAPURAM	138	546	-	563	1	1						2	1	2	2	bore dry		2		
8	KATHIRIPATTI	82	275	-	275	1		1					0						2		
9	KOLLAPATTI	108	415	-	462	2	2		1	bore repair			0	1					2		
10	PERUMALKOVILPATTI	673	2671	-	2671	1	1						4		0	3	bore dry		3	2	
11	RAJAKALLIAMMAN NAGAR	150	707	-	727	3	3						0						2		
12	VELAMPATTI	17	59	-	53	1		1	1	bore repair			0						1		
13	MURUGANPATTI	253	959	-	959	1	1						5		4	0			3	2	
	Total	2780	10642	-	10731	23	14	9	8				23	6	17	7			31	2	

Sl. No.	Name of the Village	Total Household	POPULATION						STREET LIGHT	
			Total Population	SC	ST	MBC	BC	Others	No. of SL	THAI
1	Ramanathapuram	281	1047	0	0	1047	0	0	42	
2	Nadupatti	129	486	0	0	0	486	0	17	
3	Kurumbapatti	130	476	0	0	212	264	0	24	
4	Ambathurai	601	2103	911	0	65	1127	0	84	
5	Rengasaminagar	107	422	0	0	186	236	0	8	1
6	Amalinagar	111	476	0	0	0	476	0	12	
7	Indirapuram	138	546	546	0	0	0	0	23	2
8	Kathiripatti	82	275	0	0	8	267	0	13	
9	Kollapatti	108	415	293	0	0	122	0	17	2
10	Perumalkovilpatti	673	2671	0	0	738	1933	0	58	14
11	Rajakalliamman Nagar	150	707	77	0	0	630	0	19	8
12	Velampatti	17	59	0	0	0	59	0	2	3
13	Muruganpatti	253	959	959	0	0	0	0	43	
	Total	2780	10642	2786	0	2256	5600	0	362	30

Improvement through THAI

There are 362 lights in 13 hamlets of the panchayat. Under THAI scheme 30 new street lights have been provided. As the distance of streets at Perumalkovilpatti is a longer one, 14 new street lights have been provided. Rajakalliamman Nagar is extension area where 8 new lights have been provided. Indirapuram is a small habitation with spacious streets/lanes. Hence, two lights have been provided there. At Velampatti there was no CFL. Hence, 3 new lights have been provided at Velampatti.

Status of Roads and Culvert

Velampatti to Chinnalapatti connectivity is single layer metal road and four pipeline culverts available along the road are fully damaged. On the National Highway, Perumalkovilpatti BT and road four concrete culverts are partly damaged. There are three one layered metal roads, one CC road, 8 BT roads and one earthen road in this panchayat. Of the roads, three are partly damaged and six are fully damaged (*see* Table on p. 13).

Improvement through THAI

Under the THAI scheme 10 CC roads and three BT roads were constructed.

Status of Streets and Lanes

There are 61 streets/lanes in the panchayat and of which only 12 have drainage facility. In 13 lanes there is inadequate drainage system. The surface of the streets is in good condition in 11 streets. In 19 streets surface of the streets is partially damaged and remaining 31 are fully damaged.

Status of Government Building

At 11 hamlets except Amali Nagar and Katiripatti, 38 government buildings are functioning (6 are tiled, 5 are Asbestos, 27 are CC). In 18 buildings EB facility is available and water supply and toilet facilities are available at 12 buildings, and compound wall at three buildings.

There is one Higher Secondary School at Muruganpatti, seven middle schools and six primary schools are in panchayat areas. Regarding, facilities available at schools water supply and EB connections are at seven schools, and toilet facilities are at six schools. There are seven kitchen sheds and three need minor repair, and one cycle stand is available at a school premise.

Status of Burial/Funeral Ground

There are totally 15 burial/funeral grounds in the panchayat area. Only at 6 grounds minimum facilities are available. At Muruganpatti ground the waiting hall, compound wall and cement passages are available. Water facility and street lights are available at Muruganpatti, Amali Nagar, and Ramanathapuram. Approach road to the burial ground is available for 9 hamlets. For 13 hamlets, the panchayat expects full facilities for the grounds. (*see* Table on p. 14).

Sl. No.	Name of the Village	Total Households	POPULATION						ROAD WORKS			
			Total Population						Roads			THAI
				SC	ST	MBC	BC	Others	No. of Roads	BT & WBM	Condition	CC
1	Ramanathapuram	281	1047	0	0	1047	0	0	1			
2	Nadupatti	129	486	0	0	0	486	0				
3	Kurumbapatti	130	476	0	0	212	264	0				
4	Ambathurai	601	2103	911	0	65	1127	0	3	2	1 fully 1 partly	
5	Rengasaminagar	107	422	0	0	186	236	0				2
6	Amalinagar	111	476	0	0	0	476	0				
7	Indirapuram	138	546	546	0	0	0	0				1
8	Kathiripatti	82	275	0	0	8	267	0	2	2	1 fully 1 partly	
9	Kollapatti	108	415	293	0	0	122	0	2	1	fully damaged	
10	Perumalkovilpatti	673	2671	0	0	738	1933	0	3	3	2 Partly 1 fully	1
11	Rajakalliamman Nagar	150	707	77	0	0	630	0				3
12	Velampatti	17	59	0	0	0	59	0	1	1	fully damaged	
13	Muruganpatti	253	959	959	0	0	0	0				3
	Total	2780	10642	2786	0	2256	5600	0	12	9		10

Sl. No.	Name of the Village		POPULATION						BUILDINGS								
									Burial Ground								THAI
		Total Household	Total Population	SC	ST	MBC	BC	Others	No. of BG	Burial Stage	Waiting shed	Retaining Wall	CC Path	Drinking Water	Light	Approach Road	
1	Ramanathapuram	281	1047	0	0	1047	0	0	2	1	0	0	0	0	1	2	
2	Nadupatti	129	486	0	0	0	486	0	1	1	0	0	0	0	0	0	
3	Kurumbapatti	130	476	0	0	212	264	0	1	0	0	0	0	0	0	0	
4	Ambathurai	601	2103	911	0	65	1127	0	1	1	0	0	0	0	0	0	
5	Rengasaminagar	107	422	0	0	186	236	0	1	1	0	0	0	0	0	0	
6	Amalinagar	111	476	0	0	0	476	0	1	0	0	0	0	1	1	1	
7	Indirapuram	138	546	546	0	0	0	0	1	1	0	0	0	0	0	1	
8	Kathiripatti	82	275	0	0	8	267	0	1	0	0	0	0	0	0	1	1
9	Kollapatti	108	415	293	0	0	122	0	1	0	0	0	0	0	0	1	
10	Perumalkovilpatti	673	2671	0	0	738	1933	0	2	0	0	0	0	0	1	2	
11	Rajakalliamman Nagar	150	707	77	0	0	630	0	1	0	0	0	0	0	0	1	
12	Velampatti	17	59	0	0	0	59	0	1	0	0	0	0	0	0	1	
13	Muruganpatti	253	959	959	0	0	0	0	1	1	1	1	1	1	0	1	
	Total	2780	10642	2786	0	2256	5600	0	15	6	1	1	1	2	3	11	1

Improvement through THAI

Under THAI, a full-fledged burial ground was constructed at Kathiripatti where there was a dispute over the boundary of Kathiripatti hamlet and adjacent village panchayat. Hence, preference was given to Kathiripatti.

2. Sendurai Village Panchayat

Sendurai is a larger village panchayat, having a population of 15,204 is located at Natham block. It is a BC dominated village Panchayat and the number of ST is 1945. Sendurai has 25 habitations and it is the headquarters of the village Panchayat. Of the total 1126 houses in the panchayat, 855 are huts, 942 are tiled, the remaining are CC.

Status of Water Supply

The village panchayat has 300 public taps and 447 house service connections. It has 3248 households. The village panchayat has 61 Mini Power Pump and 8 Hand Pump. There are two bore-wells which are under repair in Bodikampatti and Mamarathupatti village. There is a bore-well in Karuthanayakkanpatti completely dried up (*see* Table on p. 16).

Improvement through THAI

During the survey, it has been stated that the status of distribution of water supply was inadequate in 10 habitations. Water supply is below 50 liters per day per person. Hence, under THAI seven works have been undertaken to improve the water supply distribution. Among the seven-works undertaken three are erection of new bore-wells and four are provision of mini power pumps. Preference is given to Sendurai, the mother village as more number of HSC are in that area. At Vadakkupudur distribution is 33 liters and at Kuppandigoundanpatti the supply is 37 liters and moreover it is an SC habitation. Regarding mini power pumps, preference is given to the habitations where the distribution is below 50 liters per day per person except Pandhipomminayakkanur where no mini power pump is available.

Status of Street Lights

The village panchayat has 257 tube lights, 91 CPL lights, one high man light and one solar light. Totally it has 358 street lights. (*see* Table on p. 18).

Improvement through THAI

In 10 habitations, totally 75 street lights have been provided under THAI scheme. 25 street lights have been provided at one habitation namely Periyurpatti where the distance of street is a lengthy one (1243 meter); the next one is Sendurai, having a lengthy street (1940.5 meter).

Road Works

Under THAI scheme, six cement concrete roads have been provided where the condition of streets is not good during rainy season.

Sl. No.	Name of the Village	Total Household	Drinking Water																	
			Total Population	Public Tap	House connection	Mini Power Pump (MPP)				Conditions	THAI		Hand Pump				Conditions	THAI	Over Head Tank	
						Total	Fit for Drinking	Not Fit for Drinking	Not working		New Bore Well	New MPP	Total	Fit for Drinking	Not Fit for Drinking	Not working			No. of OHT	Conditions
1	2	3	4	5	6	7	8	9	10	11	12	13	14	15	16	17	18	19	20	21
1	Bodikkampatti	130	594	14	82	4	4	0	1	Bore damage			0						2	
2	Chitragoundanpatti	112	724	33	16	3	3	0	0				0						1	
3	Kalathupatti	192	975	12	6	1	1	0	0			1	1	0	1	1	bore dry		1	
4	Kamatchipuram	21	65	4	0	0	0		0				0						1	
5	Karuthanaickenpatti	184	630	24	0	2	2	0	0				2	0	2	2	bore dry		2	
6	Kuppandigoundanpatti	27	107	10	0	1	1	0	0		1		0						1	
7	Mallanaickanpatti	88	352	9	13	2	2	0	0				0						1	
8	Mamarathupatti	245	1210	46	30	7	7	0	1	Bore damage		1	0						1	
9	Mettupatti	55	269	9	3	2	2	0	0				2	0	2	2	1 dry 1 repair		2	
10	Nallapitchanpatti	240	1210	12	60	4	4	0	0				3	0	3	3	bore dry		1	
11	Palamalayanpatti	39	185	5	0	1	1	0	0				1	0	1	1	bore dry		1	
12	Pandhipomminaiyakanur	69	276	8	5	0	0	0	0			1	0						2	1 total damage
13	Periyurpatti	253	959	11	0	7	5	2	0				0						2	
14	Rengaiyanservaikaranpatti	162	472	17	7	3	3	0	0				2	0	2	0			1	

1	2	3	4	5	6	7	8	9	10	11	12	13	14	15	16	17	18	19	20	21
15	S. Kovilpatti	183	1001	16	12	1	1	0	0				0						2	1 total damaged
16	S. Kurumbapatti	280	1269	16	32	2	2	0	0				2	1	1	1	bore dry		1	Partially damaged
17	Thattamadaipatti	32	140	14	3	2	2	0	0				1	0	1	1	bore dry		1	
18	Sendurai	520	2606	15	150	7	7	0	0		1	1	5	0	5	3	bore dry		2	
19	Thirukalathupatti	31	139	5	0	1	1	0	0				0						0	
20	Thirunoothupatti	167	751	14	18	4	3	1	0				0						2	
21	Vadakkupudur	67	368	15	0	2	1	2	1	Bore dry	1		0						2	
22	Vettaiyankulam	21	975	4	0	2	2	0	0				0							
23	Siluvankurai	27	122	5	0	1	1	0	0				0						1	
24	Kakkan colony	114	572	12	10	2	2	0	0				1	1	0	1	bore dry		1	
	Total	3259	15971	330	447	61	57	5	3				20	2	18	15			31	

Status of Street Lights in Sendurai Village Panchayat

Sl. No.	Name of the Village	Total Household	POPULATION						STREET LIGHTS	
			Total Population	SC	ST	MBC	BC	Others	No. of SL	THAI
1	Bodikkampatti	130	594	170	0	0	424	0	12	0
2	Chitragoundanpatti	112	724	57	0	0	667	0	12	0
3	Kalathupatti	192	975	0	0	975	0	0	32	1
4	Kamatchipuram	21	65	0	0	0	65	0	6	0
5	Karuthanaickenpatti	184	630	125	0	261	244	0	18	8
6	Kuppandigoundanpatti	27	107	0	0	0	107	0	10	7
7	Mallanaickanpatti	88	352	0	0	0	352	0	9	0
8	Mamarathupatti	245	1210	0	0	930	280	0	18	6
9	Mettupatti	55	269	0	0	0	269	0	12	0
10	Nallapitchanpatti	240	1210	196	0	676	338	0	18	5
11	Palamalayanpatti	39	185	0	0	185	0	0	5	0
12	Pandhipomminaiyakanur	69	276	0	0	276	0	0	7	0
13	Periyurpatti	253	959	959	0	0	0		32	25
14	Rengaiyanservaikaranpatti	162	472	0	0	0	472	0	10	0
15	S. Kovilpatti	183	1001	0	0	1001	0	0	11	0
16	S. Kurumbapatti	280	1269	265	0	0	1004	0	22	1
17	Thattamadaipatti	32	140	0	0	140	0	0	5	0
18	Sendurai	520	2606	190	0	1279	1132	5	62	14
19	Thirukalathupatti	31	139	0	0	139	0	0	6	0
20	Thirunoothupatti	167	751	0	0	0	751	0	25	4
21	Vadakkupudur	67	368	48	0	0	320	0	8	0
22	Vettaiyankulam	21	975	0	0	975	0	0	3	0
23	Siluvankurai	27	122	35	0	0	87	0	5	0
24	Kakkan Colony	114	572	572	0	0	0	0	10	4
	Total	3259	15971	2617	0	6837	6512	5	358	75

There are 24 roads in the panchayat area. Of the roads, 11 are BT roads, two earthen roads, seven single layered metal roads and four double layered metal roads, 14 roads are in good condition, seven are partially damaged and three are fully damaged (*see* Table on p. 19).

Status of Burial/Funeral Ground and Facilities

The above facility is available in 15 out of 24 habitations. In 15 burial

Sl. No.	Name of the Village	Total Household	POPULATION								ROAD WORKS					
											Roads					THAI
			Total Population	SC	ST	MBC	BC	Others	Public Tap	House connection	No. of Roads	Earthen	Conditions	BT & WBM	Conditions	CC Road
1	2	3	4	5	6	7	8	9	10	11	12	13	14	15	16	17
1	Bodikkampatti	130	594	170	0	0	424	0	14	82	1			1	Partially damaged	
2	Chitragoundanpatti	112	724	57	0	0	667	0	33	16	1					
3	Kalathupatti	192	975	0	0	975	0	0	12	6						1
4	Kamatchipuram	21	65	0	0	0	65	0	4	0		1	Fully damaged			
5	Karuthanaickenpatti	184	630	125	0	261	244	0	24	0				1	Partially damaged	
6	Kuppandigoundanpatti	27	107	0	0	0	107	0	10	0	1					
7	Mallanaickanpatti	88	352	0	0	0	352	0	9	13				4	2 Fully damaged 2 partially damaged	
8	Mamarathupatti	245	1210	0	0	930	280	0	46	30						
9	Mettupatti	55	269	0	0	0	269	0	9	3						1
10	Nallapitchanpatti	240	1210	196	0	676	338	0	12	60						
11	Palamalayanpatti	39	185	0	0	185	0	0	5	0						
12	Pandhipomminaiyakanur	69	276	0	0	276	0	0	8	5	1					1

(Contd.)

1	2	3	4	5	6	7	8	9	10	11	12	13	14	15	16	17
13	Periyurpatti	253	959	959	0	0	0		11	0	3					
14	Rengaiyanservaikaranpatti	162	472	0	0	0	472	0	17	7	1			1	partially damaged	
15	S. Kovilpatti	183	1001	0	0	1001	0	0	16	12						
16	S. Kurumbapatti	280	1269	265	0	0	1004	0	16	32						1
17	Thattamadaipatti	32	140	0	0	140	0	0	14	3				1	partially damaged	
18	Sendurai	520	2606	190	0	1279	1132	5	15	150	5			1	partially damaged	1
19	Thirukalathupatti	31	139	0	0	139	0	0	5	0						
20	Thirunoothupatti	167	751	0	0	0	751	0	14	18	1					1
21	Vadakkupudur	67	368	48	0	0	320	0	15	0						
22	Vettaiyankulam	21	975	0	0	975	0	0	4	0						
23	Siluvankurai	27	122	35	0	0	87	0	5	0						
24	Kakkan Colony	114	572	572	0	0	0	0	12	10	1					
	Total	3259	15971	2617	0	6837	6512	5	330	447	15	1		9	0	6

Sl. No.	Name of the Village	Total Household	POPULATION						BUILDINGS								
			Total Population						Burial Ground								THAI
				SC	ST	MBC	BC	Others	No. of BG	Burial Stage	Waiting shed	Retaining Wall	CC Path	Drinking Water	Light	Approach Road	
1	Bodikkampatti	130	594	170	0	0	424	0	1	1				1	1	1	
2	Chitragoundanpatti	112	724	57	0	0	667	0	1					1			
3	Kalathupatti	192	975	0	0	975	0	0	1					1			
4	Kamatchipuram	21	65	0	0	0	65	0	1								
5	Karuthanaickenpatti	184	630	125	0	261	244	0	2					2			
6	Kuppandigoundanpatti	27	107	0	0	0	107	0	1								
7	Mallanaickanpatti	88	352	0	0	0	352	0	1					1			
8	Mamarathupatti	245	1210	0	0	930	280	0	1					1			
9	Mettupatti	55	269	0	0	0	269	0	1					1			
10	Nallapitchanpatti	240	1210	196	0	676	338	0	1								
11	Palamalayanpatti	39	185	0	0	185	0	0	1								
12	Pandhipomminaiyakanur	69	276	0	0	276	0	0	1							1	1
13	Periyurpatti	253	959	959	0	0	0		1					1			
14	Rengaiyanservaikaranpatti	162	472	0	0	0	472	0	1								
15	S. Kovilpatti	183	1001	0	0	1001	0	0	1					1			
16	S. Kurumbapatti	280	1269	265	0	0	1004	0	1								
17	Thattamadaipatti	32	140	0	0	140	0	0	1							1	

18	Sendurai	520	2606	190	0	1279	1132	5	1	1		1	1	1	1	1	
19	Thirukalathupatti	31	139	0	0	139	0	0	1								
20	Thirunoothupatti	167	751	0	0	0	751	0	1		1			1			
21	Vadakkupudur	67	368	48	0	0	320	0	1								
22	Vettaiyankulam	21	975	0	0	975	0	0	1					1		1	
23	Siluvankurai	27	122	35	0	0	87	0	1								
24	Kakkan Colony	114	572	572	0	0	0	0	1					1			
	Total	3259	15971	2617	0	6837	6512	5	25	2	1	1	1	14	2	5	1

grounds two burial stages, one waiting shed, one compound wall, and one CC path are available. In 14 burial grounds, drinking water facility, two light facility and five burial stages and one access road are available. But basic facilities are yet to be provided. People of the panchayat demanded the following facilities in the burial: funeral ground and funeral platform, compound wall, lights, water supply, waiting hall and CC passage road up to funeral platform and approach roads. (*see* Table on p. 21)

Improvement of THAI

Under THAI only one burial ground with all basic facilities were provided at Pandhipomminayakkanur

3. Villpatti Village Panchayat

Vilpatti village Panchayat is located at Kodaikanal Hills. This Panchayat is having a population of 14,357 and of them 5294 are SC. It is a BC dominated village Panchayat. Villpatti has 26 habitations and it is the headquarters of the village Panchayat. There are 4208 households in the panchayat area. Among them 438 are in huts, 493 are in tiled houses and 1104 are in CC house. Of the 1254 toilets constructed, 1202 are household and other are for public use. All are in good conditions and they are being used.

Status of Water Supply

There are 235 public taps and 136 household connections for water supply water through 12 OHT in this panchayat area. In this village panchayat 33 mini power pumps are available and out of the total pumps 25 are used for drinking purpose. Now 20 mini power pumps are in well working condition. The other four bore-wells are dried up and one bore-well is in disrepair. Out of 33 mini power pumps 13 syntex tanks are in damaged condition. There are 14 hand pumps also used for water supply, and out of 14 six used for drinking purposes. Out of 14 hand pumps five bore-wells are in working condition and others are damaged and are in dried condition. There are 23 GLR available but 21 are in usage for drinking water supply purpose. (*see* Table on p. 24)

Improvement through THAI

At Mattupatti pipeline extension work was carried out under THAI scheme. Out of total 26 hamlets available in Villpatti village panchayat

Sl. No.	Name of the Village	Total Household	DRINKING WATER																		
						Mini Power Pump (MPP)					THAI		Hand Pump					THAI	Over Head Tank	
			Total Population	Public Tap	House connection	Total	Fit for Drinking	Not Fit for Drinking	Not working	Conditions	New Bore Well	New MPP	Total	Fit for Drinking	Not Fit for Drinking	Not working	Conditions		No. of OHT	Conditions
1	2	3	4	5	6	7	8	9	10	11	12	13	14	15	16	17	18	19	20	21
1	Kovilpatti	165	837	0	0	2		2	1	bore dry			2		2	2	bore dry			
2	Thiruvalluvar Nagar	80	414	10	0															
3	Pilakkavai	30	96	0	0															
4	Puliyur	32	98	0	0															
5	Chinnapallam	142	316	8	1								2		2	2	bore dry			
6	Barathi Annanagar	65	226	9	0														2	
7	Kurunchi Nagar	591	2065			4	4		2	bore dry									2	
8	Attuvampatti	112	474	11	3	2	1	1	2										2	1 partly damage
9	Valaikattu Otai	506	976	18	22	2	2		2	1 dry 1repair			2	2		1	bore repair		2	
10	Mattupatti	200	710	14	3	2	1	1					1	1					2	
11	Uppuparaimethu	201	631	14	0															
12	Paraipatti	45	176	8	0	1	1		1	bore dry									1	
13	Peythuparai	329	1074	20	3	4	3	1	1	repair			2	1	1					
14	Kannikkadu	23	43	0	0															
15	Nagaramarathu Alai	10	38	0	0															
16	Ganeshapuram	72	249	7	0															
17	Pallangi	108	402	4	0	1	1		1				1	1						

(*Contd.*)

1	2	3	4	5	6	7	8	9	10	11	12	13	14	15	16	17	18	19	20	21
18	Annai Sathya Colony	253	974	13	9	3	3													
19	Villpatti	407	2109	30	73	2	2		2				2		2	2	bore repair			
20	Vellaparai	74	198	0	0															
21	Barathi Nagar	29	94	4	8	6	3	3	3											
22	Attuvampatti Colony	133	661	0	0	3	3						2	1	1	2	bore dry			
23	Gurusamypallam	62	239	14	3	1	1		1										1	
24	Pallangi	137	363	12	3															
25	Perumpallam	90	162	4	0															
26	Anna Ramasamy Nagar	312	732	30	8															
	Total	4208	14357	230	136	33	25	8	16				14	6	8	9			12	

at four hamlets, the supply of water is below 80 liters per day per person. At Mattupatti it is 67 liters per day a person. Moreover, out of two mini tank water supply at one is not fit for drinking. Engine of one mini power pump is under repair. One Hand pump is available there. Against this background pipe line extension work was provided under THAI, and by which all parts of the hamlets (SC, BC and MBC streets) have adequate water supply.

Status of Street light

Street light facilities at Villpatti village Panchayat is somewhat in improved condition in 24 habitations. 353 street lights are provided in the panchayat area and out of that 127 tube lights in 18 villages, 150 CFL in 20 villages, 3 ordinary pulps in three villages, 2 sodium vapour lamps in two villages and the remaining 71 solar lamps in seven habitations. Out of 72 lamps 32 in Puliyur and 30 lamps in Pilakkavai.

Sl. No.	Name of the Village	Total Households	POPULATION						STREET LIGHTS	
			Total Population	SC	ST	MBC	BC	Others	No. of SL	THAI
1	Kovilpatti	165	837	523	0	39	275	0	14	
2	Thiruvalluvar Nagar	80	414	198	0	0	216	0	7	
3	Pilakkavai	30	96	0	0	0	96	0	30	
4	Puliyur	32	98	0	0	0	98	0	32	
5	Chinnapallam	142	316	57	0	0	259	0	6	
6	Barathi Annanagar	65	226	32	102	31	61	0	20	2
7	Kurunchi Nagar	591	2065	1509	0	0	556	0	33	2
8	Attuvampatti	112	474	176	0	48	250	0	17	
9	Valaikattu Otai	506	976	121	0	0	855	0	11	
10	Mattupatti	200	710	33	0	31	646	0	9	2
11	Uppuparaimethu	201	631	499	0	0	132	0	13	
12	Paraipatti	45	176	41	0	0	135	0	3	
13	Peythuparai	329	1074	261	0	60	753	0	18	2
14	Kannikkadu	23	43	0	0	0	43	0		
15	Nagaramarathu Alai	10	38	0	0	0	38	0		

16	Ganeshapuram	72	249	103	0	47	99	0	8	
17	Pallangi	108	402	39	0	56	307	0	1	2
18	Annai Sathya Colony	253	974	507	0	71	396	0	14	
19	Villpatti	407	2109	790	0	316	1003	0	32	
20	Vellaparai	74	198	53	0	0	145	0	3	2
21	Barathi Nagar	29	94	0	0	0	94	0	16	
22	Attuvampatti Colony	133	661	158	0	99	404	0	19	
23	Gurusamypallam	62	239	0	0	0	239	0	12	
24	Pallangi	137	363	74	76	72	141	0	13	
25	Perumpallam	90	162	72	0	0	90	0	7	2
26	Anna Ramasamy Nagar	312	732	48	0	0	684	0	15	2
	Total	4208	14357	5294	178	870	8015	0	339	16

Improvement through THAI

Street lights are provided at 8 hamlets at the rate of two each (totally 16 street lights). Earlier at these hamlets number of CFL is less. In the remaining three hamlets number of CFL available is more in number; preference is given as the length of street is long. Thus, the felt needs of people of habitation is properly identified and fulfilled.

Status of Road Facilities

Pillakkavai road 3 k.m. earthen road, Kurunchi Andavarkovil road 2 k.m. earthen road, Nayudupuram to Anna Ramasamynagar 2.80 k.m. double layer metal road, Barathi Annanagar to Kovilpatti 5 k.m. earthen road, Nagaramaranthali 3 k.m. earthen road, Paraipatti to Kannikadu 1.5 k.m. earthen road, Palani junction to Uppuparai 2.70 double layer metal road, Chinnapallam to Lurthu Church 1.5 k.m. earthen road and Nayudupuram to Anna Ramasamynagar 2.80 BT road are in fully damaged condition.

Ganeshapuram 1.80 BT main road, Attuvampattiperiyaodai 3 k.m. BT road, Pethuparai to Barathi Annanagar 2.8 k.m. BT road, Villpatti 0.4 k.m. BT main road, Chinnapallam 1 k.m. BT road, Ganeshapuram 5 k.m. BT main road and Paraipatti to Kannikadu 1.5 k.m. earthen roads are in good condition. Pethuparai to Barathi Annanagar 2.8 BT road, Kovilpatti 5 k.m. earthen road and Pallangi to Kombai 8 k.m. BT road are partially damaged.

Sl. No.	Name of the Village	Total Household	POPULATION						ROAD WORKS					THAI	
			Total Population						Roads						
				SC	ST	MBC	BC	Others	No. of Roads	Earthen	Conditions	BT & WBM	Conditions	CC Road	BT & WBM
1	Kovilpatti	165	837	523	0	39	275	0	1	1	fully damaged				
2	Thiruvalluvar Nagar	80	414	198	0	0	216	0							
3	Pilakkavai	30	96	0	0	0	96	0	1	1	fully damaged				
4	Puliyur	32	98	0	0	0	98	0							
5	Chinnapallam	142	316	57	0	0	259	0	2	1	fully damaged			1	1
6	Barathi Annanagar	65	226	32	102	31	61	0						1	
7	Kurunchi Nagar	591	2065	1509	0	0	556	0							
8	Attuvampatti	112	474	176	0	48	250	0	1					1	
9	Valaikattu Otai	506	976	121	0	0	855	0							
10	Mattupatti	200	710	33	0	31	646	0							
11	Uppuparaimethu	201	631	499	0	0	132	0	1			1	fully damaged	1	
12	Paraipatti	45	176	41	0	0	135	0	2	1	fully damaged			1	
13	Peythuparai	329	1074	261	0	60	753	0	2			1	partly damaged		
14	Kannikkadu	23	43	0	0	0	43	0							
15	Nagaramarathu Alai	10	38	0	0	0	38	0	1	1	fully damaged				
16	Ganeshapuram	72	249	103	0	47	99	0	2					1	
17	Pallangi	108	402	39	0	56	307	0	1			1	partly damaged		
18	Annai Sathya Colony	253	974	507	0	71	396	0							
19	Villpatti	407	2109	790	0	316	1003	0	2	1	fully damaged				
20	Vellaparai	74	198	53	0	0	145	0							
21	Barathi Nagar	29	94	0	0	0	94	0	1	1	fully damaged				
22	Attuvampatti Colony	133	661	158	0	99	404	0						1	
23	Gurusamypallam	62	239	0	0	0	239	0							
24	Pallangi	137	363	74	76	72	141	0							
25	Perumpallam	90	162	72	0	0	90	0							
26	Anna Ramasamy Nagar	312	732	48	0	0	684	0	2			2	fully damaged	1	
	Total	4208	14357	5294	178	870	8015	0	19	7		5		8	1

Improvement through THAI

There are fifteen earthen roads in this panchayat area. Hence under THAI scheme nine cement concrete roads have been provided to replace the earthen roads which are fully damaged and connecting more than two habitation important locations like school and PDS shops. BT road is being provided only to the newly emerging habitations and commercial complexes.

Status of Burial/Funeral Ground

The burial and funeral facility is available in 14 out of 26 habitations. In all the 14 burial grounds, there is no burial stage. But three waiting sheds are available. There is no compound wall, no CC path in the above grounds. In one burial ground (Barathi Annanagar), the drinking water and light facility are not available. Seven burial grounds have no access road. Yet basic facilities are yet to be provided. Public demanded the following basic facilities in the burial/funeral ground: funeral platform, compound wall, lights, water supply, waiting hall and CC passage road up to funeral platform and approach roads.

Improvement through THAI

There are 24 burial grounds in 19 hamlets but with limited facilities. At hilly area finding out a suitable government owned site for burial ground is the challenging task. At Peithuparai habitation, the burial ground is located at the lower side of a hillock. Moreover, it is a barrowed land. Villagers had a fear over the possibility of mud-sliding during the rainy season. There is no other site. Hence under THAI, a retaining wall was approved to ensure the safety of the site of the burial ground. Steps to climb up to the platform have been provided; street lights and water supply have also been provided. Public of this remote village, feel happy as the safety and strength of the burial ground site was ensured. People are extremely happy over the facilities provided under this scheme.

Building Facilities

There are 12 Primary Schools, one Middle School and one High School in this village panchayat. Out of 12 schools, eight schools

Sl. No.	Name of the Village	Total Household	POPULATION						BUILDINGS								
			Total Population						Burial Ground								THAI
				SC	ST	MBC	BC	Others	No. of BG	Burial Stage	Waiting shed	Retaining Wall	CC Path	Drinking Water	Light	Approach Road	
1	Kovilpatti	165	837	523	0	39	275	0	1							1	
2	Thiruvalluvar Nagar	80	414	198	0	0	216	0	1								
3	Pilakkavai	30	96	0	0	0	96	0	1								
4	Puliyur	32	98	0	0	0	98	0	1								
5	Chinnapallam	142	316	57	0	0	259	0	2							1	
6	Barathi Annanagar	65	226	32	102	31	61	0	2					1	1		
7	Kurunchi Nagar	591	2065	1509	0	0	556	0	1								
8	Attuvampatti	112	474	176	0	48	250	0	1								
9	Valaikattu Otai	506	976	121	0	0	855	0	1								
10	Mattupatti	200	710	33	0	31	646	0									
11	Uppuparaimethu	201	631	499	0	0	132	0	1		1					1	
12	Paraipatti	45	176	41	0	0	135	0									
13	Peythuparai	329	1074	261	0	60	753	0	1							1	1
14	Kannikkadu	23	43	0	0	0	43	0									
15	Nagaramarathu Alai	10	38	0	0	0	38	0									
16	Ganeshapuram	72	249	103	0	47	99	0	1								

17	Pallangi	108	402	39	0	56	307	0	2							1	
18	Annai Sathya Colony	253	974	507	0	71	396	0									
19	Villpatti	407	2109	790	0	316	1003	0	3		2					1	
20	Vellaparai	74	198	53	0	0	145	0	1								
21	Barathi Nagar	29	94	0	0	0	94	0									
22	Attuvampatti Colony	133	661	158	0	99	404	0	1								
23	Gurusamypallam	62	239	0	0	0	239	0									
24	Pallangi	137	363	74	76	72	141	0	1							1	
25	Perumpallam	90	162	72	0	0	90	0	1								
26	Anna Ramasamy Nagar	312	732	48	0	0	684	0	1								
	Total	4208	14357	5294	178	870	8015	0	24	0	3			1	1	7	1

have drinking water facility and four schools have electricity facility and three schools have kitchen shed and toilet facilities are available. School students have demanded cycle stand and play ground.

4. Kasavanampatti Village Panchayat

Kasavanampatti is a small village having 11 hamlets. BC is the numerically higher caste, SC is in the second order and MBC population is very small in number. The total population is 4175. In this village panchayat, out of total 1225 houses, RC houses are 173 and other types of houses are 284.

Status of Water Supply

Status of water supply in the village Panchayat during summer is not adequate due to poor storage in the water sources namely wells, bore wells and mini power pumps. There are 15 OHTs in this village panchayat and out of 15 OHT 7 bore-wells supply of drinking water through 285 public taps and 178 household connections are in operation. Barring other bore-wells are working in good conditions. There are 12 hand pumps available for water supply and out of 12, six HP are in working condition. Out of 6, two are used for drinking water purpose. One mini power pump is also used for water supply in this village panchayat.

Improvement through THAI

Under THAI scheme four mini power pumps have been provided at four hamlets where water distribution was uneven. Seven pipeline extension works have been undertaken at six hamlets to reach unconnected area. Among the six hamlets at Kasavanampatti, the mother village pipeline extension works in two streets and at four hamlets it was in one street at each hamlet have been provided.

Status of Street light

Street light facilities at Kasavanampatti village Panchayat is somewhat in improved condition in 11 habitations. There are 215 street lights provided and out of that 180 tube lights in all villages, 21 ordinary pulps in five villages, 12 sodium vapour lamps in seven villages and the remaining two mercury lamps in Bothinayakkanpatti habitation.

Sl. No.	Name of the Village	Total Household	Total Population	DRINKING WATER																
						Mini Power Pump (MPP)					THAI		Hand Pump					THAI	Over Head Tank	
				Public Tap	House connection	Total	Fit for Drinking	Not Fit for Drinking	Not working	Conditions	New Bore Well	New MPP	Total	Fit for Drinking	Not Fit for Drinking	Not working	Conditions		No. of OHT	Conditions
1	Pothinayakkanpatti	110	338	35	25	2		2					0	1					1	partly damaged
2	Govindapuram	64	215	25	6	1	1					1	2						1	partly damaged
3	Kuyavanayakkanpatti	137	405	32	13	1		1				1	1	1					1	partly damaged
4	Karattupatti	45	210	15	3	1		1	1	bore dry			1	1					1	partly damaged
5	Kittampatti	23	165	15	4	1	1						1	1					2	partly damaged
6	Koralampatti	110	358	27	8	2		2	1	bore dry		1	1	1					2	partly damaged
7	Kurumbapatti	164	540	26	4	3	3					1	1						2	partly damaged
8	Malayandipattipuram	78	310	15	4	1		1					0						1	partly damaged
9	Pappankulam	141	414	32	15	2		2					2	1	1				1	partly damaged
10	Kasavanampatti	287	890	40	87	2		2	1	bore repair			2	2					1	partly damaged
11	Thirumalpatti	66	330	23	3	3	2	1					1						1	partly damaged
	Total	1225	4175	285	172	19	7	12	3				12	8	1	0			14	

Sl. No.	Name of the Village	Total Household	Total Population	STREET LIGHTS	
				No. of SL	THAI
1	Pothinayakkanpatti	110	338	20	1
2	Govindapuram	64	215	14	
3	Kuyavanayakkanpatti	137	405	24	2
4	Karattupatti	45	210	5	1
5	Kittampatti	23	165	10	
6	Koralampatti	110	358	20	1
7	Kurumbapatti	164	540	34	
8	Malayandipattipuram	78	310	21	
9	Pappankulam	141	414	24	1
10	Kasavanampatti	287	890	27	3
11	Thirumalpatti	66	330	16	
	Total	1225	4175	215	9

Improvement through THAI

There were nine street lights provided under THAI scheme at six hamlets. Kasavanampatti being a mother village as well as a spiritual centre three street lights were provided; at Kuyavanayakkanpatti two lights and in the remaining four hamlets one at each hamlet was provided. Along with the distance of streets other factors like public places like temple, school and shops and establishment located at hamlets were also taken into consideration while taking decision.

Status of Road Works

Sl. No.	Name of the Village	POPULATION		ROAD WORKS					
				Roads					THAI
		Total Households	Total Population	No. of Roads	Earthen	Conditions	BT & WBM	Conditions	BT & WBM
1	Pothinayakkanpatti	110	338						1
2	Govindapuram	64	215						
3	Kuyavanayakkanpatti	137	405						
4	Karattupatti	45	210						
5	Kittampatti	23	165						

(*Contd.*)

6	Koralampatti	110	358						1
7	Kurumbapatti	164	540						
8	Malayandipattipuram	78	310						
9	Pappankulam	141	414						
10	Kasavanampatti	287	890						1
11	Thirumalpatti	66	330						
	Total	**1225**	**4175**						**3**

Improvement through THAI

Three BT roads were provided under THAI scheme. Preference was given to BT roads as it served as a multi-purpose, connecting burial ground, nearby hamlets and agricultural lands. Such a way public discussed and put-forth their demands during the survey, it is learnt.

Status of Burial Ground

Sl. No.	*Name of the Village*	*Total Households*	*BUILDINGS*									
				Burial Ground								*THAI*
			Total Population	*No. of BG*	*Burial Stage*	*Waiting shed*	*Retaining Wall*	*CC Path*	*Drinking Water*	*Light*	*Approach Road*	*Burial Ground*
1	Pothinayakkanpatti	110	338									
2	Govindapuram	64	215									
3	Kuyavanayakkanpatti	137	405									
4	Karattupatti	45	210									
5	Kittampatti	23	165									
6	Koralampatti	110	358									
7	Kurumbapatti	164	540									
8	Malayandipattipuram	78	310									
9	Pappankulam	141	414									
10	Kasavanampatti	287	890									1
11	Thirumalpatti	66	330									
12	Total	1225	4175									1

Improvement through THAI

At Kasavanampatti village with all facilities at burial ground have been improved. It is a demand put forth by the villagers long ago.

PUDUKOTTAI DISTRICT

1. Thulayanur Village Panchayat

(1) Total number of habitations: 26; (2) Total population of the village Panchayat: 6229; (3) Total number of houses: 1270.

Status of Water Supply

The village panchayat has 145 public taps, 227 house service connections. Out of 26 habitations, 22 habitations have got adequate drinking water supply (above 40 liters). In 6 habitations provision of water is below 40 liters per day. There are 16 mini power pumps and 15 hand pumps in the panchayat. All mini and hand pumps are functioning well and in working condition.

Improvement through THAI

Out of 24 habitations in the panchayat supply of water less than 40 liters is at six habitations only. Under THAI scheme six mini power pumps were provided in four habitations. Preference is given to these four habitations due to non-availability of any mini power pump. (In Thulayanaur four mini power pumps are already functioning but water supply is inadequate as the habitation has more population).

Status of Street Lights

There are 252 tube lights, 4 sodium vapour lamps and one mercury lamp and totally 257 lights in the entire village panchayat. Public demanded 194 additional street lights. More demand is from Samathuvapuram (29), Kulathupatti (13), Chinnakulathuvayal (13), Adukkampatti (16) Malaikudipatti (12) and Besant Nagar (10). Public reported that the distance of street at their habitation is more than 300 meters. At remaining habitations, the demand of new street light is in single digit.

Sl. No.	Name of the Village	Total Household	Total Population	Public Tap	House connection	DRINKING WATER														
						Mini Power Pump (MPP)					THAI		Hand Pump					THAI	Over Head Tank	
						Total	Fit for Drinking	Not Fit for Drinking	Not working	Conditions	New Bore Well	New MPP	Total	Fit for Drinking	Not Fit for Drinking	Not working	Conditions		No. of OHT	Conditions
1	Kunnathupatti	14	77	0	0	1							0							
2	Mavoor	89	547	14	0	0					3		1							
3	Thulayanur	204	1282	22	36	4					1		1							
4	Kulathupatti	76	376	5	1	2					1		0							
5	Puduparali	10	39	0	0	0							1							
6	Pesant nagar	19	87	3	4	0					1		1							
	Total	412	2408	44	41	7	0	0	0		6		4	0	0	0			0	

Sl. No.	Name of the Village	Total Household	STREET LIGHTS		
			Total Population	No. of SL	THAI
1	Kunnathupatti	14	77	2	
2	Mavoor	89	547	10	
3	Thulayanur	204	1282	17	
4	Kulathupatti	76	376	17	2
5	Puduparali	10	39	2	1
6	Pesant Nagar	19	87	2	2
7	Adukkappatti	164	757	32	3
8	Ammapatti	25	90	6	3
9	Andakkudipatti	25	52	2	
10	Ayyanarpuram	25	117	4	
11	Settiyur	10	43	2	
12	Chinnakalluvayal	10	43	11	
13	Solathavayal	18	124	6	
14	Kollakattupatti	16	49	6	2
15	Malaikkudipatti	50	252	19	
16	Melaviduthi	27	112	6	
17	Mettupatti	31	154	6	
18	Munkithappatti	22	78	8	
19	Papathi Oorani	9	45	3	
20	Pankondanviduthi	14	61	2	
21	Samathuvapuram	100	332	24	
22	Sandanaviduthi	58	281	21	
23	Valayanvayal	106	469	10	3
24	Parali	90	389	24	
25	Periyakalluvayal	30	247	3	
26	Pudukudyiruppy	22	77	3	2
	Total	1242	6103	358	18

Improvement through THAI

During the survey more demand for street lights came from six habitations. Under THAI scheme, out of these six habitations at five habitations street lights were provided. Totally 18 street lights have been provided.

Status of Road Facility

As the habitations of Thulayanur village Panchayat are more in number and they located in faraway places they are connected with 39 earthen roads. Public requested to improve the condition of these roads as about 31 earthen roads were fully damaged. At Ammapatti, there is a cement concrete road but as it is partially damaged and hence public demanded to repair it.

Sl. No.	Name of the Village	Total Households	Total Population	ROAD WORKS						
				Roads					THAI	
				No. of Roads	Earthen	Conditions	BT & WBM	Conditions	CC Road	WBM & BT
1.	Kunnathupatti	14	77							
2.	Mavoor	89	547		2	partly damaged				1
3.	Thulayanur	204	1282		3	fully damaged				
4.	Kulathupatti	76	376		1	fully damaged				
5.	Puduparali	10	39		1	fully damaged			1	
6.	Pesant Nagar	19	87		1	fully damaged				
7.	Adukkappatti	164	757		6	fully damaged			1	
8.	Ammapatti	25	90		1	fully damaged				1
9.	Andakkudipatti	25	52		3	partly damaged				1
10	Ayyanarpuram	25	117		1	fully damaged				
11.	Settiyur	10	43							
12.	Chinnakalluvayal	10	43		2	fully damaged				
13.	Solathavayal	18	124		1	fully damaged				1
14.	Kollakattupatti	16	49							1
15.	Malaikkudipatti	50	252		1	fully damaged				
16.	Melaviduthi	27	112		2	fully damaged			1	
17.	Mettupatti	31	154		1	fully damaged			1	
18.	Munkithappatti	22	78		1	fully damaged			1	
19.	Papathi Oorani	9	45							
20.	Pankondanviduthi	14	61		1	fully damaged				
21.	Samathuvapuram	100	332		1	fully damaged				
22.	Sandanaviduthi	58	281		3	fully damaged			1	
23.	Valayanvayal	106	469							
24.	Parali	90	389		2	fully damaged				
25.	Periyakalluvayal	30	247		1	fully damaged				
26.	Pudukudyiruppy	22	77							
	Total	1264	6180	0	34		0	0	6	5

Improvement through THAI

There are more number of earthen roads at Thulayanur village panchayat. Under THAI scheme in 19 habitations various works have been carried out, and of which road works have been carried out (eight cement concrete roads and five BT roads) in 13 habitations. Preference was given to the habitations where more number of earthen roads are existed and the condition of these earthen roads are fully damaged. It is the significance of habitation-based planning by which real need and priority could be fairly done.

Status of Burial/Funeral Ground

The above facility is available in 24 habitations. But basic facilities are yet to be provided to all those places. Public requested to provide the following basic facilities in the burial/funeral ground: funeral platform, compound wall, lights, water supply, waiting hall and CC passage road up to funeral platform.

Sl. No.	Name of the Village	Total Households	Total Population	BUILDINGS											
				Burial Ground								THAI			
				No. of BG	Burial Stage	Waiting shed	Retaining Wall	CC Path	Drinking Water	Light	Approach Road	Burial Ground	Threshing Floor	Retaining wall	Pathing Gate
1	Kunnathupatti	14	77	1	0	0	0	0	0	0	1				
2	Mavoor	89	547	1	0	0	0	0	0	0	1	1			
3	Thulayanur	204	1282	2	0	0	0	0	0	0	2				
4	Kulathupatti	76	376	1	0	0	0	0	0	0	1			1	
5	Puduparali	10	39	0	0	0	0	0	0	0	0				
6	Pesant nagar	19	87	0	0	0	0	0	0	0	0				
7	Adukkappatti	164	757	1	0	0	0	0	0	0	1				
8	Ammapatti	25	90	1	0	0	0	0	0	0	1				
9	Andakkudipatti	25	52	1	0	0	0	0	0	0	1				1
10	Ayyanarpuram	25	117	1	0	0	0	0	0	0	1			1	
11	Settiyur	10	43	1	0	0	0	0	0	0	1				
12	Chinnakalluvayal	10	43	1	0	0	0	0	0	0	1				
13	Solathavayal	18	124	1	0	0	0	0	0	0	1		1		
14	Kollakattupatti	16	49	1	0	0	0	0	0	0	1				

(*Contd.*)

15	Malaikkudipatti	50	252	0	0	0	0	0	0	0	0				1
16	Melaviduthi	27	112	1	0	0	0	0	0	0	1				
17	Mettupatti	31	154	1	0	0	0	0	0	0	1				
18	Munkithappatti	22	78	1	0	0	0	0	0	0	1				
19	Papathi Oorani	9	45	1	0	0	0	0	0	0	1				
20	Pankondanviduthi	14	61	2	0	0	0	0	0	0	2				
21	Samathuvapuram	100	332	1	0	0	0	0	0	0	1				
22	Sandanaviduthi	58	281	1	0	0	0	0	0	0	1		1		1
23	Valayanvayal	106	469	1	0	0	0	0	0	0	1				
24	Parali	90	389												
25	Periyakalluvayal	30	247	1	0	0	0	0	0	0	1				
26	Pudukudyiruppy	22	77												
	Total	1264	6180	22	0	0	0	0	0	0	23	1*	2	2	3

*Burial ground with all facilities

Improvement through THAI

Under THAI scheme burial ground with all facilities were provided at Maavur. Maavur is the third thickly populated habitat of the village panchayat. Hence, preference was given to Maavur also other construction work two retaining wall, two floors and three number of bathing ghats have been provided.

2. Vagavasal Village Panchayat

Vagavasal is a larger village panchayat, having the population of 7813. There are 29 hamlets in the panchayat. It is a multi-caste village panchayat

Status of Water Supply

In 9 hamlets water supply is not adequate. The water supply is below 40 liters per day per head. In 15 hamlets water distribution is only below 10 liters per day. Only in remaining 5 hamlets water supply is more than adequate.

Sl. No	Name of the Village	Total Household	Total Population	Public Tap	DRINKING WATER																
					House connection	Mini Power Pump (MPP)				Conditions	THAI		Hand Pump					THAI	Over Head Tank		THAI
						Total	Fit for Drinking	Not Fit for Drinking	Not working		New Bore Well	New MPP	Total	Fit for Drinking	Not Fit for Drinking	Not working	Conditions		No. of OHT	Conditions	OHT
1	Ayyavayal	61	18	1	0	0							2								
2	Idayapatti	580	127	51	6	0						1	8								
3	Janakipatti	57	30	6	0	1							1								
4	Kalluvayal	24	11	1	0	0							1								
5	Rajapatti	921	171	30	7	1						1	2								
6	Thattampatti	216	62	13	0	0							3					1			
7	Viswakarmanagar	874	219	34	68	3							0								
8	Vagavasal	597	158	55	24	2							8								1
9	Kanthiranthanaya ki Amman Nagar	67	13	1	0	0						1	1								
	Total	3397	809	192	105	7						3	26					1			1

Improvement through THAI

During the survey it was reported that water distribution was not adequate at 17 habitations. Hence, during the implementation of THAI scheme more attention was given to ease out the issue of scarcity of water. Eight works (5 mini power pumps, one pipeline extension, one construction of OHT and provision of one hand pump) have been undertaken during the implementation of THAI scheme. Water scarcity was reported at many habitations. Hence, preference was given based on the following factors: population size, and the non-availability of water source (i.e. mini power pumps/hand pump).

Status of Street Lights

There are 234 tube lights, one vapour-light and 12 CFL lights and totally 247 street lights in the panchayat areas. Public demanded 97 new tube lights. 12 street lights at Rajapatti South Street, 12 street lights from 4th street of Viswakarma Nagar, one street light from Vaduganvayal and four lights from Kanthirantha Nayagi Amman Street came as demand in the entire panchayat area.

Sl. No.	*Name of the Village*	*Total Household*	*Total Population*	*STREET LIGHTS*		
				No. of SL	*Need*	*THAI*
1	Ayyavayal	61	18	3	7	
2	Idayapatti	580	127	25	5	
3	Janakipatti	57	30	5	2	
4	Kalluvayal	24	11	9	8	
5	Rajapatti	921	171	14	20	20
6	Thattampatti	216	62	11	1	
7	Viswakarmanagar	874	219	45	23	
8	Vagavasal	597	158	68	2	4
9	Kanthiranthanayaki Amman Nagar	67	13	3	7	7
10	Kedayapatti	96	434	90	4	
11	Vadugampatti	44	187	11	6	
12	Vaduganvayal	19	38	4	9	
13	Kandravayal	9	23	4	1	1
14	Arasan Nagar	4	12	7	1	
15	Ulaganathapuram	5	9	6	1	
	Total	3574	1512	305	97	32

Improvement through THAI

Under THAI scheme 32 new street lights have been provided at four hamlets. 20 tube lights have been provided at Rengapatti south street and west street and seven street lights have been provided at Sri Kanthiranthanayaki Nagar (extension area) and four lights have been provided at Vagavasal the mother village. Whatever have been demanded during the survey, under THAI scheme, all have been complied with.

Status of Roads

There are 7 BT roads, 14 earthen roads, 7 one layered metal roads and only 6 CC roads available at the village Panchayat. 9 earthen roads were partly damaged and one was fully damaged. All CC roads are also partly damaged. Public demanded 29 small culverts in 13 hamlets and repair the roads.

Improvement through THAI

Under THAI scheme, one CC road (at Rajapatti) and three BT roads were formed (at Vagavasal, at Edayapatti and at Ayyanvayal).

Status of Burial Ground

Improvement through THAI

At Janakipatti, needed facilities have been provided at the funeral ground. A retaining wall has been constructed at Rajapatti as per the demand of public during the survey for THAI scheme.

3. Viralur Village Panchayat

Viralur is a multicaste village panchayat with a population of 5914. There are 18 habitations with 1126 houses in the panchayat.

Status of Water Supply

In this panchayat there are 129 public taps and 155 house water service

Sl. No.	Name of the Village	Total Households	Total Population	ROAD WORKS								
				Roads							THAI	
				No. of Roads	Earthen	Conditions	CC Road	Conditions	BT & WBM	Conditions	CC Road	WBM & BT
1	Ayyavayal	61	18		1	partly damaged						1
2	Idayapatti	580	127									1
3	Janakipatti	57	30		1	partly damaged						
4	Kalluvayal	24	11			partly damaged						
5	Rajapatti	921	171		1	partly damaged	1	partly damaged			1	
6	Thattampatti	216	62		2	partly damaged	1	partly damaged				
7	Viswakarmanagar	874	219		2	partly damaged						
8	Vagavasal	597	158		1	partly damaged	1	partly damaged				
9	Kanthiranthanayaki Amman Nagar	67	13		1	fully damaged						
10	Kedayapatti	96	434				2	partly damaged				1
11	Vadugampatti	44	187		1							
12	Vaduganvayal	19	38									
13	Kandravayal	9	23									
14	Arasan Nagar	4	12									
15	Ulaganathapuram	5	9									
16	Vijayapuram	41	129				1	partly damaged				
	Total	3615	1641	0	10		6		0		1	3

Sl. No.	Name of the Village	Total House hold	Total Population	BUILDINGS								
				Burial Ground								THAI
				No. of BG	Burial Stage	Waiting shed	Retaining Wall	CC Path	Drinking Water	Light	Approach Road	
1	Ayyavayal	61	18									
2	Idayapatti	580	127	1	1	0	0	0	0	0	0	
3	Janakipatti	57	30	1	1	0	0	0	0	0	1	1
4	kalluvayal	24	11									
5	Rajapatti	921	171	1	1	0	0	0	0	0	1	
6	Thattampatti	216	62	1	1	0	0	0	0	0	1	
7	Viswakarmanagar	874	219									
8	Vagavasal	597	158									
9	Kanthiranthanayaki Amman Nagar	67	13									
10	Kedayapatti	96	434	1	1	0	0	0	0	0	0	
11	Vadugampatti	44	187	1	1	0	0	0	0	0	1	
12	Vaduganvayal	19	38									
13	Kandravayal	9	23									
14	Arasannagar	4	12									
15	Ulaganathapuram	5	9									
16	Vijayapuram	41	129	1	1	0	0	0	0	0	0	
	Total	3615	1641	7	7	0	0	0	0	0	4	1

connections. In 12 streets water supply is below 40 liters per day. In seven habitations water supply is between 20 to 40 liters and at one habitation it is very low between 11 to 20 liters. At one street of Pallanatham ACS Nagar there is no provision for water supply. The households used to fetch water from the nearby street. The households of 15 habitations are receiving above 40 liters per day even during summer. But, among the above habitations in 5 streets water supply is below 40 liters during summer.

DRINKING WATER																			
Sl. No.	Name of the Village			Mini Power Pump (MPP)								Hand Pump						Over Head Tank	
		Total Households	Total Population	Public Tap	House Connection	Total	Fit for Drinking	Not Fit for Drinking	Not Working	Conditions	THAI	Total	Fit for Drinking	Not Fit for Drinking	Not Working	Conditions	THAI	No. of OHT	Conditions
1	Kaaniyaalampatti	79	353	17	28	1					1	1					-		
2	Viralur	137	546	20	22	1					1						-		
3	Pallarnatham	8	35	0	0						1						-		
4	Purasankaalpatti	17	69	3	4	1					-						-		
5	Pillampatti	44	176	9	2						-						-		
6	Sankampatti	43	238	8	7						-						-		
7	Kotikaalpatti	122	578	17	3						2						1		
8	Nathakadu	10	82	3	2						-	1					-		
9	Vadakkipatti	60	240	13	9	1					-						-		
10	Ponnikulathupatti	7	25	1	0						-						1		
11	Kumaradinatham	36	130	0	0						1						-		
12	Iramakkavundanpatti	149	746	10	18	1					-	8					-		

DRINKING WATER																			
Sl. No.	Name of the Village			Mini Power Pump (MPP)								Hand Pump						Over Head Tank	
		Total Households	Total Population	Public Tap	House Connection	Total	Fit for Drinking	Not Fit for Drinking	Not Working	Conditions	THAI	Total	Fit for Drinking	Not Fit for Drinking	Not Working	Conditions	THAI	No. of OHT	Conditions
13	Muthampatti	27	106	4	3	0					0	2					0		
14	Medukattampatti	14	56	0	0	1										–			
15	Narchandupatti	38	148	2	0	2						2							
16	Parapatti	22	78	4	4							1							
17	Pagavanpatti	64	256	6	9														
	Total	813	3606	101	95	8					6	12					2		

Improvement through THAI

Kaniyalampatti is one of the seven hamlets where water supply is below 40 liters. There is only one mini-power pump and one hand pump are in operation. Under THAI scheme six mini power pumps have been provided in five hamlets one at each hamlet except Kodikalpatti where there are five streets with total population of 578. Moreover, there is no house service connection. At Ponnikulathupatti, one hand pump was provided under THAI scheme. At this hamlet also water supply is below 40 liters per day per person.

Status of Street lights

There are 78 tube lights, 6 CFL and totally 84 lights in the panchayat area. In order to reduce the distance between street lights public demanded new street lights. Total number of demand for tube lights are 103. The households demanded additional street lights.

Sl. No.	*Name of the Village*	*Total Households*	*Total Population*	*Street Lights*		
				No. of SL	*Need*	*THAI*
1	Kaaniyaalampatti	79	353	1	6	
2	Viralur	137	546	12	19	
3	Pallarnatham	8	35		7	
4	Purasankaalpatti	17	69	3	3	
5	Pillampatti	44	176	10		3
6	Sankampatti	43	238			
7	Kotikaalpatti	122	578	14	8	8
8	Nathakadu	10	82			
9	Vadakkipatti	60	240	7	17	
10	Ponnikulathupatti	7	25	1	12	
11	Kumaradinatham	36	130			
12	Iramakkavundanpatti	149	746	11	20	9
13	Muthampatti	27	106			
14	Medukattampatti	14	56	4	4	
15	Narchandupatti	38	148			
16	Parapatti	22	78	6	6	
17	Pagavanpatti	64	256	15	4	
	Total	877	3862	84	106	20

Improvement through THAI

Twenty street lights were provided under THAI scheme at Pallarnatham (3), Kodikkapatti (8) and Ramagoundanpatti (9). Earlier at Theppakulam at Keelatheru of Ramagoundanpatti there was no street light. Hence, new street lights were provided under THAI scheme.

Status of Road works

There are 18 earthen roads in the panchayat areas. Only at two roads repair was done during 1999/2010. Seven earthen roads are partly damaged and 10 earthen roads are damaged fully. Public demanded the improvement of roads. Drainage facility is available only in 2 streets. In 16 streets people demanded drainage facilities. There are 11 CC roads without drainage facility in the panchayat area. Among them 8 CC roads are fully damaged. Hence people demanded the repair works of the damaged roads or with new CC roads.

Improvement through THAI

Under THAI scheme four new CC roads have been provided at Viralur, Kotikkalpatti, Nathakadu and Ramagoundanpatti one each. Repair work is not permitted under THAI. At Vadakkipatti one BT road was provided. Earlier, the road was single layered metal road. As the condition of the road was fully damaged, new BT road was formed under THAI scheme.

Out of 19 habitations, in 6 habitations there is no burial ground. The villagers of 5 habitations except pirate habitations, they buried the dead bodies at their own grounds. Facilities like water supply, street lights, funeral platform, compound wall, CC road, approach road have been demanded. There are approach roads available for 14 funeral grounds.

Improvement through THAI

Under THAI scheme at six burial grounds the needed facilities have been provided. Though there are 13 burial grounds, preference was given to six hamlets where the population is more than other hamlets.

Sl. No.	Name of the Village	Total Households	Total Population	ROAD WORKS								
				Roads							THAI	
				No. of Roads	Earthen	Conditions	CC Road	Conditions	BT & WBM	Conditions	CC Road	WBM & BT
1	Kaaniyaalampatti	79	353	5	2	1 fully damaged	2	1 fully 1 partly	1	single layer		
2	Viralur	137	546	6	4	3 fully 1 partly	2	partly damaged			1	
3	Pallarnatham	8	35	5	2	1 partly 1 fully	3	partly damaged				
4	Purasankaalpatti	17	69	2	1	partly damaged			1	BT road		
5	Pillampatti	44	176	2	1	fully damaged			1	BT road		
6	Sankampatti	43	238	4	1	fully damaged			3	2 single layer 1 BT		
7	Kotikaalpatti	122	578	4	2	1 fully damaged 1 partly damaged	1	partly damaged	2	1 BT road 1 single layer	1	
8	Nathakadu	10	82	1	1	fully damaged					1	
9	Vadakkipatti	60	240	2					2	single layer		1
10	Ponnikulathupatti	7	25	1	1	partly damaged						
11	Kumaradinatham	36	130									
12	Iramakkavundanpatti	149	746	3	1	fully damaged	1	fully damaged	1	BT road	1	
13	Muthampatti	27	106	2	1	partly damaged	1	fully damaged				
14	Medukattampatti	14	56									
15	Narchandupatti	38	148									
16	Parapatti	22	78	1	1	partly damaged						
17	Pagavanpatti	64	256	1			1	partly damaged				
	Total	877	3862	39	18		11		11		4	1

Sl. No.	Name of the Village	Total Households	Total Population	Burial Ground								THAI
				No. of BG	Burial Stage	Waiting Shed	Retaining Wall	CC Path	Drinking Water	Light	Approach Road	
1	Kaaniyaalampatti	79	353	1							1	1
2	Viralur	137	546	1							1	1
3	Pallarnatham	8	35	1							1	1
4	Purasankaalpatti	17	69	1							1	1
5	Pillampatti	44	176	1								1
6	Sankampatti	43	238	1							1	1
7	Kotikaalpatti	122	578	2	1	1	1	1	1	0	1	
8	Nathakadu	10	82									
9	Vadakkipatti	60	240	1							1	
10	Ponnikulathupatti	7	25	1								
11	Kumaradinatham	36	130								1	
12	Iramakkavundanpatti	149	746	1							1	
13	Muthampatti	27	106								1	
14	Medukattampatti	14	56								1	
15	Narchandupatti	38	148	1							1	
16	Parapatti	22	78								1	
17	Pagavanpatti	64	256	1							1	
	Total	877	3862	13	1	1	1	1	1	0	14	6

4. Mimisal Village Panchayat

It is a medium sized village Panchayat located at sea shore area—of East Coast Road. It is a multi-caste village Panchayat. Total population of the Panchayat is 2926. There are about 21 habitations and number of total houses is 754. There are 6 hamlets in this panchayat.

Status of Water Supply

There are 49 public taps and 47 house service connections in this panchayat. Water is not adequate to distribute to all habitations. In 19 habitations, the distribution of water is below 20 liters per day per head. Water scarcity is severe during the summer season. Once in two days only water was supplied. Non-availability of hand pumps and mini-pump systems added the crisis. 13 habitations are severely affected. In Alathur, Kammaikarai Kudiyiruppu, Chatirampatinam, V.O.C. Nagar and Mimisal hamlets supply of water is below 13 liters per day per head.

Improvement through THAI

During the survey it was reported that water supply at all 13 habitations was less than 40 liters per day per person. During the implementation of THAI scheme, pipeline extension works (8) at six hamlets were carried out. Mimisal being the sea-shore area safety water is the issue. It needs a special project to ensure adequate water supply in all 13 habitations.

Status of Road

There are 33 earthen roads in this panchayat area and of which 28 are in fully damaged condition. Two CC roads are partly damaged in the panchayat area. Drainage facility is yet to be provided.

There are eight BT roads in the panchayat and of which only two roads are in good condition. Three BT roads are partly damaged and the remaining three are fully damaged. Of the four metal roads three roads are in good condition in this panchayat area.

DRINKING WATER																		
Sl. No.	Name of the Village	Total Households	Total Population			Mini Power Pump (MPP)					THAI		Hand Pump				Conditions	THAI
				Public Tap	House Connection	Total	Fit for Drinking	Not Fit for Drinking	Not Working	Conditions	Pipeline Extension	New MPP	Total	Fit for Drinking	Not Fit for Drinking	Not Working		
1	Alathur	68	335	1805	9						3							
2	Sathirampattinam	367	1320	4	10						1							
3	Thappankkottai	33	111															
4	Kanmaykkarai Kudieruppu	37	113	3	5						1							
5	Mimisal	509	1934	26	21													
6	Mimisal Kudieryppu	66	295															
7	Va. Vu.Si. Nagar	36	151	3	2						1							
8	Eambakkottai	43	179															
9	Muruginivayal	9	40															
	Total	1168	4478	1841	47						6							

Sl. No.	Name of the Village	Roads							THAI	
		No. of Roads	Earthen Road	Conditions	CC Road	Conditions	BT & WBM	Conditions	CC Road	BT & WBM
1	Alathur						1	fully damaged		1
2	Sathirampattinam	7	7	6 fully 1 partly					1	
3	Thappankkottai						2	fully damaged		
4	Kanmaykkarai Kudieruppu	1	1	fully damaged						1
5	Mimisal	10	10	8 fully 2 partly	1	partly damaged			1	
6	Mimisal Kudieryppu	7	7	fully damaged						1
7	Va. Vu.Si. Nagar	1	1	partly damaged	1	partly damaged				
8	Eambakkottai	4	4	fully damaged						
9	Muruginivayal	2	2	fully damaged						
	Total	32	32		2		3		2	3

Improved through THAI

Under THAI scheme two CC roads at Sathirapattinam and Mimisal were provided. Priority was given to these hamlets due to bad condition of existing BT roads and CC roads. Three BT roads have been provided at Alathur, Kammakarai Kudiyerppu, as the existing BT roads were two fully damaged and one partly damaged.

Status of Street Lights

There are 47 tube lights, 134 CFL and 4 Sodium Vapour lamps in the panchayat. Being located at sea-shore area at a tail end fluctuation of voltage is frequent which resulted in frequent power failures and power cuts. Hence, the public demanded the high powered transformer. Public demanded 125 new street lights. There is no lighting facility at Mimisal (main village) habitation namely sea-shore street and Bharathi Nagar.

Sl. No.	*Name of the Village*	*Total Households*	*Total Population*	*No. of SL*	*Need*	*THAI*
1	Alathur	68	335	14	33	3
2	Sathirampattinam	367	1320	48	17	
3	Thappankkottai	33	111	5	8	1
4	Kanmaykkarai Kudieruppu	37	113	2	11	1
5	Mimisal	509	1934	15	29	
6	Mimisal Kudieryppu	66	295	21	17	
7	Va. Vu.Si. Nagar	36	151	7	1	
8	Eambakkottai	43	179			
9	Muruginivayal	9	40	4	2	
10	S.P. Madam	45	199	63	7	
	Total	1213	4677	179	125	5

Improvement through THAI

Five street lights have been provided under THAI scheme. Three at Alathur, one each at Thappankottai and Kanmaikarai Kudiyeruppu have been provided.

Status of Burial Ground Facility

There are totally 22 burial grounds at these village panchayats. And the highest number of burial ground is at Alathur, 7 habitations funeral/ burial grounds are in seven habitations. But basic facilities are not available in all the grounds. At Embakkottai two burial grounds but facilities are yet to be provided. Public demanded funeral platform, waiting hall, compound wall, water supply and lighting facilities in all 22 grounds. They also demanded approach roads for all funeral grounds. Approach road at Allathur are 5 in number but all are earthen roads, needs improvement.

Sl. No.	Name of the Village	Burial Ground								THAI
		No. of BG	Burial Stage	Waiting shed	Retaining Wall	CC Path	Drinking Water	Light	Approach Road	Burial Ground
1	Alathur	7	0	0	0	0	0	0	7	1
2	Sathirampattinam	2	0	0	0	0	0	0	0	
3	Thappankkottai	1	0	0	0	0	0	0	0	
4	Kanmaykkarai Kudieruppu	1	0	0	0	0	0	0	0	
5	Mimisal	2	0	0	0	0	0	0	0	
6	Mimisal Kudieryppu	2	0	0	0	0	0	0	0	
7	Va. Vu.Si. Nagar	1	0	0	0	0	0	0	0	
8	Eambakkottai	2	0	0	0	0	0	0	0	
9	Muruginivayal	1	0	0	0	0	0	0	0	
10	S.P. Madam	3	0	0	0	0	0	0	0	
	Total	22	0	0	0	0	0	0	7	1

Improvement through THAI

At Alathur one burial ground has been improved with all facilities. One culvert has also been constructed.

VILLUPURAM DISTRICT

1. Singanur Village Panchayat

Singanur is a medium sized village panchayat having three hamlets namely Singanur Puthiya Colony, Singanur Old Colony and Singanur. It has 29 streets. Though it is a multi-caste village panchayat, majority is SC. MBC, BC and ST are the remaining communities in the gram panchayat. The percentage of SC among the total population is 79.24. In respect of status of their housing condition, it is found that out of 726 houses, 269 houses are hutments, occupied by SC community. From this statistics one can understand the economic status of SC families. There is no toilet facility in 50 per cent of houses. It is noted that special drive is very much needed on 'Swachh Bharat' in this panchayat.

Status of Water Supply

Distribution of water supply to the villagers was done satisfactorily. Distribution of water supply per head per day is adequate in all three hamlets. Severe scarcity of water is not reported after the provision of OHT by TWAD in all three hamlets one each during early 2000. There are 69 public taps and 118 house service connections in this gram panchayat. There are 9 mini power pumps and the water is fit to drink as it is tested.

There are seven hand pumps in operation in the panchayat. But four hand pumps are not functioning due to want of some minor repair and proper maintenance. Hence, public demanded repairing of two bore wells, and the motors. There are no Rain Water Harvest (RWH) arrangements near the water bodies.

Considering the severe scarcity of water due to failure of monsoon consequently for past three years, RWH system has to be established wherever possible so that each drop of water is successfully harvested and stored.

Improvement through THAI

At this village Panchayat among all three hamlets, distribution of water supply was adequate during the survey. But due to lack of rain, the householders faced water scarcity. During the implementation of

Sl. No.	Name of the Village	DRINKING WATER																							
									Mini Power Pump								Hand Pump						Over Head Tank		
		Total Households	Total Population	SC	ST	MBC	BC	Others	Public Tap	House Connection	Total	Fit for Drinking	Not Fit for Drinking	Not Working	Conditions	THAI	Total	Fit for Drinking	Not Fit for Drinking	Not Working	Conditions	THAI	No. of OHT	Condi-tions	THAI
1	Singanur New Colony	220	1243	1243	0	0	0	0	19	64	3	3		3	1 pipeline 1 Motor 1 borewell		3	3		3	3 Hand Pump 3 borewell		1	Good	1
2	Singanur	140	825	0	23	696	106	0	30	0	3	0				2	1	1		1			1	Good	
3	Singanur Old Colony	357	2018	1995	0	0	23	0	20	54	6	6		2	1 borewell 1 Motor		3	3		2	1 Hand pump 1 borewell		1	Good	

THAI, at Singanur more numbers of households are in the hamlet. Two mini power pumps and one OHT was constructed, because more number of house connections are only in that panchayat area.

Status of Street light

There are 130 lights available at streets and other public places. Public demanded additional street lights.

Sl. No.	Name of the Village	Total Households	Total Population						STREET LIGHTS							
				SC	ST	MBC	BC	Others	Tube	CFL	Sodium	HML	Solar	No. of SL	Need	THAI
1	Singanur New Colony	220	1243	1243	0	0	0	0	23	22	0	0	0	45		6
2	Singanur	140	825	0	23	696	106	0	2	12	12	0	0	26		0
3	Singanur Old Colony	357	2018	1995	0	0	23	0	8	51	0	0	0	59		4
	Total	**717**	**4086**	**3238**	**23**	**696**	**129**	**0**	**33**	**85**	**12**	**0**	**0**	**130**		**10**

Improvement through THAI

At the mother village Singanur status of street lights facility is adequate. Under THAI, 10 street lights were provided at the SC hamlets Singanur old colony (4) and Singanur New Colony (6) where number of street lights are less than new colony.

Status of Road Works

There are 29 streets in this village panchayat. In all these streets drainage facility is not available. Out of 29 only at two streets the surface of road is in good condition, and the condition of 9 streets CC roads are reported as partly damaged whereas condition of 18 roads are fully damaged. Hence, public demanded CC roads where fully damaged.

Improvement through THAI

There are 20 streets and the surface of the 18 street is fully damaged.

Sl. No.	Name of the Village	Total Household	Total Population	SC	ST	MBC	BC	Others	ROAD WORKS: No. of Roads	Earthen	Conditions	CC Road	Conditions	BT & WBM	Conditions	THAI: CC Road	THAI: WBM & BT
1	Singanur New Colony	220	1243	1243	0	0	0	0	9			9	2 partly 7 fully damaged			1	
2	Singanur	140	825	0	23	696	106	0	6			6	4 partly 1 fully damaged			1	
3	Singanur Old Colony	357	2018	1995	0	0	23	0	14			14	3 partly 10 fully damaged			1	
	Total	717	4086	3238	23	696	129	0	29			29				3	

Hence during the implementation of THAI three CC roads one at each hamlet was provided.

Status of Buildings Belongs to Government/Local Bodies

Totally there are 10 buildings and all of them are having RCC roofing. Facilities like EB connection, drinking water, toilets and compound wall are demanded by the public. The primary school is functioning at Singanur, and important facilities like drinking water, EB service connection, toilet, kitchen shed have been demanded by the public.

Status of Burial/Funeral Ground

Burial ground is in all three hamlets. In respect of basic amenities provided at burial ground, Singanur New Colony burial ground needs such facilities. At remaining two hamlets platform for burial and compound wall are available. Hence in all three burial grounds, water supply, electricity, public waiting shed, CC pavement, and approach road to the burial ground are the demands of villagers.

Improvement through THAI

Among all three hamlets, burial ground facility is available. But at Singanur Old Colony facilities are less than the remaining two hamlets. Under THAI at Singanur and Singanur Old Colony needed facilities have been provided there which two burial grounds are fully equipped with all facilities. At Singanur New Colony dovetailing was in attempt, the Panchayat President reported.

2. Thennamadevi Village Panchayat

Thennamadevi is a small village having four hamlets. Families of MBC are more in number next to SC. BC is less in number in this panchayat area. The total population is 2726. Out of total 629 houses, RC houses are 63 and other types of houses are 71. Toilet facility is available only in 15 houses.

Status of Water Facility

There are 70 public taps and 400 house service connections have

Sl. No.	Name of the Village	Total Households	POPULATION						BUILDINGS									
									Burial Ground									THAI
			Total Population	SC	ST	MBC	BC	Others	No. of BG	Burial Stage	Waiting shed	Retaining Wall	CC Path	Drinking Water	Light	Approach Road	
1	Singanur New Colony	220	1243	1243	0	0	0	0	1								
2	Singanur	140	825	0	23	696	106	0	1	1		1	1	1	1	1	1
3	Singanur Old Colony	357	2018	1995	0	0	23	0	1	1		1	1	1	1	1	1
	Total	717	4086	3238	23	696	129	0	3	2		2	2	2	2	2	2

been given to the public. But supply of water is not adequate in all public taps. Supply through HSC is more than adequate. Supply from mini power pump (10 in number) and from 13 hand pumps are inadequate. Out of total four hamlets Poothamedu hamlet families have 55 liters water per head. There are nine overhead tanks at Thennamadevimedu hamlets. The condition of one OHT is partly damaged, and another one is fully damaged at Thennamadevi hamlet. Public demanded there pairs of the OHT. Four pump rooms need repair as they are partly damaged. In respect of 11 mini power pumps available, only one power pump is available at Thennamadevi colony which supplies drinking water. Bore well of Poothamedu, Thennamedevi and T. Devimedu were dried and two needed repair. Water comes out from 17 Hand Pumps is consumable.

Improvement through THAI

There are four hamlets where water supply is more than adequate, i.e. above 200 liters per day per person. At Poothamedu, the number of house service connection is second to Thennamadevi where it is 137. Hence, under THAI one mini power pump was provided to Thennamadevi.

Status of Street Light

Totally, there are 207 lights. Of them tube lights are 152; sodium vapour lights are 41 and CFL are 14. Public demanded additional tube lights in all hamlets. There are twenty streets at Thennamadevi village panchayat. But drainage facility is not available in any street. The surface condition of 13 streets is good whereas CC road at five streets is partly damaged, the CC is fully damaged in two streets at Poothamedu.

Improvement through THAI

Under THAI four street lights were provided at Poothamedu where the distance of street is larger than the streets of remaining three hamlets.

Status of Road Works

At Thennamadevi, the mother village one BT road was provided under

Sl. No.	Name of the Village	DRINKING WATER																							
											Mini Power Pump						Hand Pump						Over Head Tank		
		Total Household	Total Population	SC	ST	MBC	BC	Others	Public Tap	House connection	Total	Fit for Drinking	Not Fit for Drinking	Not working	Conditions	THAI	Total	Fit for Drinking	Not Fit for Drinking	Not working	Conditions	THAI	No. of OHT	Conditions	THAI
1	Thennamadevi	142	640	0	0	640	0	0	16	137			2				4	1	4		2 dry		3	1 totally damaged	
2	Thennamadevi Colony	252	1226	1226	0	0	0	0	23	75		1	4				4	1	4		2 bore repair 1 dry		3	1 partially damaged	
3	Thennamadevi Medu	94	406	0	0	406	0	0	11	85			2				2		5		2 dry		1		
4.	Poothamedu	141	524	0	0	475	49	0	20	103	2		2				3	1	1				1		2
	Total	717	4086	1226	0	1521	49	0	70	400	2	1	10				13	1	14				8		2

Sl. No.	Name of the Village	Total Households	Total Population	POPULATION					STREET LIGHTS							
				SC	ST	MBC	BC	Others	Tube	CFL	Sodium	HML	Solar	No. of SL	Need	THAI
1	Thennamadevi	142	640	0	0	640	0	0	27	4	15	0	0	46		
2	Thennamadevi Colony	252	1226	1226	0	0	0	0	38	0	10	0	0	48		
3	Thennamadevi Medu	94	406	0	0	406	0	0	16	6	7	0	0	29		
4	Poothamedu	141	524	0	0	475	49	0	71	4	9	0	0	84		4
	Total	717	4086	1226	0	1521	49	0	152	14	41	0	0	207		4

THAI. It connects the main road where buses are flying. Also, road from the remaining hamlets also get connected through this newly formed BT road. As this BT road is essential, fund is not allotted to provide CC roads.

One BT road is available connecting Thennamadevi and Thennamadevi Poothamedu. The BT road was constructed in the year 1998/99 and the condition of the road is good.

Sl. No.	Name of the Village	Total Households	Total Population						ROAD WORKS								
									Roads							THAI	
				SC	ST	MBC	BC	Others	No. of Roads	Earthen	Condi-tions	CC Road	Condi-tions	BT & WBM	Condi-tions	CC Road	WBM & BT
1	Thennamadevi	142	640	0	0	640	0	0									1
2	Thennamadevi Colony	252	1226	1226	0	0	0	0									
3	Thennamadevi Medu	94	406	0	0	406	0	0									
4	Poothamedu	141	524	0	0	475	49	0									
	Total	717	4086	1226	0	1521	49	0									1

Status of Burial/Funeral Ground

Burial ground/funeral ground facilities are somewhat better compared to other panchayats. Burial ground is available in each hamlet. At three burial grounds funeral platform and waiting hall are not available. Compound wall is constructed at three hamlets. The need of approach road is not taken into consideration earlier. Hence, Thennamadevi Medu residents demanded all basic facilities to their hamlet.

Sl. No.	Name of the Village		POPULATION						BUILDINGS								
									Burial Ground								THAI
		Total Households	Total Population	SC	ST	MBC	BC	Others	No. of BG	Burial Stage	Waiting Shed	Retaining Wall	CC Path	Drinking Water	Light	Approach Road	
1	Thennamadevi	142	640	0	0	640	0	0	1	1	0	1	1	1	1	1	1
2	Thennamadevi Colony	252	1226	1226	0	0	0	0	1	1	0	1	1	1	1	1	1
3	Thennamadevi Medu	94	406	0	0	406	0	0	1	0	0	0	0	0	0	1	0
4	Poothamedu	141	524	0	0	475	49	0	1	1	0	1	1	1	1	1	1
	Total	**717**	**4086**	**1226**	**0**	**1521**	**49**	**0**	**4**	**3**	**0**	**3**	**3**	**3**	**3**	**4**	**3**

Improvement through THAI

At three hamlets (one SC hamlet and two MBC hamlets) all facilities have been provided at burial ground during the implementation of THAI.

Status of Government Buildings

There are 24 government buildings in the panchayat and of which 22 have CC roof, and 11 have EB connections. Toilet and water supply facilities are available at two buildings.

In respect of school, two primary schools and one higher secondary school are functioning in this panchayat. Cycle stand is not available in any school in the panchayat.

Status of Small Ponds

There are 6 small ponds but three ponds have been encroached. In-let channel is needed for two tanks and out-let channel is needed for five tanks.

Other Activities

Public play ground is available but youth group is not functioning. Youth prefer to play volley ball and cricket.

In respect of women welfare, there are 18 SHGs with 325 members were affiliated with Tamil Nadu Mahalir Thittam.

3. Bommaiyarpalayam Village Panchayat

Bommayarpalayam is located along the sea-shore of Bay of Bengal. It is in Vanur Union which is located in the border of Puducherry Union Territory. There are seven hamlets in this village panchayat. At the hamlet of Pillaichavadi fishermen colony is located. Yet another fishermen habitation is in Pommayarpalayam, the main village. There are 2363 houses in the panchayat and of which 558 are hutments. 1338 are cemented concrete houses and the remaining are mixed roofing houses. Regarding toilet facilities at 1100 houses toilets are available and in usage. In 1244 houses, there is no toilet facility.

Pommayarpalayam is a multi-caste village panchayat. Among the total population of 7524, MBCs are 6958 and SCs are 566. There is no family from BC and ST.

Status of Water Supply

Total number of public taps is 145. Total number of house service connections in this panchayat is 844. The highest number of HSC is at Kuyilampalayam hamlet, i.e. 259 where the total number of houses is 582. Supply of water is not even. Daily distribution of water is available at Kuyilampalayam, Bommayarpalayam, Pillaichavadi and fishermen colony of Bommayarpalayam. More than 40 liters per day per person is required, but Pillaichavadi is reported to have water scarcity. Hence, the public demanded improve in distribution of water.

It is noted that at Pillaichavadi only one mini power pump is provided. There is no hand pump even leading to severe scarcity in summer. Available 11 mini power pumps with sintex and 12 hand pumps are very much useful.

There are 14 OHTs of which 10 are functioning well, and 4 are in partly damaged condition. All OHTs are constructed by TWAD.

Sl. No.	Name of the Village	DRINKING WATER																							
											Mini Power Pump						Hand Pump						Over Head Tank		
		Total Household	Total Population	SC	ST	MBC	BC	Others	Public Tap	House connection	Total	Fit for Drinking	Not Fit for Drinking	Not working	Conditions	THAI	Total	Fit for Drinking	Not Fit for Drinking	Not working	Conditions	THAI	No. of OHT	Conditions	THAI
1.	Kuilampalayam	582	2332	0	0	2332	0	0	45	259	4	1				1	1						2	1 partly damage	
2.	Bommaiyarpalayam Colony	154	450	450	0	0	0	0	11	110	0						3								
3.	Pillaichavadi Fishermen Kudiyiruppu	187	431	0	0	431	0	0	15	54	0	1					1						1	1 partly damage	
4.	Bommayarpalayam Fishermen Kudiyiruppu	437	984	0	0	984	0	0	25	127	0	1					1						2		
5.	Pillaichavadi Village	1261	943	0	0	943	0	0	8	134	2						2								
6.	Pillachavadi colony	30	116	116	0	0	0	0	2	0	1					1	0						1		
7.	Bommaiyarpalayam	712	2268	0	0	2268	0	0	39	160	4	3	1		Borewell & motordamage		4						5	1 Partly damage	
	Total	2363	7524	566	0	6958	0	0	145	844	11	3	1			1	12						6		

Improvement through THAI

During the survey, the public of Pillaichavadi colony of Bommaiyarpalayam panchayat reported water scarcity. Hence, one mini power pump was provided under THAI. At Kuyilampalayam, house service connection is more in number (259) and the total number of houses is 582. More than 50 per cent of total houses have water service and so the supply of water was not even. Hence, under THAI one mini power pump was provided. Thus, the felt needs were identified by the families in respect of water supply was fulfilled.

Status of Street Lights

There are 447 tube lights, 18 CFL and 72 sodium vapour lamps, and totally 537 street lights.

Sl. No.	Name of the Village	Total Households	Total Population	POPULATION					STREET LIGHTS							
				SC	ST	MBC	BC	Others	Tube	CFL	Sodium	HML	Solar	No. of SL	Need	THAI
1.	Kuilampalayam	582	2332	0	0	2332	0	0	126	0	31	0	0	157		2
2.	Bommaiyarpalayam Colony	154	450	450	0	0			21	0	6	0	0	27		0
3.	Pillaichavadi Fishermen Kudiyiruppu	187	431	0	0	431			43	4	1	0	0	48		0
4.	Bommayarpalayam Fishermen Kudiyiruppu	437	984	0	0	984			75	6	0	0	0	81		0
5.	Pillaichavadi Village	1261	943	0	0	943			50	8	10	0	0	68		0
6.	Pillaichavadi Colony	30	116	116	0	0			5	0	0	0	0	5		0
7.	Bommaiyarpalayam	712	2268	0	0	2268			127	0	24	0	0	151		11
	Total	2363	7524	566	0	6958	0	0	447	18	72	0	0	537		13

Improvement through THAI

There was a demand for street lights in all the hamlets. But during the implementation of THAI, only at two hamlets namely Kuyilampalayam two street lights and Bommaiyarpalayam and

Bommaiyarpalayam Colony 11 street lights have been provided. Based on the population strength it was decided.

Status of Roads

There are 114 streets/lanes in this village panchayat. There is no drainage facility in this panchayat. The surfaces of 49 streets are in good condition, and in 52 streets surface is partially damaged and in 13 fully damaged.

There are 2 BT roads and 2 earthen roads. BT roads are in fully damaged condition and 2 mud roads are fully damaged.

Sl. No.	*Name of the Village*	*Total Households*	*Total Population*	*ROAD WORKS*								
				Roads							*THAI*	
				No. of Roads	*Earthen*	*Conditions*	*CC Road*	*Conditions*	*BT & WBM*	*Conditions*	*CC Road*	*WBM & BT*
1.	Kuilampalayam	582	2332	22			22	14 partly 1 totally damaged			1	1
2.	Bommaiyar-palayam Colony	154	450	8			8	3 partly 1 totally damaged			0	
3.	Pillaichavadi Fishermen Kudiyiruppu	187	431	12			12	5 partly damaged			0	
4.	Bommayar-palayam Fishermen Kudiyiruppu	437	984	12			12	2 partly 3 totally damaged			0	
5.	Pillaichavadi Village	1261	943	24			24	11 partly 5 totally damaged			2	
6.	Pillaichavadi Colony	30	116	1			1				1	
7.	Bommaiyar-palayam	712	2268	39	2	1 partly 1 fully damaged	35	17 partly 3 totally damaged	2	2 fully damaged	3	
	Total	2363	7524	118	2		114		2		7	1

Improvement through THAI

As public identified during the survey partly damaged earthen roads under THAI scheme, seven CC roads one each at Kuyilampalyam and Pillaichavadi colony, two at Pillaichavadi village and three at Bommaiyarpalayam have been provided. Regarding BT road one at

Kuyilampalayam was formed.

Status of Burial/Funeral Faculties

Burial/Funeral ground is available at all seven hamlets. But the following facilities have to be provided: funeral platform 4; waiting hall 7; compound wall and CC passage 4 each; water and EB facility 5 each. Approach road to funeral ground is available.

Sl. No.	Name of the Village	Total Households	Total Population	BUILDINGS								
				Burial Ground								THAI
				No. of BG	Burial Stage	Waiting shed	Retaining Wall	CC Path	Drinking Water	Light	Approach Road	
1.	Kuilampalayam	582	2332	1	1	0	1	1	1	1	1	0
2.	Bommaiyarpalayam Colony	154	450	1	1	0	1	1	1		1	0
3.	Pillaichavadi Fishermen Kudiyiruppu	187	431	1		0					1	0
4.	Bommayarpalayam Fishermen Kudiyiruppu	437	984	1		0					1	0
5.	Pillaichavadi Village	1261	943	1		0					1	0
6.	Pillachavadi Colony	30	116	1		0					1	0
7.	Bommaiyarpalayam	712	2268	1	1	0	1	1		1	1	0
	Total	2363	7524	7	3	0	3	3	2	2	7	0

Improvement through THAI

At Bommayarpalayam village Panchayat, the burial ground with all basic facilities were already provided under various schemes. During the survey at Bommayarpalayam, the mother village public demanded culvert and drainage facility. Considering their felt need through THAI three culverts/drainage facilities was provided.

Status of Buildings

There are 41 government buildings in the panchayat. 38 are CC building and others are AC sheets.

Status of School Buildings

HSS and high school are located away from Bommayarpalayam. Two middle schools are at Bommayarpalayam, one at Kuyilampalyam, Primary school is at Pillaichavadi and Kuyilampalayam. Toilet is needed for middle school. Other facilities like EB services, Water supply, kitchen sheds are available.

Status of Small Ponds/Tanks

There are five ponds in the panchayat area. Three at Bommayarpalayam and two at Kuyilampalayam, but they are encroached. Compound wall is needed for 4 ponds. Bathing ghats are needed at three. In-let channel is needed at 3 and out-let channel is needed for 3 ponds.

Status of Other Facility

There is no playground, no bus stands, and no marketing facility in the panchayat. Three SHGs are functioning in Bommiyarpalayam. 271 women members are affiliated to Government women development centres and 371 women were enrolled with other NGOs.

4. Vellimalai Village Panchayat

Vellimalai Village Panchayat is located at Kalvarayan Hills. It is a big Panchayat having a population of 6484. It is a tribal dominated village Panchayat and the number of SC is only five. The families belong to BC and MBC are not living here. Vellimalai has 29 habitations located north, south and eastern side of Vellimalai, and the headquarters of the village Panchayat.

There are 1501 houses in the panchayat area. Of which 453 are hutments, 662 are tiled, 258 are cement concrete and 128 are mixed type. There are 46 public taps and 16 service connections.

Status of Water Supply

Status of water supply in the village Panchayat during summer is not adequate due to poor storage in the water sources namely wells, bore wells and mini power pumps. There are 15 OHTs which have been

Sl. No.	Name of the Village	DRINKING WATER																									
											Mini Power Pump								Hand Pump						Over Head Tank		
		Total Household	Total Population	SC	ST	MBC	BC	Others	Public Tap	House connection	Total	Fit for Drinking	Not Fit for Drinking	Not working	Condi-tions	THAI	GLR	THAI	Total	Fit for Drinking	Not Fit for Drinking	Not working	Condi-tions	THAI	No. of OHT	Conditions	THAI
1.	Gangappadi	87	280	0	280	0	0	0	2	0	0	0	0	0			0		0	0	0	0			0		
2.	Kannumathivalavu	21	54	0	54	0	0	0	2	0	0	0	0	0			0		1	1	0	1			1	Good	
3.	Konakkadu	18	97	0	97	0	0	0	2	0	0	0	0	0		1	0		2	2	0	2			1	Good	
4.	Kotta Puthur	18	60	0	60	0	0	0	4	0	0	0	0	0			0	1	2	2	0	1	BW repair		1	Good	
5.	Mel Molipattu	84	194	0	194	0	0	0	0	0	0	0	0	0			0	1	2	2	0	2			0		
6.	Melvenniur	43	190	0	190	0	0	0	4	0	0	0	0	0			0		0	0	0	0			1	Good	
7.	Vellimalai	93	302	0	302	0	0	0	5	7	2	2	0	0			2		2	2	0	1	BW dry		1	Good	
8.	Mel Kendikkal	84	302	0	302	0	0	0	0	0	1	1	0	1	BW repair	1	0		3	3	0	0			1	Good	
9.	Melvazapadi	92	505	0	505	0	0	0	0	0	0	0	0	0			0	1	4	1	3	1	HP repair		0		
10.	Mela Thevanur	39	142	0	142	0	0	0	0	0	0	0	0	0			0		2	2	0	1	BW repair		0		
11.	Nadumathur	109	553	0	553	0	0	0	4	0	0	0	0	0			0		3	3	0	3			1	Good	
12.	Thazh Mathur	63	340	0	340	0	0	0	2	0	0	0	0	0			0		0	0	0	0			1	Good	
13.	Thazh Sathanur	39	110	0	110	0	0	0	2	0	1	1	0	1	Pipe-line repair		0		2	2	0	1	BW repair		1	Good	
14.	Thazh Thevanur	55	28	231	0	231	0	0	0	0	0	0	0	0		1	0		2	2	0	0			0		
15.	Thazh Vazappadi	53	370	0	370	0	0	0	0	0	0	0	0	0			0		3	3	0	0			0		
16.	Uthukadu	21	69	0	69	0	0	0	0	0	0	0	0	0			0		1	1	0	1	BW repair		0		
17.	Thoranangkattivalavu	25	90	0	90	0	0		0	0	0	0	0	0		1	0		1	1	0	0			0		
18.	Thazh Kendikkal	108	450	0	450	0	0	0	3	0	0	0	0	0			0		3	3	0	0			1	Good	
19.	Kattumozhipattu	5	16	0	16	0	0	0	0	0	0	0	0	0			0		0	0	0	0			0		
20.	Kora Mozhipattu	3	9	0	9	0	0	0	0	0	0	0	0	0			0		0	0	0	0			0		

21.	Thazh Mathur	63	340	0	340	0	0	0	2	0	0	0	0	0			0		4	4	0	0			0		
22.	Thazh Molipattu	51	157	0	157	0	0	0	4	0	0	0	0	0			0		1	1	0	1			1	Good	
23.	Nadu Molipattu	13	116	0	116	0	0	0	0	0	0	0	0	0			0		1	1	0	0			1	Good	
24.	Thazh Vellimalai	125	333	5	328	0	0	0	7	9	1	1	0	0			1		5	5	0	1	HP repair		1	Partly damaged	
25.	Mel Sathanur	43	158	0	158	0	0	0	2	0	0	0	0	0			0		0	0	0	0			1	Good	
26.	Uthukadu	21	69	0	69	0	0	0	0	0	0	0	0	0			0		0	0	0	0			0		
27.	Koil Moilipattu	26	505	0	505	0	0	0	0	0	0	0	0	0			0		2	2	0	0			0		
28.	Thazh Kottapudur	24	73	0	73	0	0	0	0	0	1	1	0	1	Motor repair		0		2	2	0	1	BW repair		0		
29.	Mel Mathur	32	358	0	358	0	0	0	3	0	0	0	0	0			0		2	2	0	0			1	Good	
30.	Kottapudu (Ka. Ko)	18	60	0	60	0	0	0	0	0	1	0	1	1	Pipeline & BWI repair		0		1	1	0	1			0		
31.	Thazh Venniyur	41	180	0	180	0	0	0	0	0	0	0	0	0			0		2	2	0	1	HP repair		0		
	Total	1476	5912	236	5879	231	0	0	48	16	7	6	1	4		4	3	3	53	50	3	19			15		

constructed during the year 1997 to 2012. Out of 15 OHTs, 14 are established under TWAD and remaining one is constructed from panchayat union fund. There are 7 mini pumps and water comes out of them fit to drink but only two mini pumps are functioning well. Remaining five need repair in syntax, pipe line, bore well and motor. There is only one GLR but not in usage. In all water resource area RWH arrangement is yet to be constructed. There are 53 hand pumps, the water from these pumps is fit to drink. Among these HPs which are in function 9 are not functioning and borewells of these HPs need repair works. RWH is provided only at one point. Only in 13 habitations water supply per day is 40 liters and above. In 14 habitations, it is less than 40 liters. At two habitations there is no water supply.

Improvement through THAI

During the survey it was reported that water scarcity was experienced in summer season. Out of 29 habitations, at 14 habitations distribution of water was below 40 liters per day per person. Hence during the implementation of THAI, four mini power pumps, one ground level reservoir and deepening of one well have been undertaken. Preference was given to the habitations namely Melakendikkal and Thoranamkattivalavu water distribution was 13 liters and 11 liters respectively. And at Kottapudur population is more and Thazh Tazhanur is very remote where remaining two mini power pumps were provided.

Status of Street Lights

Street light facilities at Vellimalai village Panchayat are in somewhat improved condition. At eight habitations there is no street light. There are 200 tube lights in the remaining 21 habitations. Public demanded light facility for eight habitations.

Improvement through THAI

Only tube lights are in the panchayat before implementation of the THAI public demanded additional lights. Under THAI seven tube lights were provided at seven habitations one each at six habitations and one additional tube light at Vellimalai the mother village

Sl. No.	Name of the Village	Total Households	Total Population	POPULATION					STREET LIGHTS							
				SC	ST	MBC	BC	Others	Tube	CFL	Sodium	HML	Solar	No. of SL	Need	THAI
1.	Gangappadi	87	280	0	280	0	0	0	7	0	0	0	0	7		0
2.	Kannumathivalavu	21	54	0	54	0	0	0	0	0	0	0	0	0		1
3.	Konakkadu	18	97	0	97	0	0	0	0	0	0	0	0	0		1
4.	Kotta Puthur	18	60	0	60	0	0	0	13	0	0	0	0	13		0
5.	Mel Molipattu	84	194	0	194	0	0	0	13	0	0	0	0	13		0
6.	Melvenniur	43	190	0	190	0	0	0	7	0	0	0	0	7		0
7.	Vellimalai	93	302	0	302	0	0	0	10	0	0	0	0	10		2
8.	Mel Kendikkal	84	302	0	302	0	0	0	11	0	0	0	0	11		0
9.	Melvazapadi	92	505	0	505	0	0	0	16	0	0	0	0	16		0
10.	Mela Thevanur	39	142	0	142	0	0	0	0	0	0	0	0	0		1
11.	Nadumathur	109	553	0	553	0	0	0	13	0	0	0	0	13		0
12.	Thazh Mathur	63	340	0	340	0	0	0	9	0	0	0	0	9		0

13.	Thazh Sathanur	39	110	0	110	0	0	0	5	0	0	0	0	5		0
14.	Thazh Thevanur	55	28	231	0	231	0	0	0	0	0	0	0	0		1
15.	Thazh Vazappadi	53	370	0	370	0	0	0	7	0	0	0	0	7		0
16.	Uthukadu	21	69	0	69	0	0	0	0	0	0	0	0	0		1
17.	Thoranangkatttivalavu	25	90	0	90	0	0	0	0	0	0	0	0	0		0
18.	Thazh Kendikkal	108	450	0	450	0	0	0	16	0	0	0	0	16		0
19.	Kattumozhipattu	5	16	0	16	0	0	0	0	0	0	0	0	0		0
20.	Kora Mozhipattu	3	9	0	9	0	0	0	0	0	0	0	0	0		0
21.	Thazh Mathur	63	340	0	340	0	0	0	9	0	0	0	0	9		0
22.	Thazh Molipattu	51	157	0	157	0	0	0	9	0	0	0	0	9		0
23.	Nadu Molipattu	13	116	0	116	0	0	0	10	0	0	0	0	10		0
24.	Thazh Vellimalai	125	333	5	328	0	0	0	26	0	0	0	0	26		0
25.	Mel Sathanur	43	158	0	158	0	0	0	9	0	0	0	0	9		0
26.	Uthukadu	21	69	0	69	0	0	0	0	0	0	0	0	0		0
27.	Koil Moilipattu	26	505	0	505	0	0	0	9	0	0	0	0	9		0
28.	Thazh Kottapudur	24	73	0	73	0	0	0	2	0	0	0	0	2		0
29.	Mel Mathur	32	358	0	358	0	0	0	7	0	0	0	0	7		0
30.	Kottapudu (Ka. ko)	18	60	0	60	0	0	0	2	0	0	0	0	2		0
31.	Thazh Venniyur	41	180	0	180	0	0	0	7	0	0	0	0	7		0
	Total	1476	5912	236	5879	231	0	0	217	0	0	0	0	217		7

preference is given to the habitations where there is no light.

Status of Roads

There are 14 BT roads one earthen road and three roads which are one-layer metal road are in this panchayat. The condition of two BT roads is good, 10 roads are partly damaged and four roads are in fully damaged condition. Regarding the condition of streets/lanes there is no drainage facility; the surface of the many streets/lanes is not in good condition. Only in 6 streets, the surface is not damaged. In 12 streets, the condition of CC road is partly damaged and 22 number of CC roads, it is fully damaged.

Improvement through THAI

There are 18 roads and among them 10 are partly damaged, five are fully damaged and only two are in good condition. Under THAI eight CC roads and one BT road were provided considering the condition of the roads.

Status of Drainage

Drainage facilities are not available in 39 lanes. Six street roads are in good condition, partly damaged in 12 streets. Being a hilly area, road and drainages are very much needed, the villagers opined. They demanded the same during the survey, the Panchayat President told.

Status of Buildings

The condition of 35 government buildings located at 18 habitations are not in use, due to various reasons like non-availability of electricity service, lack of water supply, toilet and compound wall.

There are 7 schools of HSS, one High School, one Middle School and five primary schools. In respect of schools' infrastructure facilities there is lack of facilities like water, electricity connection, toilet and some minor repair only at Higher Secondary School at Vellimalai. Cycle stand facility is needed at High School located at Kattupudur and Middle School functioning at Melavazhapadi hamlet. Kitchen shed facility is available in three schools, minor repair is needed at Vellimalai and major repair is needed at Kattupudur school.

Sl. No.	Name of the Village	Total Households	Total Population	ROAD WORKS								
				Roads							THAI	
				No. of Roads	Earthen	Conditions	CC Road	Conditions	BT & WBM	Conditions	CC Road	WBM & BT
1.	Gangappadi	87	280	2			2	Fully damaged			1	
2.	Kannumathivalavu	21	54	1			1	Fully damaged			1	
3.	Konakkadu	18	97	1			1	Partly damaged				
4.	Kotta Puthur	18	60	2			2	1 fully damaged				
5.	Mel Molipattu	84	194	2			2	1 partly 1 fully damaged			1	
6.	Melvenniur	43	190	1			1	Partly damaged			1	
7.	Vellimalai	93	302	1			1	1 partly damaged				
8.	Mel Kendikkal	84	302	2			1	Fully damaged	1	Fully damaged	1	
9.	Melvazapadi	92	505	2			2	1 fully damaged				
10.	Mela Thevanur	39	142	2			2	1 fully damaged				
11.	Nadumathur	109	553	3			2	1 partly 1 fully damaged	1	Partly damaged	1	
12.	Thazh Mathur	63	340	1			1				1	
13.	Thazh Sathanur	39	110	2			2	Fully damaged				
14.	Thazh Thevanur	55	28	1			1	1 partly damaged			1	
15.	Thazh Vazappadi	53	370	2			2	1 partly 1 fully damaged				1
16.	Uthukadu	21	69	1			1	Fully damaged				
17.	Thoranangkatttivalavu	25	90	1			1					
18.	Thazh Kendikkal	108	450	3			2	Fully damaged	1	Fully damaged	1	

19.	Kattumozhipattu	5	16	1			1	Fully damaged				
20.	Kora Mozhipattu	3	9	1			1	Fully damaged				
21.	Thazh Mathur	63	340	2			2	Fully damaged				
22.	Thazh Molipattu	51	157	2			2	1 partly damaged				
23.	Nadu Molipattu	13	116	1			1	1 fully damaged				
24.	Thazh Vellimalai	125	333	2			1	Fully damaged	1	Fully damaged		
25.	Mel Sathanur	43	158	2			2	Fully damaged				
26.	Uthukadu	21	69	1			1					
27.	Koil Moilipattu	26	505	1			1	Partly damaged				
28.	Thazh Kottapudur	24	73	1			1	Fully damaged				
29.	Mel Mathur	32	358	2			1	Partly damaged	1	Partly damaged		
30.	Kottapudu (Ka. Ko)	18	60	1			1	Fully damaged				
31.	Thazh Venniyur	41	180	1			1	Partly damaged				
	Total	1476	5912	48			43		5		8	1

Playground facility is available at Vellimalai Higher Secondary School only. Kabaddi is the main game students play. A hand pump is available near the playground. There is no youth group existed to maintain the playground. It is the school students who do maintenance.

There is no bus stand facility. There is one weekly market available at Vellimalai, where the Panchayat office is located.

Regarding the functioning of SHGs, out of 29 hamlets at 26 hamlets (40 streets) 39 SHG are functioning under Mahalir Thittam. Totally 498 women are empowering themselves through the SHG activities.

Status of Burial Ground

Burial ground is available only at Vellimalai, and in 28 habitations there is no burial/funeral ground. It is told that the tribal families bury the dead bodies at their own agriculture land site.

Sl. No.	Name of the Village	Total Households	Total Population	BUILDINGS								
				Burial Ground								THAI
				No. of BG	Burial Stage	Waiting Shed	Retaining Wall	CC Path	Drinking Water	Light	Approach Road	
1.	Gangappadi	87	280	0								
2.	Kannumathivalavu	21	54	1								
3.	Konakkadu	18	97	1								
4.	Kotta Puthur	18	60	1								
5.	Mel Molipattu	84	194	1								
6.	Melvenniur	43	190	1								
7.	Vellimalai	93	302	1								1
8.	Mel Kendikkal	84	302	1								
9.	Melvazapadi	92	505	2								
10.	Mela Thevanur	39	142	1								
11.	Nadumathur	109	553	1								
12.	Thazh Mathur	63	340	1								
13.	Thazh Sathanur	39	110	1								
14.	Thazh Thevanur	55	28	1								
15.	Thazh Vazappadi	53	370	1								
16.	Uthukadu	21	69	0								
17.	Thoranangkatttivalavu	25	90	1								
18.	Thazh Kendikkal	108	450	1	1	1	1	1	1	1	1	

19.	Kattumozhipattu	5	16	1								
20.	Kora Mozhipattu	3	9	1								
21.	Thazh Mathur	63	340	1								
22.	Thazh Molipattu	51	157	1								
23.	Nadu molipattu	13	116	1								
24.	Thazh Vellimalai	125	333	1								
25.	Mel sathanur	43	158	1								
26.	Uthukadu	21	69	1								
27.	Koil Moilipattu	26	505	1								
28.	Thazh Kottapudur	24	73	1								
29.	Mel Mathur	32	358	1								
30.	Kottapudu (ka. ko)	18	60	1								
31.	Thazh Venniyur	41	180	1								
	Total	1476	5912	30	1	1	1	1	1	1	1	1

Improvement through THAI

Out of 27 habitations only at one habitation namely Thazhl Kendikkal burial ground is available. At remaining habitations, the villagers use their own land site for burial. Hence under THAI at Vellimalai being the mother village and more number of families settled in the hamlet basic facilities have been provided. Besides the above works, one culvert and drainage work and one threshing floor have been provided. Threshing floor is very much useful to dry out minor forest products.

2
Planning and Implementation Process

2.1. Introduction

After the introduction of New Panchayat Raj System, expectation of the public from the institution has been increased exponentially. Development experts criticized the top-down approach of planning as it not only bypasses the rural poor and other social groups, but also some locations within a Village Panchayat. They advocate for local level planning as it seeks to look into the aspirations and requirements of specific local areas and communities which have been neglected for a long time.

In framing the development planning for rural development, the government agencies have the practice of projecting phenomena like total population, the availability of infrastructure and other basic facilities total for village rather than considering the status and issues in respect of facilities available at hamlet/habitation level. Further in the context of power control by traditional authorities and elite in respect of utilizing available resources resulting into uneven development in rural areas, and hence there is a strong case for people's participation.

Government of Tamil Nadu observed that in implementing development schemes, village panchayat is considered as the basic unit for fund allotment. But in people's perception habitation is considered as basic unit for their socio-economic development. As programme capture is the phenomenon that works in villages due to hierarchical nature of the village community.

Under this scheme, the above referred factors are at considerable extent taken into account as the habitation based planning involving people is initiated. It is found that participatory planning principles like analysis of existing conditions, determining the needs, decision of appropriate action, fixing of roles and responsibilities, a consensus on a plan more relevant to local needs and conditions including vulnerable section namely women and families belong to SC and ST have been featured under the scheme. Hence, attention is given in the study to understand and analyse the planning process.

A unique survey was conducted in the villages for the first time in the state, under the scheme for assessing the actual facilities available in each habitation and actual requirements needed to ensure all minimum facilities at the micro level. It is an effective tool for micro planning. It is an extensively designed format having 37 pages intended to collect the following basic details: (i) water supply, (ii) street lights, (iii) streets and lanes, (iv) burial ground, (v) government and local body buildings (except school buildings), (vi) government and local body school buildings, (vii) small tanks and ponds, (viii) playground, (ix) bus stand, (x) market, (xi) SHGs, (xii) village roads, (xiii) panchayat union roads and other structures. The detailed format is in the annexure.

2.2. Process Analysis in Sample Villages

Dindigul District

Sendurai Village Panchayat

During the field visit, the researchers made enquiry on the administration of survey. Many respondents of the hamlets told that they felt extremely happy in involving themselves in the survey as it was such a detailed enquiry never administered at any point of time by the government. It is reported that the expectation of the villagers was very high. People shared that the elected president preferred to implement various development works mainly in one or two hamlets where he/she got many votes. Many presidents are not treating all hamlets equally and failed to give priority to those hamlets where the very basic infrastructure facilities have not been provided so far, villagers observed. The inhabitants of remote hamlets involved in the survey with a high expectation as the scheme have more promises to them. But the process of habitation-based planning was not properly informed to the public. The villagers have the opinion that many felt needs expressed by them during the survey have not been taken into consideration and the officials and the presidents not properly consulted the villagers in finalizing the works. During the Gram Sabha convened specially for the scheme, the presidents read out the works selected under the scheme based on the budget allotted to the village panchayat by the government. Further, the villagers reported that they were not informed of the follow-up action to fill the gaps in the scheme implementation.

It is reported that in the year 2011-12 during the survey was undertaken, there was no scarcity of water at Sendurai Village Panchayat. Water supply was distributed everyday at many habitations. At some habitations the water supply was twice a day. But in some habitations to ensure adequate supply during the summer, under the scheme three number of new bore wells each at Kuppandi Goundanpatti, Sendurai Amman Koil Street, and Vadakkupudur have been planned and provided. Further four number of mini power pumps were also planned and accordingly provided at four habitations each one at Thirukulathupatti, Mamarathupatti, Pandhipomminaickenpatti and Chinnakulam where the population of SC is more. Further under the dovetailing one mini power pump and one new bore well were demanded and the same was fulfilled. In respect of street lights, the habitations are scattered around 20 km. radius and so more number of new street lights have been demanded. Accordingly, street lights have been provided at 17 habitations, under the scheme. The demand for CC road is usually very high. At many habitations there are mud roads which were replaced with CC road under dovetail besides new CC roads were provided, under the scheme. In respect of burial ground, villagers reported that at many habitations, approach road and other facilities are not available at burial ground. Burial ground facilities have been provided under the scheme only at one habitation namely Panthipomminaickenpatti due to limitation of fund. People informed that in many number of cremation grounds basic facilities have yet to be provided.

Reaching the Unreached

It is to be underscored that despite certain limitations in the planning process due to administrative constraints, basic needs of the excluded or marginalized communities have been provided. In this context, it is to be mentioned that the unmet needs of the SC Colony have been attended to through this scheme. It is really reaching the unreached. Because of the intervention of the officials in the gram panchayat planning exercise, prioritization of works has been done judicially and equity issue is being addressed. It is because of the professionals' involvement in the planning process.

Ambathurai Village Panchayat

There are 13 hamlets at village panchayat of Ambathurai. It is a multi-caste village; under the scheme the total allocation is Rs. 30 lakhs as the village falls under the habitation range of 5-15. Out of the 13 habitations, in 9 habitations THAI works have been selected. The types of works carried out are provision of street lights (total 30) in 7 habitations, BT roads in 2 habitations, CC road in 6 habitations and burial ground facility at only one habitation.

The panchayat president recollected that as Ambathurai was one of the five village panchayats in Athoor Union selected under THAI, in the year 2011-12. Being a new project, focusing habitation based planning, the district level officials and union officials made frequent visit to Ambathurai and conducted orientation on the survey work by which the rapport between officials and elected representatives was strengthened, he added.

During the survey all needs demanded by the villagers have been recorded. But during the finalization priority was given to street lights, BT road, CC road and burial ground, the president informed. In respect of water supply no work was selected under the scheme as many bore wells dug already were failed due to poor yield. During the field visit of the research team, the villagers of Perumalkoilpatti, one of a hamlet village reported that the distribution of water supply were not adequate. Also they pointed out that at many habitations equal distribution of water supply could not be ensured due to failure of bore-wells. The panchayat president informed that it was decided to identify the new water source after the arrival of monsoon in subsequent years. In this respect, the district administration has been informed and special sanction was expected, he reported.

The vice-president and ward members belong to SC habitations informed that during the survey many women requested to plan for improving the conditions of school for their children. They further told that the survey work helped the elected representatives and officials to understand the expectation of rural people especially the economically poor families. They expected more than basic amenities from the government.

The Village Panchayat President expected that the government has to specify the role of elected representatives in the implementation of all development programmes. In the context of participatory democracy, in action the government officials have to orient the ward members of the panchayat to participate in the scheme implementation at the hamlet level. At Indirapuram SC habitation demand of villagers' (actual felt need) is a double layer WBM BT road was provided from Indirapuram to Mayanam road. Also, a single layer BT road from Indirapuram to Ambathurai is provided. A Cement Concrete (CC) road at North Street of Indirpuram was also in the demand list of villagers. These demands are fulfilled under the scheme. In another SC hamlet namely Muruganpatti, three CC roads were demanded and the same were provided. A double layer WBM BT road was demanded by the villagers of Kathirpatti up to the burial ground road and the same was provided. Cremation facilities were also provided at Kathirpatti.

The President reported that to ensure fruitful utilization of the burial ground facilities improved under the scheme, additional fund from dovetailing had to be provided. By which the works like raising the level of the ground by filling with loose soil suitable to dig pits for burying dead bodies could be undertaken, he added. In three habitations namely, Perumalkovilpatti, Rajakaliamman Nagar and Rengasamy Nagar public demanded CC road. Because the existing gravel road was not useful due to stagnation of drainage and rain-water and posed a threat to safe mobility especially to children and elders. This issue was taken and priority is given in providing CC roads in the above referred habitations.

Here also one could notice the works carried out in that panchayat are also helpful to SC community. All the works carried out in this panchayat were also the felt needs of the SC community. It comes out unequivocally the provision of facility to SC colony as per the demand and prioritized in the planning process and it was possible because of the active intervention of the officials. The interaction between officials and representatives of the people enabled the gramsabha to understand the logic behind the prioritization of works for the benefits of the SC community.

Kasavanampatti Village Panchayat

At Kasavanampatti the scheme was implemented in the year 2012-13. The panchayat secretary of that period was transferred who is now the secretary of Mangarai Village Panchayat. The researchers met him and collected details of the planning and implementation process from him. He told that he along with Ward Members, Vice-President and the President of Kasavanampatti village panchayat went to each street in all wards/habitations, collected details from each family and habitants. He informed that it was a labourious task as many details in each aspect of basic needs have to be recorded. For example, he cited that the number of EB service connections and service of each meter box had to be filled in the survey format. But service numbers of all EB connections were not properly registered and these details have been collected from the EB department, he added. Such a minute details have been properly collected, verified and filled in the format.

He further informed that it was an eye opener. The panchayat vice-president who was fully involved in the survey work shared that giving priority to the needs like drinking water facility, street lights, formation of CC roads, and improving the facilities at burial/cremation ground was the salient features of the scheme. Fund allocation to Kasavanampatti village panchayat is Rs. 30 lakhs. Though it is not adequate to fulfil all the basic needs, about 50 per cent of the issues in the supply of drinking water were solved; and the need of street lights to the newly extended areas was fulfilled he pointed out. It was reported that residents of all 10 hamlets of Kasavanampatti village panchayat demanded drainage facilities, and play cum recreation center for youth along with sports equipment. In respect of demand of CC road, about 70 per cent of that need was fulfilled. The survey helped to have a vision to the panchayat council on the gap in the basic infrastructure facilities and how to draft plan to fill the gap, many ward members reported.

The demand of providing approach road to the cremation ground at Kasavanampatti main village was duly fulfilled under the scheme. Earlier the road was gravel, and so its condition was very bad during rainy season. Moreover, on the two sides of the road one would find cultivable agricultural lands and for cultivation of the lands tractors and other vehicles are moving to transport inputs and outputs related to farming exercises. Hence, the condition of the gravel road becomes deplorable. Now the BT road was provided which is very useful to reach easily to the burial ground and to the agriculture field also. The facility of platform for funeral stage at an elevated level was provided under the scheme. It removed the hardship faced by villagers in safe burial/cremation of dead bodies during the rainy season. Further, the Hand Pump provided at the burial ground, helped a lot in conducting the funeral ceremony. All these facilities provided under the scheme are very useful, the local farmers reported.

The burial ground at Pothunaickanpatti is located on the tank of Kumanankulam. It is the Panchayat Union tank. A BT road, a CC road from the main road to burial ground and a waiting hall were provided under THAI scheme. The villagers have the habit of both funeral and burial. But there was no funeral platform in the ground. The burial ground is in low lying area though it is located on the tank bund. The ward member Mr. Shanmugam reported that during the raining season, the flood water used to drain through the burial ground. Hence, sufficient space has to be earmarked for cremation and the same has to be levelled up for safe disposal of dead bodies, he added.

At Kurumbapatti the stage for funeral was provided along with a compound wall. It is properly utilized. But the nearby farmer encroaches a small area of burial ground, it is found. Though he was compelled to give away the encroached area, he did not come forward to remove, the concerned ward member told. It is learnt that local villagers joined with the encroacher and demanded that all encroachments in all hamlets have to be verified and removed. Then the encroached area at the burial ground, was cleared, the vice-president informed.

It is observed that the rationale behind the THAI scheme had been properly taken into consideration by all the stakeholders concerned. In the village panchayat of Kasavanampatti there are 10 hamlets and the major issue in the panchayat is distribution of drinking water adequately to all the habitants. This issue was properly identified during the survey work and then during the finalization, priority was also properly given to 'water supply' for implementation with the cost of Rs.11.83 lakhs.

A comprehensive water supply scheme covering two village panchayats Karisalpatti, a nearby village panchayat and Kasavanampatti is in operation. Generally, that source is adequate but due to severe drought for the past three to four years, the yield from that source is not adequate to meet the needs of both the village panchayats. Moreover, there is an agreement between these two village panchayats that four by seven measurement out of water earmarked to Karisalpatti and 3/7 portion is to Kasavanampatti, the village taken for the study. Comparing the no. of hamlets, Karisalpatti has only four hamlets whereas Kasavanampatti has 10 hamlets. The aim of providing minimum basic infrastructure facility under water supply to all the habitants was though attempted under the scheme, but still the need for adequate water in two/three hamlets is yet to be fulfilled.

Yet there is a concern. In some small habitations pipe line extension work was carried out to new mini syntax tank to fulfil the demand of small numbers of families though they could fetch water from other nearby syntax tank. Because of this and due to drought also, adequate water would not reach all syntax tanks in the same habitation. And it is observed that in one mini tank water taps are in loosen condition and the provision for closing the taps is not available. During our discussion with the nearby families they shared that it was the play of children. Accountability of proper maintenance of the water structures is yet to be inculcated to villagers, especially of remote habitation. By reviving standing committees especially, the water and sanitation committee and by orienting its members, the distribution of water supply could be improved further, the vice-president and the secretary jointly emphasized.

The villagers suggested that the main water source meant for two village panchayat has to be deepened further. The vice-president informed that the villagers of Karisalpatti mobilized themselves money to do the deepening and the villagers of Kasavanampatti were informed about that. In the meantime, the AD panchayat during his visit to Kasavanampatti agreed to allot a minimum of Rs. 3 lakhs considering the drought. It shows the district officials has the proper follow-up on the implementation of the scheme and coming forward to dovetail other scheme fund to fill the gap. There are 6 new bore wells with syntax tank facilities provided where the water supply is not adequate which was reported during the survey. Further at five habitations due to demand of more public taps, extension of pipe line work was undertaken under the scheme.

At six habitations new street lights were provided. Out of above six at two habitations additional street lights were provided as it was demanded during the survey. Further it is the mother village. Only one CC road connecting the burial ground site was provided though there were many demands from more than six habitations. But two

BT roads were provided. One road improved the connectivity to burial ground and another BT road up to the burial ground at Pothinaickenpatti hamlet solved the long pending demands of the villagers.

Vilpatti Village Panchayat

The residents of Anna Ramasamy Nagar, Bharathi Nagar, Mattupatti, Peythuparai and Vellaparrai have expressed happiness over giving priority to their demand of provision of street lights to their habitations under the THAI scheme. Many houses at Anna Rangasamynagar did not get electricity connection due to non-availability of adequate number of poles to reduce the distance between poles but now they were able to get the EB service connection to their houses. It is possible due to habitation-wise approach taken under the scheme, they added. Travellers of Peythuparai and Vellaparai habitation informed that they could come out on their houses safely during the night as their demand for street lights have been fulfilled. Since it is a hilly region houses have been constructed long back and they were awaiting for electricity connection to their houses. Electricity department asked them to pay for the poles to cover the long distance. They are unable to pay. They waited for a long period. This scheme enables them to have electricity connection to their houses. Normally during night, they won't come out of their houses as there was no electricity and street light. Now they have street lights and house connected with electricity.

In respect of provision of CC road under the scheme was very much useful, the villagers of Ganeshapuram a remote area under ward No. 3 shared. The CC road connected ration shop as well as primary school which are located at the top area of Ganeshapuram. Earlier the path was a mud road and so the students faced lot of problems, during rainy season. And the ration commodities have not been transported to the ration shop. Now that problem is solved as their demand of CC road provided under the scheme is a strong and weatherproof one and so the vehicle could easily reach the ration shop and primary school. There are about 35 ST Irular families living at Ganeshapuram. They demanded drainage and retaining wall to arrest the soil erosion and land slide during rainy season. It is noted that their houses are constructed in unplanned manner and streets/ lanes are also very narrow.

Joint Effort of Key Stakeholders

Peythuparai village burial ground was improved and facilities were given under this scheme and hence people expressed that their long pending demands have been considered positively by the government through this scheme. The burial ground is located at top near the side of a patta land. Moreover, during the rainy season due to soil erosion the burial ground site could not be used, the ward member informed. Hence in consultation with the engineers, a suitable design was prepared to prevent the soil erosion as well as to extend the burial site area. Accordingly, a retaining wall was provided along with a waiting shed, for the convenience of participants who attend funeral. The waiting shed is used as bus shelter as it is located at the side of the road. It is a case for successful joint effort of the key stakeholders of habitation based planning. The ward member and villagers of Peythuparai informed that though the space at burial ground was not adequate, after providing retaining wall cum compound wall, and waiting shed under the scheme, funeral is being done safely. As street lights are available there is no fear over wild animals in the case of delay in completion of funeral ceremony, they added.

Provision of CC road at eight habitations is very useful work, as it ensures safety mobility from mud and thorny bushes, and easy for vehicle movement, the villagers reported.

The people of Ganeshapuram informed that issue of water supply was considered in this scheme. The ward member reported that the bore-well and the motor are located at the patta land and with the help of landowner only the pumping could be possible. Sometime it was delayed to pump water due to non-availability of the farm owner. The ward member further informed that the issue was discussed during the planning process with the farm owner and he assured to be available to switch on the motor for pumping out water to the people of that habitation.

It is reported that the GLR provided under the scheme at Mattupatti is not functioning due to leakage. The Panchayat Secretary and the President informed that the issue was discussed with the Union Officials and they agreed to do the needed modification to ensure proper storage of water at the GLR. The President further said that more than three years have been passed but the union officials are yet to address the issue and so it was decided to rectify the problem using village panchayat fund than waiting for union effort, he added.

It is found during the survey that at 6 hamlet villages, distribution of water supply per day is below 40 liters per person. It is told that though water is distributed everyday, the supply is not equal and adequate for the above habitations. Hence there were many demands for provision of water supply during the survey work. But under the scheme only one work namely provisions of GLR and pipe line extension was given priority and undertaken at Mattupatti one of the 6 hamlets, where water is distributed below 40 liters per person per day. It is told that water supply would be improved in other remaining habitations using the village panchayat fund and 14th Finance Commission Fund.

In respect of street lights, being a hilly village and having more than 25 habitations, the demand from all habitations for provision of street lights have been reported during the survey. The total demand for street light was projected as 785. But the scheme preference was given to very needy and to remote streets. The demand for CC road was high as the habitations are located at high and low level area, the President told. The mobility of villagers during the rainy season on the mud road is not a safety one. Moreover, the runaway water during the raining days cause damage to the existing mud road, hence more demands he added. It is reported under the scheme preference is given to needier habitations and CC road was provided at 10 habitations. It is told that during the survey public reported that about 20 number of CC roads which have been formed earlier were in damaged condition. But under the scheme no work for repairing the damaged CC road was undertaken as it is not a permitted work.

In fourteen habitations, during the survey it was reported that no proper facilities were available at burial ground site. There was no proper approach road to six burial grounds. Under the scheme only one habitation namely Pethuparai all facilities were provided which are very much useful, the villagers reported. The BT road laid between Chinnapallam to Lurthupuram is serving as a road for connectivity. It is always a problem to achieve equity in providing infrastructural facilities to the villages' panchayats with more number of habitations because programme capture was a culture. Through this scheme, the state government wants to address the problem with the active participation of the local bodies. Though it is difficult, the deliberative process enabled the panchayats to prioritise the works and carried out the same. Since there is an assurance for providing facilities for all the hamlets, people have come forward to accept the prioritization officials have helped the deliberative process to arrive consensus decisions.

Pudukottai District

Vagavasal Village Panchayat

Viswakarma Nagar is one of the 16 hamlets in the Vagavasal village panchayat. Though it is one of the old settlements it was a well-planned settlement. There are 225 houses at Viswakarma Nagar, and its streets and lanes are widely designed. During the planning process, the habitants of Viswakarma Nagar demanded mini tank facility even though there are four mini tanks at the hamlet. The villagers informed that due to severe drought, the groundwater level has gone down and so the mini power pump mini tanks provided earlier were not functioning.

Participatory Management

Under THAI two new mini tank facilities have been provided. Out of two, one mini tank, constructed at the first street is not functioning due to poor yield. Another one located at the 5th street is functioning well and the yield as well as quality of water is very good. Hence, families living in other streets also used to come over to the Fifth Street and fetch water for cooking from the new mini tank provided under THAI. The habitants informed that mini tank facilities are very useful especially at the time of panchayat administration takes time to do repair of motors of OHT. The women are oriented properly in the operation and maintenance of the mini tank, the ward member reported. The women involved themselves in monitoring and regulating the distribution of water through mini-tank. The level of groundwater is adequate as the undue exploitation is prevented by the women team. Further everyday morning and evening water is distributed equally to all families. It is a model to the participatory approach in distribution of water through mini tank, it is noted.

The habitants of Viswakarma Nagar told that they made demand of drainage facility during the survey taken under the scheme. They reported that topography of the Viswakarma Nagar is suitable for construction of drainage. The drainage water could be easily drained out. Moreover, the width of streets and lanes is sufficient enough for the construction of drainage, they expressed. Under the scheme, there is a clear guidance for dovetailing in the case of the felt needs identified by the villagers are not able to cover under the scheme. The officials remarked that the concept of dovetailing/convergence was the right approach, but bringing together various stakeholders/ source of fund could be possible only by district administration.

At Thattampatti hamlet a hand pump is provided under THAI. During the field visit, the habitants informed that "though there is sufficient arrangement for water supply at Thattampatti, the taste of water is not good as well as the yield become less in the hand pump. During the survey an additional hand pump has been demanded near the Kailasa Muni Temple where the water source is good. The Panchayat Secretary informed that accordingly a Hand Pump was provided and the yield is good and the taste of the water is good. For cooking and drinking purposes, the villagers used to come over to the Hand Pump located near the temple site in spite of distance they have to cover, he added.

The demand of two BT roads, one from the primary school to Avudayar Oorani and another one is approach road to burial ground has been fulfilled under the scheme. The villagers informed that both roads are very useful. The road towards Avudayar Oorani is useful to about 25 householders as well as to larger number of farmers who have to transport materials and equipment to their field easily. The families made a further demand, that provision of drainage facility. It is found that after laying of new BT road under the scheme, the level of road is raised and during the raining season the flood water is logged along the road side and around the houses. Hence, the villagers made a new demand of providing drainage facility along the road side to ensure environmental sanitation.

New Demand Made

At Thattampatti hamlet, the habitants demanded one additional OHT/ bore-well at the AD colony area. It is reported that there are about 130 households and the supply of drinking water equally to all could not be possible due to poor yield. Hence, the need of one new bore/ OHT at AD Colony area is referred by the habitants. The villagers after the implementation of the scheme had the realization that all basic needs in each hamlet have to be fulfilled instead of addressing one or two basic needs in each hamlet. They expected allocation of more fund under the scheme in future considering fulfilling all basic demands made by villagers. Further they suggested that works selected for implementation by union have to be in tune with the demands already made by the villagers.

The public of Kedayapatti informed that the land sites/buildings belong to village panchayats and union panchayats have to be properly protected or utilized. They suggested that efforts have to be taken during the survey under the scheme and in consultation with the villagers during special gram sabha meeting, suitable plans have to be drafted to make use these properties for constructive purposes. Necessary allocation has to be made through the scheme accordingly, as there is no any special scheme in existence at present. At Vagavasal, where the village panchayat office is located, villagers demanded a new OHT/bore-well to ensure adequate water supply. One new OHT with the capacity of 10,000 liters is provided under the scheme. Now adequate water supply is ensured to all 150 householders at Vagavasal.

The villagers further informed that during the scheme survey exercise, they made a demand of providing a new road from the existing road between Vagavasal and Rajapatti. The new road would serve two purposes namely to take the Goddess during the festival celebration and could connect the other side of village road. The present condition of the road is a gravel one. Considering the felt need under the scheme, it was listed but due to objection from some families, the work was not being carried out. The families made objection that it is not a public path whereas according to the revenue record "it is a public passage". Hence, the villagers requested that the village panchayat administration must prove the ownership of the passage under reference through court (as the dispute is in the court) and provide a *pucca* road under the scheme or any other funding source. Such facts and figures are shared by villagers during the survey under the scheme. It is an opportunity to closely look into the felt needs/other important issues of the local people. Hence, the district administration must extend help to find solution to issues emerged during survey and the felt need demanded had to be fulfilled, they reported.

At Vagavasal, the burial ground has adequate space and the funeral stage has been already provided under other scheme. During the survey, the villagers demanded other facilities like compound wall, CC road up to funeral stage, and a hand pump at the burial ground site. It is a common burial ground to all the communities of

Vagavasal. Hence, their demand had been fulfilled under the scheme. In respect of provision of street lights, under the scheme, four new lights were provided at the rate of each one in four hamlets. These street lights are located at appropriate places and in proper usage. But villagers told that due to poor voltage many number of street lights available at remote habitations are not functioning and requested to provide a new transformer. Under road work a two layer WBM+BT road planned and sanctioned under the scheme. But it is found during the field visit the said road work is not executed due to disputes among the habitants in respect of ownership of the passage and the fund earmarked is kept in the account of DRDA.

It is found that in all 9 hamlets, totally in 17 streets distribution of water was below 40 liters per day per person. Except in three habitations of Viswakarma Nagar hamlet, water is supplied every day whereas at Viswakarma Nagar once in two days, though the population is comparatively larger than other habitations. Hence during the planning, priority was given to Viswakarma Nagar and other three hamlets. Accordingly, at Viswakarma Nagar two mini power pumps were provided. At Rajapatti habitation one mini power pump is provided by which the need of adequate water supply is fulfilled completely. At Thattampatti habitation one hand pump was provided. At Vagavasal one OHT and at Edyapatti pipeline extension was provided.

Cent Percent Street Light Facility Ensured

In respect of provision of street lights, the total number of street lights demanded during the survey was 97. During the planning process preference is given to three hamlets. At Rajapatti the total demand is 20 street lights as poles are already there. The need was fixing of street lights at 20 poles. And so all the 20 lights demanded by the public of Rajapatti hamlet was provided by which 100 per cent fulfilled in respect of street lights. The remaining two hamlets are Goundrajavayal and Edyapatti where the demand of one new pole and street lights and 8 new poles with street lights were provided.

In respect of CC road, it is found that there are 10 number of mud roads needed improvement of which one road was fully damaged and remaining 9 roads were partially damaged. Hence at Rajapatti, Edayapatti and Ayyavayal hamlets 3 CC roads were formed one at each. A BT road was provided at Thattampatti hamlet to improve the connectivity to the main road. Though facilities demanded at five burial grounds in five hamlets, priority was given to Vagavasal which is the mother village. A retaining wall was provided at Rajapatti, where two tanks are available. Facility of retaining wall is provided at one tank considering the need of the public hailing from Rajapatti.

Functioning with Rationality

It is interesting to note that the villagers have demanded facilities for their hamlets based on their requirements and the provisions available in the scheme. Once survey was over and prioritization takes place, with the involvement of the officials, basic needs of the underprivileged are met and for which all the caste groups gave their approval. There is a yet another issue namely the arrest of wastage of money. On all scheme implementation one can notice the wastage of money as they have to spend the earmarked money whether it would be useful or not. But in this scheme people decide that not even single paisa is wasted. In the planning and implementation both elected representatives and officials are involved, every act is being done rationally.

Viralur Village Panchayat

The panchayat president had orientation through SHG movement. Her name is Mrs. Parvathi, her husband is a socially conscious and oriented person and so he encourages and facilitates in the activities of the village panchayat. The president and ward members shared that the major problem in the village is the non-availability of adequate space for burial ground. Improvement of basic facilities like water supply and street lights were the felt needs of the people of the village panchayat.

At Pallar Natham habitation, the villagers faced hardship in taking the dead bodies to the burial ground. There was no proper pathway to the burial ground. The villagers had to pass through private land and the owners of land most of the occasions refused to permit them. As all the families live in that habitation belongs to same caste, there is no serious conflict among them seen. The villagers had to walk over about one kilometer to reach the burial ground. The villagers even agreed to pay money to the patta holding farmers but the farmers are not ready to sell their land. All the efforts taken to find solution to the issue were failed. The villagers felt very much on their fate.

The announcement of the scheme by the Chief Minister was a boon to them as it aimed to address the issues in the infrastructure gap at habitation level, the president told. In the scheme specific activities like water supply, street light and improvement in burial ground have been listed, villagers involved in the survey work very seriously. Among the needs demanded by public, priority was given to burial ground, water supply and street lights.

The Success of Consultative Process

Accordingly, under the scheme at the burial ground facilities like CC road, platform for burial, and hand pump were provided. In respect of provision of proper road connectivity, a new pathway is suggested along the bund of a panchayat tank. When the panchayat administration took effort to form a gravel road up to burial ground, the villagers immediately refused to alter the pathway traditionally used. Later they all have been persuaded and agreed to join with the panchayat administration in the formation of gravel road along the bund of panchayat tank. Accordingly, the gravel road at a distance of 700 meter was formed to reach the burial ground easily. At the site of the burial ground, the shed, the CC road and the hand pump facilities have been provided under the scheme. The villagers shared that provision of hand pump at the burial ground was a good activity. Earlier to fetch water for the various purposes at the burial site, the villagers have to go over to private farm and fetch water from their wells. Now that hardship had been done away with as the hand pump provided at burial ground was functioning well, they added.

During the survey, the villagers from three hamlets namely Kodikkalpatti, Kumaradi Natham and Ponnikulathupatti made demand to improve the distribution of drinking water. At that time, among these habitations the distribution was only 20 liters, 14 liters and 24 liters per day per person respectively. Hence, during the planning process priority was given to these hamlets and also to Pallarnatham and Viralur. Except Ponnikulathupatti mini power pump at each above referred villages, were provided. The main reason for including additional two above referred habitations is, that they too used to receive below 40 liters. Further at Ponnikulathanpatti and Kodikkalpatti one hand pump each was provided to reduce the rush in public taps.

Regarding street lights the total demand is for 103 numbers. But only 20 street lights was provided under THAI. The criteria observed during the planning process was that priority was accorded to those hamlets with more population, and long distance. Hence at Pallarnatham against the total demand of seven street lights, three street lights, at Kodikkalpatti eight street lights against the total demand of 18 lights and at Ramayagoundanpatti nine street lights out of total demand of 21 lights were provided to meet the immediate requirements.

There are eight mud roads which need improvement. But four CC roads two roads at Kodikkalpatti, one road at Ramayagoundanpatti and the remaining one at Viralur (the mother village) were provided. The BT road was provided at Vadakkipatti to improve the connectivity to other habitations.

Balance Maintained in Fixing Priority

In respect of provision of basic facilities at burial ground, it is reported during the survey that at four hamlets, for six habitations new burial ground was demanded. Out of these six habitations at five habitations the resident used to do burial at their own land. And in the remaining one habitation the residents have the permission to bury dead bodies at the burial ground available in the nearby hamlet. At the remaining 13 habitations burial grounds are there but without basic facilities. In six hamlets where common burial grounds are existed but without facilities, hence priority was given to those six hamlets.

Information Empowerment of Villagers

In the whole process of planning people have not only involved themselves in planning and implementation of the scheme but they learnt a lot about water management. Normally villagers on burial ground issues, they try to go with traditional. Shifting of place and change of pathway to burial ground are unacceptable to them. But here people accept the collective decision taken by the gram sabha. Community is with the gram panchayat. It is a welcome move, as rational decision-making process convincing everyone to respond to the request of the gram panchayats. Meeting the basic needs of the people from this scheme fund raises hope that they will get continuously such a kind of fund through this scheme.

Thulaiyanur Village Panchayat

During the survey, the public of six hamlets out of total 28 hamlets of Thulayanur village panchayat reported that the distribution of drinking water was not adequate. It was also reported that the availability of water per person per day, in these hamlets was below 40 liters. Among the above six hamlets at one hamlet namely Mavur, in two habitations the water supply was below 40 liters. Hence, the demand was from seven habitations. In remaining 21 habitations there was no scarcity of water. Under the scheme, 5 mini power pumps were provided at four hamlets where the quality of water supply was very poor.

Regarding the provision of street lights, the total no. of demand was 194, from 26 habitations. More number of street lights demanded from 8 habitations out of those 26. Under the scheme among the above mentioned 8 habitations five street lights were provided at three streets. The remaining 13 street lights were not provided to other hamlets where the demand for street lights was very minimum, hence by providing one or two street lights in those hamlets it became cent per cent completion in respect of street lights. Such a balanced view was possible because of habitation based planning.

The Strength of Deliberative Democracy

During the survey it was noticed that there were 39 mud roads and of which 6 are partially damaged and two are in good condition. Under the scheme CC road was given to 8 habitations at 8 hamlets where the existing mud roads were very bad. Four BT roads were formed at four hamlets by which those hamlets get easy connectivity to main road, which is leading to the district headquarters, Puthukkottai. In respect of provision of facilities at the burial ground, it was found during the survey that all 24 burial grounds have approach roads. Facilities are not available there. Under THAI at one hamlet namely Mavur all facilities were provided where the approach road was very bad.

During the survey, many other felt needs were reported. Among those needs by considering the priorities, bathing ghat was constructed at three tanks which is very much useful to women folk and children. Further two retaining walls were constructed along with the two bathing ghats to strengthen the bund of the tanks. One threshing floor and three culverts were also provided, under the scheme. As it is evident from other village panchayats, particularly decision making play an important role in prioritizing the works based on the consensus evolved through a discourse process in a multi-hamlet village panchayat. It has been noticed that despite their higher quantum of needs, villagers have been oriented to take a radical decision through a consensual way. Deliberative democracy provides rich dividend. It also raises hope among all and this scheme keeps the tempo as it has got assurance to all that the scheme would provide all basic needs to all the hamlets.

Mimisal Village Panchayat

Being a coastal village panchayat supply of water below 40 liters per person per day was reported by the residents of 13 habitations during the survey. In all the above habitations once in two days only water was distributed. Under the scheme pipeline extension was provided at 8 habitations. Demand for provision of street light was from three hamlets only. Under the scheme totally 5 street lights were provided against the demand of 36 numbers at the three hamlets.

In respect of provision of CC road only at two hamlets CC roads were provided though the number of mud roads in Mimisal is ten and in another hamlet namely Chathirapattinam the number of mud road is six. Hence two CC roads one at each above referred hamlets was provided considering the condition of the mud roads. BT roads were provided at three hamlets namely Alathur, Kanmaikarai Kudiyiruppu and Mimisal Kudiyeruppu where the need was very necessary, it was reported. With regard to provision of facilities at burial ground, it was found during the survey in all 10 habitations there were 22 burial grounds. Except Alathur, all the remaining habitations there is no approach road. And in all 22 burial grounds other basic facilities are not available.

Under the scheme at Alathur burial ground with all facilities were provided, considering the number of families who are going to be benefited. It is to be noted here as we have seen that people in the village have been oriented to take a collective decision based on the rationality. The involvement of the officials in the planning process helped the panchayats to take a decision after convincing the people about to fulfil the felt needs of the people.

Villupuram District

Vellimalai Village Panchayat

It is found that during the survey for planning, number of 20 hamlets have been identified where water distribution is below 40 liters per person per day. Out of above hamlets, it is noted that at 9 hamlets villagers use to receive only below 10 liters at 7 hamlets below 10 to 20 liters and at remaining 4 hamlets 20 to 35 liters. Hence under THAI preference is given to address the water supply issue in those habitations. Accordingly, deepening of well was taken in 3 hamlets and mini power pump was provided at 4 hamlets. All these works were successfully executed and availability of water has been improved in those habitations.

In respect of street light, it is found that during the survey all 29 habitations were listed out where street lights are needed. Among those 29 habitations priority is given to the streets where the distance between electricity poles is longer. Accordingly, at 7 habitations street lights were provided. Among the above 7 habitations, one namely Mel-vellimalai more number of street lights were provided as there were many small habitations located in remote area that too scattered over the Mel-vellimalai area. In respect of provision of CC road, it is reported during the survey that at 28 hamlets more number of mud roads are there where CC roads have to be provided. Under THAI scheme 7 number of CC roads were provided to 7 habitations. The BT road was provided at Thazha-valapadi by which 5 hamlets get connectivity.

Attending Felt Needs than Sending Fund

Another important activity implemented under THAI is provision of basic facilities at the site of burial ground. At Vellimalai village panchayat, it is found during the survey that at 27 hamlets, there is no common burial ground available and so families used to bury the dead bodies at their own land. But those who have small extent of land bury the dead bodies. Others those who do not have land found it very difficult. It was a pitiable condition. Unless people who have lands permitted in their lands to bury dead bodies, landless people face volley of troubles. Under THAI scheme due to limitation of fund, only at Vellimalai, the mother village, with all basic facilities a new burial ground was provided. Preference is given to Vellimalai which is the headquarters where the Block office and other Field offices of line departments are located. Moreover, many outsiders are migrated to Vellimalai for income generation activities. It is a common burial ground that can be used by all. It is considered as one of the important steps taken by the panchayat in this scheme.

Singanur Village Panchayat

There are three hamlets, having 15 habitations. Supply of drinking water in all the fifteen habitations was only below 40 liters per day per person. Under the scheme preference was given to Singanur old colony where the daily distribution of water is comparatively lower than the mother village Singanur and another hamlet namely Singanur new colony. Accordingly, one OHT and two mini power pumps were provided at old colony.

In respect of street light facility preference is given to Singanur old as well as new colony. 10 new poles were provided in the area where the distance between street lights was more. At the Athikulam habitation of Singanur old colony, the demand for street lights was pending for the past 40 years. It is fulfilled only through THAI (Read case study-1 for more information). Regarding CC road preference was given to Singanur new colony, being an extension area.

Peoples' Sentiment Respected

In respect of making improvement at burial ground site, it was found that at two hamlets, the villagers made demand for waiting hall. It is reported that, many persons—friends and relatives are visiting during the post-funeral ceremonies. Hence "Kariya Kottagai" (Waiting Hall) was demanded. Accordingly, under the scheme at two hamlets—Singanur and Singanur old colony waiting halls were provided. Also, an approach road and CC road to burial ground located at Singanur and to a burial platform at the burial ground of Singanur old colony were provided.

It is to be noted here, because of the meticulous survey conducted for data collection, people at the villages are aware of the conditions of the village. They are further oriented to prioritize their needs based on the urgency and the funds available. Now they have been oriented to take collective decision based on not number but on consensus basis.

Thennamadevi Village Panchayat

In this village panchayat at Poothamedu hamlet distribution of drinking water was below 40 liters per person per day. In other three hamlets, the position of water supply is comparatively better than Poothamedu. Hence during the planning, preference was given to Poothamedu. Accordingly, two mini power pumps and one hand pump were provided under the scheme.

In respect of street lights, it was reported that the total demand was 7 in numbers. Hence, under the scheme 4 street lights were provided at Poothamedu hamlet by which the need was fulfilled completely.

In respect of burial ground facilities during the survey, waiting hall for all four hamlets have been demanded. Accordingly, at three hamlets waiting hall was provided. In respect of demand under road work, at Thennamadevi hamlet as an approach road to burial ground, a BT road was provided. The felt needs demanded by the people dwelling in three habitations have been fulfilled because of this scheme. Otherwise it is not possible due to poor income of this small village panchayat, president reported. Many of the small village panchayats are suffering because of the insufficient resources and poor fund allocation due to population size. As a result, many of the felt needs and basic needs could not be met. But THAI scheme is a boom to this type of small villages. While planning for this village, other schemes can be used through the plan implementation. It all depends on the panchayat presidents and the officials involved in implementation of the scheme.

Bommaiyarpalayam Village Panchayat

It is a coastal village panchayat. There are four hamlets. At two hamlets, the supply of water is below the average 40 liters per person per day (up to 20 liter) and in the remaining two hamlets it is up to 30 liters. Hence preference is given to the first two hamlets namely, Pillaichavadi and Kuyilampalayam. A new bore well, motor and new pipe line at Pillaichavadi and one mini power pump at Kuyilampalayam were provided under this scheme. In respect of street lights, the demand was very high. At Fishermen habitation demand for street lights was more. At Bommaiyarpalayam hamlet there are 5 small habitations, and so totally 13 street lights were provided there.

Many numbers of roads are muddy and hence demand for CC roads is high from all habitations. Four CC roads have been given to Bommaiyarpalayam and at Kuyilampalayam one CC road was provided. Since Bommaiyarpalayam has more number of habitation, the needs of that village was considered positively. Regarding BT road, a connectivity road between Kuyilampalayam to Periya Muthaliyar Chavadi was provided. Approach roads to burial ground located in 5 habitations were provided as in the burial ground other minimum facilities are available already.

2.3. District-wise Analysis

The sample districts have been selected from various regions. In this context an attempt is made to do district-wise analysis for having better understanding on the planning and implementation process within the district and among the districts.

Dindigul District

Table 2.1: No. of works completed in sample Village Panchayats in Dindigul District

Sl. No	Name of the Village Panchayat	Total No. of Habitation	No. of Habitation Work done	Water						Road		S L	Building				
				NB	MPP	PLE	OHT	HP	GLR	CCR	BT & WBM	SL	BG	C&D	TF	RW	BG
1.	Sendurai	24	13	3	4	-	-	-	-	6	-	75	1	-	-	-	-
2.	Ambathurai	11	9	-	-	-	-	-	-	10	3	34	1	-	-	-	-
3.	Kasavanampatti	11	10	-	4	7	-	-	-	-	3	9	1	-	-	-	-
4.	Vilpatti	26	15	-	-	-	-	-	1	7	1	16	1	-	-	-	-
	Total	72	47	3	8	7	0	0	1	23	7	134	4	0	0	0	0

NB: New Bore well, MPP—Mini Power Pump, PLE—Pipe Line Extension, OHT—Over Head Tank, HP—Hand Pump, GLR&DW—GLR Deepening Well, CCR—Cement Concrete Road, BT&WBM—Block Thar & With Blue Metal Road, SL—Street Light, BG—Burial Ground, C&D—Culvert and Drainage, TF—Threshing Floor, RW—Retaining Wall, BG—Bathing Ghat.

Source: Computed.

The scheme was introduced in the year 2011/12. At that time of introduction, those village panchayats, which are coming under habitation, range of 26 and above and 16 to 25 have been identified under the scheme. During the survey at Sendurai (habitation range 16-25) there were no serious issues in the distribution of water supply as the rainfall was adequate. But during the time of evaluation study which is initiated only in the year 2015/16, villagers from many hamlets reported that they suffered a lot due to failure of monsoon since 2011/12 consecutively. During the field visit of the Research Team, villagers from many habitations whom used to receive more than 40 liters per day per person earlier reported severe scarcity of water. Hence, during the planning process sensitization of people on water management has to be considered, they suggested.

It is learnt that priorities were given to CC road, burial ground and street lights, no other works under water supply was undertaken, due to depletion of groundwater and failure of many bore-wells dug in earlier period, the President of Ambathurai reported.

It is learnt that the residents of many habitations of Vilpatti Village Panchayat expected that under the scheme many no. of CC roads would be provided. They told that due to ups and downs, the mobility through the mud roads was a risky one. Hence their major demand is provision of CC roads and retaining wall along the major passage to prevent the soil erosion.

Their next demand is street lights and facilities at all burial grounds. The villagers of Vilpatti enforced that common land is hardly available in the hilly villages. Also habitations are located scatter. During the planning for the improvement of all basic needs, special attention has to be exercised for hilly villages, as the situations are different from villages which are located at plain area.

In habitation based planning process, the basic needs have been identified and listed out. During fund allocation felt needs of SC habitation got priorities. Accordingly, different works like new bore-well, mini power pump, GLR and pipe line extensions were undertaken. These are the specific felt needs of residents of habitations than the needs projected for overall village panchayat.

Another interesting finding is that instead of providing CC roads in two hamlets at Kasavanampatti sample village panchayat, BT roads were provided improving the existing metal road which serve as the road for connectivity to farm area as well as to nearby habitation. It is possible because public identified the right type of works as well as the survey team was able to finalize those works within the guidelines.

Yet another important observation is that at one of the sample villages Ambathurai, none of work under water supply is undertaken under the scheme. Though water scarcity was reported during the survey in four habitations, due to non-availability of groundwater and failure of many bore-wells dug earlier, the village panchayat administration in consultation with the block officials decided not to take water service work under the scheme and so the fund was utilized for other felt needs namely CC roads and street lights. This is the merit of habitation based planning, permitting flexibility in selection and prioritization.

It is also observed that preference is given to habitation where SC population is more where water supply improvement and provision of street lights and CC road were provided under the scheme.

Pudukottai District

Table 2.2: No. of works completed in sample Village Panchayats in Pudukottai District

Sl. No.	Name of the Village Panchayat	Total No. of Habitation	No. of Habitation Work done	Water						Road		S L	Building				
				NB	MPP	PLE	OHT	HP	GLR	CCR	BT & WBM	SL	BG	C&D	TF	RW	BG
1.	Thulaiyanur	29	19	-	6	-	-	-	-	8	5	18	1	-	2	2	3
2.	Mimisal	10	7	-		8	-	-	-	2	3	5	1	1	-	-	-
3.	Vagavasal	16	10	-	5	1	1	1	-	1	3	32	1	-	-	1	-
4.	Viralur	18	12	-	6	-	-	2	-	4	1	20	6	-	-	-	-

NB: New Bore well, MPP—Mini Power Pump, PLE—Pipe Line Extension, OHT—Over Head Tank, HP—Hand Pump, GLR&DW—GLR Deepening Well, CCR—Cement Concrete Road, BT&WBM—Block Thar & With Blue Metal Road, SL—Street Light, BG—Burial Ground, C&D—Culvert and Drainage, TF—Threshing Floor, RW—Retaining Wall, BG—Bathing Ghat.

Source: Computed.

Public participation was very good at Thulaianur Village Panchayat, by which many felt needs were identified and priority was given to the real needs though other needs are grouped under the scheme. Balanced view was taken in providing street lights and CC road considering condition of street in the hamlet villages. Works have been distributed to many habitations than concentrating a few. The BT roads provided under the scheme are very much useful as it connects main roads which lead to district headquarters and other important places.

At Mimisal, the available fund was fruitfully distributed to those habitations where the public were encouraged to discuss and to decide priority by themselves, it is learnt.

At Vagavasal Village Panchayat, in spite of many hamlets demanded many felt needs apart from the work type earmarked under the scheme, the villagers were able to identify prioritized needs and successfully finalized the needier works during the planning process. The habitation based planning enriched the view of micro planning among the general public and enabling the key stakeholders to sustain their spirit in initiating micro level planning, it is found.

Strength of Collective Responsibilities

At Viralur Village Panchayat, attention was given in analyzing the issues and fixing priority so as the fund could be spared to fulfil the demand of other habitations. Being an affair of one-year duration, the scheme has to be completed within the duration of the financial year earmarked for each village panchayat. All the officials of concerned level maintained the time schedule earmarked for each frame of the scheme namely survey, selection and gram sabha approval, super check, scrutiny and administrative sanction, tender call, issue of work order, supervision inspection and review and completion. As clean guidelines are available besides quick response of the higher officials pertaining to clarifications, and fixing of responsibility and accountability, the scheme has been completed successfully without any carry over to next financial year. This is possible thanks to officials and public involvement.

Flexibility than Uniformity

In respect of variations among the sample districts appropriate approaches were taken to fulfil the felt needs under each category of works namely water, street lights, roads and buildings (burial ground). In respect of habitation coverage, in the district of Pudukottai more habitations covered than other two districts. Pipeline extension work did not get priority in the district of Villupuram as adequate mini power pumps are provided under the scheme. In the district of Dindigul more number of street lights (124) are provided comparing Pudukkottai (75) and Villupuram (34). This shows that felt needs of habitations at Dindigul district, i.e. about 50 per cent of the total habitations at Dindigul district has been covered in respect of provision of street lights. In the district of Villupuram, the habitation range is up to 3 in many numbers of villages. Hence, it is reported the demand for street lights is not high.

Regarding provision of roads and more no. of BT roads more no. of CC roads (25) and (26) respectively are provided in Dindigul district. The next district in this respect is Villupuram (18).

It is observed that hill villages namely Vilpatti of Dindigul district and Vellimalai of Villupuram district in more number of habitations (9 nos. and 8 nos.) respectively compared to other sample villages, more no. of CC roads are provided, i.e. 10 nos. and 8 nos. respectively. In respect of providing facilities at burial ground, in the district of Pudukottai, more no. of habitation (9 nos.) has been covered than Dindigul and Villupuram districts (4 nos. and 6 nos. respectively). In the district of Pudukottai, more no. of other building works namely bathing ghat (3 nos.), threshing floor (3 nos.), retaining wall (2 nos.) and culvert (3 nos.) have been undertaken at one sample village namely Thulayanur. Being the most felt needs of the public of Thulayanur these works were permitted, it is learnt.

Villupuram District

Though there are issues in the provision of water supply, street lights and CC road in many habitations at Vellimalai Village Panchayat, due to habitation based planning, most needed habitations are identified and preference is given to address the above issues. The BT road is provided at a crucial habitation namely Thalvalapadi by which more than five habitations located around and upper level area get connectivity. Further, a drainage and CC road were provided at Vellimalai where the Block Office, Village Panchayat Office and Ration shop are located in the higher level. Hence, the mobility of vehicle especially heavy vehicles could not be possible during the rainy season. Transporting ration commodities is a challenging task. In that circumstances under the scheme, a drainage and CC road were provided considering the seriousness of the issue. Such felt needs were reported and included in the habitation based planning.

Table 2.3: No. of works completed in sample Village Panchayats in Villupuram District

Sl. No	Name of the Village Panchayat	Total No. of Habitations	No. of Habitations Work done	Water						Road		SL	Building				
				NB	MPP	PLE	OHT	HP	GLR	CCR	BT & WBM	SL	BG	C&D	TF	RW	BG
1.	Bommaiyarpalayam	4	4	-	2	-	-	-	-	7	1	13	5	3	-	-	-
2.	Singanur	3	3	-	2	-	1	-	-	3	-	10	2	-	-	-	-
3.	Thennamadevi	4	3	-	2	-	-	-	-	-	1	4	3	-	-	-	-
4.	Vellimalai	20	18	-	4	-	-	-	3	8	1	7	1	1	-	-	-
	Total	176	123	3	35	16	2	3	4	56	22	243	24	5	2	3	3

NB: New Bore-well, MPP—Mini Power Pump, PLE—Pipe Line Extension, OHT—Over Head Tank, HP—Hand Pump, GLR&DW—GLR Deepening Well, CCR—Cement Concrete Road, BT&WBM—Block Thar & With Blue Metal Road, SL—Street Light, BG—Burial Ground, C&D—Culvert and Drainage, TF—Threshing Floor, RW—Retaining Wall, BG—Bathing Ghat.

Source: Computed.

Within the available fund, at Singanur Village Panchayat preference is given to water supply, street lights and CC road. Further providing basic amenities at burial ground, the real felt needs of the public were taken to consideration than to spend money for other needs, demanded by public. During the habitation based planning public of Thennamadevi Village Panchayat reported water supply, street lights, CC road and facilities at the site for burial ground. Except CC road, all the other felt needs demanded by the villagers have been fulfilled. Because of habitation based planning at Bommaiyarpalayam Village Panchayat, water supply, street light, and CC road have been provided at the neediest habitations. BT road is serving connectivity to main bazar area. At all habitations many basic facilities are available at burial ground except approach road. Hence, approach road only provided under at burial grounds.

2.4. Role of Local Bodies

The village panchayat administration has the responsibility of administering the survey format as per the guidance of block officials. Then the panchayat president along with the block officials involve in prioritizing the need, put before the gram sabha convened exclusively for THAI work.

It is learnt in some cases, there could be a change in the village panchayat administration, it is told. It is learnt from the villagers/ ward members that the demands made by them even though at a minimum cost were set aside and work of a heavy cost has been taken in some hamlets. The villagers shared that instead of diverting a large sum for road works like two-layer WBM+BT road under THAI, other source of fund like MLA/MP area development fund could be sanctioned. By which many number of small felt needs demanded by villagers could be successfully fulfilled under THAI.

The village panchayat president informed that the works under THAI were implemented by the union administration. Even the details of tender finalized for the execution has not been officially informed to the village panchayat administration. The contractors if are informed about any deficiency in respect of quality, they do not give their ear to the village panchayat president/ward member, they added. The panchayat presidents remarked that even without verifying the functioning of water supply works like pumping of water/storage of water without any leakages, the amount due to contractor has been paid and the assets created are handed over to the village panchayat administration. The village panchayat administration could not have power/resource to rectify if any deficiency is found in the assets handed over to them by the block panchayat administration, they added.

2.5 Conclusion

The project appears to be conventional infrastructure facility creation. It is totally construction of culverts, laying of roads, giving electricity connection and providing street lights, creating connectivity to cremation grounds, providing facilities to the same and a few others. But all are infrastructure building activities. These facilities have been given to the villages over a period of six decades. Enormous amount of resources has been spent over them and as a result one cannot argue that almost all basic needs of the villages are being provided. Of course, continuously such facilities have been given to the villages gradually. Yet one cannot argue that every segment of the rural communities is having access to all those basic facilities created in the rural areas. Because each and every village panchayat has many hamlets ranging from 3 to 37 and it varies from village to village. Villages affiliated with the caste hierarchy which acted as a barrier to the deprived communities to have access with the facilities created in the villages. To respond to the above problem an unconventional scheme has been evolved namely 'THAI'. It is a scheme of reaching the unreached. It is both target and process oriented. It touches the life of the neglected poor and marginalized poor in the rural areas. While touching the poor through this scheme, their dignity is intact. People those who are in periphery mostly marginalized have not been accessing the facilities created for the entire village. Neither it is being highlighted nor is it being solved. People who are deprived have internalized and they have not projected as an issue in the rural area. It is only 'THAI' which tries to solve the unmet needs of the deprived communities through a new mechanism. Even after two decades of experience, the local bodies have not solved this issue and not even made it an issue to the state government.

Under 'THAI' scheme, an amount ranging from 20 to 50 lakhs of rupees spent for infrastructure creation especially for creation of basic minimum facilities to lead a decent and dignified human life. Having seen the weaknesses of the Panchayati Raj system and its politics, the scheme has been entrusted to the panchayats. The responsibility of planning has been entrusted to the panchayats. The synergy between panchayats and local body officials which enabled the deliberative democracy to work better in prioritizing the works to be implemented in the rural areas for the benefit of the marginalized and neglected. 'THAI' scheme further advocated that the needs of the people have to be assessed scientifically and the works are to be prioritized through a deliberation process to strengthen local body system. It made it mandatory that it should be done through a participatory planning. In this process, a tool has been developed very comprehensively and by using the tool data have been collected. For that purpose, a team has been formed and they are oriented in data collection and they have been validated. Based on the need, menu of activities chosen from the scheme and from the perspective of the marginalized, works to be attended with the money under this scheme is decided through a gram sabha meeting. Since the officials participated in the gram sabha meeting, by giving convincing argument, decision have been taken to attend to the needs of the marginalized communities. Further, the scheme relies on dovetailing of the schemes to attend to the basic needs has worked to some extent.

This scheme raised hope among the hopeless families in the villages to evince interest in the scheme that they are the main stakeholders. The money spent in this scheme has been judicially used. Since the scheme worked on the long felt needs of the neglected, the utility of the scheme is maximum. People have been oriented to speak in scientific terms in water governance. Through this process water governance issues have reached the more remote corner of the villages. Water has been used rationally and judicially. While evaluating the impact one could see the happiness and joy of the poor, women, aged and *dalit* in enjoying the benefits of the scheme people who lived without any hope of getting all these facilities, have been provided, at their door steps, with all these facilities have created unfathomable joy. These facilities, most of them, are gap filling one. They really served the people to lead their life with dignity. It has been given a sense to the poor that the government will attend to the last man's need as it is people's, government. The scheme is unequivocally an innovative, creative and pro-poor.

3

Benefits Acquired by the People

Habitation based planning not only improved the status of basic amenities and infrastructure facilities but also brought a change in the mindset and behaviour of the rural population. It is learnt from the key stakeholders the sequential listing of works component in this scheme is very meaningful and justifiable. Under the frame of categorization of priorities provision of minimum basic requirements is in the top then only follows additional requirements and other works.

Further under provision of minimum requirement there is an ordering of priorities, helped in distributing the works in many habitations rather than concentrating in a few villages. This framework helped them to act quickly and based on consensus during the decision making process in the panchayats.

In this chapter, the major utility of the scheme found in the study is reported in five major categories—namely Water, Street light, Road, Burial ground, and Building. It is as shown as in Table 3.1.

In Dindigul district Sendurai Gram panchayat, out of total 24 habitations 6 habitations are under water supply provision, 3 new bore-wells and 4 mini power pumps have been provided. It is learnt that there is no scarcity of water during the survey time. But to meet out any challenge during the summer the above referred water supply works have been provided. At Sendurai being the main village as well as a centre of enterprises and business activities, a new bore-well and one mini power pump were provided considering its local and floating population. In three hamlet villages namely, Kalathupatti, Mamarathupatti and Pandhipommi Nayackanur at the rate of one mini power pump (totally 3 mini power pumps) has been provided. Preference is given to mini power pump as habitations are distantly located, and the topography is ups and downs, arrangement of pipe

Table 3.1: No. of works completed under water supply in sample Village Panchayats

Sl. No.	*Name of the Village Panchayat*	*Total No. of Habitations*	*No. of Habitations Work done*	*Water Supply*					
				NB	*MPP*	*PLE*	*HP*	*GLR/OHT*	*DW*
1.	Sendurai	24	6	3	4	0	0	0	0
2.	Ambathurai	11	0	0	0	0	0	0	0
3.	Vilpatti	26	1	0	0	0	0	1*	0
4.	Kasavanampati	11	9	0	4	7	0	0	0
5.	Thulayanur	29	4	0	5	0	0	0	0
6.	Mimisal	10	5	0	0	8	0	0	0
7.	Vagavasal	16	6	0	5	1	1	1	0
8.	Viralur	18	5	0	6	0	2	0	0
9.	Bommaiyarpalayam	4	2	0	2	0	0	0	0
10.	Singanur	3	1	0	2	0	0	1	0
11.	Thannamadevi	4	1	0	2	0	0	0	0
12.	Vellimalai	20	6	0	4	0	0	0	3
	Total	176	46	3	34	17	3	3	3

NB: New Bore well, MPP—Mini Power Pump, PLE—Pipe Line Extension, OHT—Over Head Tank, HP—Hand Pump, GLR&DW—GLR Deepening Well.

Source: Computed.

There are 62 works under water supply were carried out in 46 hebitations of the sample villages.

* GLR

More attention is given to provide Mini power pump (34 nos.) and provision of Pipe Line Extension (17 nos.).

line extension from existing OHTs are not possible. Against this backdrop provision of the above works is meaningful and very much benefited to the households of these habitations.

In the village panchayat of Villpatti, out of 26 habitations at only one habitation namely Mattupatti, a GLR with pipeline extension was provided. But water supply through GLR is not succeeded due to leakage. The Union and Village Panchayat administration assured to address the issue. It is reported that the water supply needs planned for various habitations would be fulfilled through dovetailing the panchayat fund.

In the village panchayat of Ambathurai, in respect of water supply no work was selected under the scheme as many bore-wells dug already were failed due to very poor yield or no yield at all.

In the Village panchayat of Kasavanampatti, out of 11 habitations in 9 habitations, 19 works have been undertaken. Accordingly, 3 new bore-wells, 8 mini power pumps and 8 pipeline extensions were provided. It is reported that the main source of water at Kombai Hilly area are being shared with one of a neighbouring village panchayat namely, Karisalpatti. To ensure adequate water, the above referred works were carried out as priority to the above referred habitations.

In Pudukottai district in the village panchayat of Thulaynur out of 29 habitations in 4 habitations, 5 mini power pumps were provided.

Mini power pump near the Middle School at Kulathupatti habitation.

In all the above habitations, the supply of water per head per day is below 40 liters. Now the inadequacy in Mini power pump near the Middle School at Kulathupatti habitation, the supply is addressed successfully through this scheme. The School children are now cleaning of hands and plates before and after having the noon-meal.

In the village panchayat of Mimisal, out of 10 habitations at 5 habitations, 8 pipeline extension works were carried out. It is learnt that due to coastal area deep bore-well is not successful. Hence, preference is given to pipeline extension from the successful mini power pump already existed.

At Vagavasal village panchayat, out of 16 habitations at 6 habitations, 8 works were carried out. 5 mini power pumps, a pipeline extension and a new OHT were provided under the scheme which addressed the issue of very poor quantity of water 6-25 liter per head per day in the above habitations.

At Viralur village panchayat out of 18 habitations at 5 habitations, 8 works were carried out. There are 6 mini power pumps, two hand pumps were provided under this scheme which addressed the issue of very poor quantity of water 12-26 liter per head per day in the above habitations.

In Villupuram district at Bommaiyarpalayam village panchayat there are 4 hamlets and in two hamlets namely Kuilampalayam hamlet which have more number of habitations and at Pillaichavadi colony due to SC habitation priority given in this respect. Accordingly, at each of the above referred hamlets two mini power pumps were provided. At Singanur village panchayat out of 3 hamlets at one hamlet in two habitations, 3 works were undertaken and OHT at Singanur which is the main village and 2 mini power pumps at Singanur extension area. Hence, the issue of inadequacy of water 29-38 liter per head per day in the above habitations was addressed successfully. At Thennamadevi village panchayat out of 3 hamlets at one hamlet namely, Poothamedu, 2 mini power pumps were provided to meet the challenge in the distribution during the summer.

At Vellimalai village panchayat out of 20 hamlets in 6 hamlets, 4 mini power pumps were provided and 3 wells were deepened. Earlier women living in the above hamlets were used to get less than 40 liters per day and went to distantly located private farm lands to fetch water. The issue of inadequacy in the distribution of water and more time spending to fetch water are successfully addressed.

It is mentioned that in the process of planning and implementing the water supply scheme to the habitations which have been neglected for long one will find not only the service delivery but also the sensitivity on water governance. People started realizing

the importance of water governance. They speak accurately the need of water in terms of quantity and availability of water. By fixing the mini pump, water problem has been solved. People those who got these benefits are immensely pleased and happy.

Table 3.2: No. of works completed under street light in sample Village Panchayats

Sl. No	Name of the Village Panchayat	Total No. of Habitation	No. of Habitation where Work done	Street Light
1.	Sendurai	24	10	75
2.	Ambathurai	11	7	34
3.	Vilpatti	26	8	16
4.	Kasavanampati	11	6	9
5.	Thulayanur	29	8	18
6.	Mimisal	10	3	5
7.	Vagavasal	16	4	32
8.	Viralur	18	3	20
9.	Bommaiyarpalayam	4	2	13
10.	Singanur	3	2	10
11.	Thannamadevi	4	1	4
12.	Vellimalai	20	6	7
	Total	176	60	243

Source: Computed.

There are 243 no. of new street lights provided in the 60 habitations in the sample villages.

In Sendurai panchayat at Dindigul district, 75 street lights have been provided in ten habitations out of 24 habitations.

In the Village panchayat of Ambathurai, 34 street lights have been provided in 7 habitations out of 11 habitations. In the village panchayat of Vilpatti, 16 street lights have been provided in 8 habitations out of 26 habitations. In the Village panchayat of Kasavanampatti, 9 street lights have been provided in 6 habitations out of 11 habitations.

In the district of Pudukottai, in the village panchayat of Thulaynur out of 29 habitations at 8 habitations, 18 street lights were provided. In the village panchayat of Mimisal out of 10 habitations at 3 habitations, 5 street light work were provided. At Vagavasal village panchayat out of 16 habitations at 4 habitations, 32 were provided. At Viralur village panchayat out of 18 habitations at 3 habitations, 20 street lights were provided.

In the district of Villupuram, at Bommaiyarpalayam village panchayat there are 4 hamlets and in two hamlets 13 street lights were provided. At Singanur village panchayat out of 3 hamlets at 2 hamlets, 10 street lights were provided. At Thennamadevi village panchayat out of 4 hamlets at one hamlet 4 street lights were provided. At Vellimalai village panchayat out of 20 hamlets at 6 hamlets 7 street lights were provided.

Street light and CC road at Konakkadu-Vellimalai Pt.

Street lights at Thazdevanur habitation-Vellimalai Pt.

Almost all the street lights are provided only to the hamlets which are considered essential for the people by the panchayats with the approval of gram sabha members. When other hamlets have been enjoying these benefits for several years, the hamlet which have been neglected these street lights for long. Whenever the panchayats got such facilities, the main villages have captured them. But this scheme reached out the needy and neglected because the scheme guidelines have been devised in such a way that they cannot be captured by the powerful and dominant groups. All deficiencies in the panchayat system have been realized and hence the state government has integrated the officials into the panchayats for planning and implementation of the scheme (Table 3.3).

Table 3.3: No. of works completed under Road works in sample Village Panchayats

Sl. No.	*Name of the Village Panchayat*	*Total No. of Habitation*	*No. of Habitation where Works done*	*Road*	
				CC	*WBM & BT*
1.	Sendurai	24	6	6 (6)	0 (0)
2.	Ambathurai	11	6	10 (5)	3 (2)
3.	Vilpatti	26	9	10 (9)	1 (1)
4.	Kasavanampatti	11	3	0 (0)	3 (3)
5.	Thulayanur	29	13	8 (8)	5 (5)
6.	Mimisal	10	5	2 (2)	3 (3)
7.	Vagavasal	16	4	1 (1)	3 (3)
8.	Viralur	18	5	4 (4)	1 (1)
9.	Bommaiyarpalayam	4	4	7 (4)	1 (1)
10.	Singanur	3	3	3 (3)	0 (0)
11.	Thannamadevi	4	1	0 (0)	1 (1)
12.	Vellimalai	20	9	8 (8)	1 (1)
	Total	**176**	**68**	**59 (50)**	**22 (21)**

* Number inside the parentheses shows total no. of habitation.

CCR — Cement Concrete Road,

BT&WBM— Block Thar & With Blue Metal Road.

There are 59 no. of CC roads, were provided in 50 no. of habitations.

There are 22 no. of WBM&BT roads and 2 layer WBM BT road provided under THAI in 21 no. of habitations.

Source: Computed.

In the district of Dindigul, in the village panchayat of Sendurai out of total 24 habitations at 6 habitations, 6 CC roads one at each habitation are provided.

In the Village panchayat of Ambathurai, in respect of road works out of 11 habitations there are 10 CC roads provided in 5 habitations and 3 WBM&BT road provided in 2 habitations.

In the village panchayat of Vilpatti, out of 26 habitations at 9 habitations, 10 CC roads and 1 WBM&BT road were provided. In the Village panchayat of Kasavanampatti, out of 11 habitations at 3 habitations, 3 CC roads have been undertaken. In Pudukottai district at Thulaynur village panchayat out of 29 habitations at 13 habitations, 8 CC roads and 5 WBM&BT roads were provided. In the village panchayat of Mimisal out of 10 habitations at 5 habitations, 2 CC roads and 2 WBM&BT roads work were carried out.

At Vagavasal village panchayat out of 16 habitations at 4 habitations one CC road and 3 WBM&BT roads were provided. At Viralur village panchayat out of 18 habitations at 5 habitations, 4 CC road works and one WBM&BT road were provided.

In Villupuram district, at Bommaiyarpalayam village panchayat there are 4 hamlets and in 4 habitations, 4 CC roads and one WBM&BT road were provided. At Singanur village panchayat out of 3 hamlets at two habitations, 3 CC road works were undertaken.

At Thennamadevi village panchayat out of 4 hamlets at one hamlet one WBM&BT road was provided which connects State Highways lead to National Highways.

At Vellimalai village panchayat out of 20 hamlets at 9 hamlets, 8 CC roads and one WBM&BT road were provided.

For many, providing a road facility is nothing as in Tamil Nadu even remotest places are connected through roads and mini buses are being operated. People those who are enjoying the facilities may not know the importance. Despite the fact many of the habitations are well connected, a few are neglected. People those who are not having such facilities now got that facility. When we hear the observation from a beneficiary that these roads are not only connected the hamlets with main roads, the roads are really a place for us to sleep in the nights, sit together for hours and discuss, dry our agriculture produces. He further lamented that the girls who got bicycles are now freely riding them on the roads joyfully to reach the school.

Table 3.4: No. of works completed under Building works in sample Village Panchayats

Sl. No	Name of the Village Panchayat	Total No. of Habitation	No. of Habitation Work done	Buildings					
				Burial ground	Bathing Ghat	Threshing Floor	Retaining Wall	Culvert	Drainage
1.	Sendurai	24	1	1 (1)	0	0	0	0	0
2.	Ambathurai	11	1	1 (1)	0	0	0	0	0
3.	Vilpatti	26	1	1 (1)	0	0	0	0	0
4.	Kasavanampatti	11	1	2 (2)	0	0	0	0	0
5.	Thulayanur	29	11	1 (1)	3	3	2	3	0
6.	Mimisal	10	2	1 (1)	0	0	0	1	0
7.	Vagavasal	16	2	1 (1)	0	0	1	0	0
8.	Viralur	18	6	6 (6)	0	0	0	0	0
9.	Bommaiyarpalayam	4	1	0 (0)	0	0	0	3	0
10.	Singanur	3	2	2 (2)	0	0	0	0	0
11.	Thannamadevi	4	3	3 (3)	0	0	0	0	0
12.	Vellimalai	20	1	1 (1)	0	1	0	0	1
	Total	176	32	19(19)	3	4	3	7	1

BG—Burial Ground, C&D—Culvert and Drainage, TF—Threshing Floor, RW—Retaining Wall, BG—Bathing Ghat.

* Number inside the parentheses shows total no. of habitations.

– There are 19 no. of burial ground in 19 no. of habitations.

– There are 3 no. of bathing ghats, 4 no. of threshing floor, 3 no. of retaining wall at Oorani, 7 no. of culverts and 1 no. of drainage/culvert, provided under THAI.

Source: Computed.

In Dindigul district at Sendurai village panchayat out of total 24 habitations at one habitation, one burial ground was provided. In the Village panchayat of Ambathurai, out of total 11 habitations at one habitation one burial ground works was undertaken. In the village panchayat of Vilpatti, out of total 26 habitations at one habitation, facilities at one burial ground were provided.

In the Village panchayat of Kasavanampatti, out of total 11 habitations at two habitations, at two burial ground facilities were provided.

In Pudukottai district at Thulayanur, out of total 26 habitations at one habitation, facilities in a burial ground were provided. There are other building works, namely 3 bathing ghats, 3 retaining walls, 2 threshing floors and 3 culverts have been provided in this village panchayat. The bathing ghats and retaining walls are provided at three

Threshing Floor

water tanks which are used by the villagers for bathing and washing. To ensure safety and convenience at the above water source, the villagers referred the above demands as their felt needs during the survey. Hence, these facilities were provided under the category of 'other works'.

Retaining Wall and bathing ghat.

At Vagavasal, out of total 10 habitations at one habitation, facilities at one burial ground and a retaining wall were provided.

In the Village panchayat of Viralur, in respect of buildings out of total 18 habitations at 6 habitation facilities at 6 burial ground works were undertaken.

Burial ground at Pallamatham habitation in Viralur Pt.

In the village panchayat of Mimisal, out of total 10 habitations at one habitation, a burial ground was provided. There is one more building work, namely culvert which serves as drainage was provided in this village panchayat.

In Villupuram district at Bommaiyarpalayam village panchayat at three habitations at the rate of one each three culverts were provided. At Singanur village panchayat at two habitations, facilities in two burial grounds were provided.

'Kariyakottagai' (place for post funeral ceremony) at Thennamadevi Pt.

At Thennamadevi at three habitation facilities at burial ground were provided, by which all four hamlets in this village panchayat have burial ground with all minimum facilities.

At Vellimalai main village facilities at the burial ground and drainage were provided. At a remote habitation a threshing floor is provided which is very much useful to dry agriculture commodities by farmers.

Threshing floor at Mel-vellimalai.

CC road with drainage at Vellimalai.

Burial ground is the birth-place of many social conflicts in the villages. At one point of time Government of Tamil Nadu announced an award for the villages which maintain common ground for all caste groups. Very few panchayats got awards. In most of the villages, the burial grounds are maintained for different social groups separately. In a same village panchayat some burial grounds with needed facilities, others did not have such facilities. Sometimes road facility to reach the burial ground. Through this scheme, the felt needs of some neglected social groups in getting such facilities have been provided with burial ground with all needed facilities. People expressed happiness that they are free from the mental tension whenever they face problem in burning the dead bodies in their villages by getting these facilities. Panchayat is also free from tension as it has to intervene every time to solve the conflicts between communities. People considered that it is a major achievement in their panchayat.

4
Integrated Analysis

4.1 Introduction

Addressing the issues of equity in the process of development in the rural areas is a challenging task. In spite of the efforts of six decades of planned development, the expected development has not been percolated equally to all villages and communities. Even in provision of minimum facilities and basic infrastructure at every village panchayat many state governments are struggling to reach success. But the conditions in the State of Tamil Nadu are a different one. The Government of Tamil Nadu has realized that about 50 per cent of total population living in rural area and in its policy on rural development focuses to bridge the gap between urban and rural divide. In this respect, the state government takes the needed care in availing RD schemes, funds of Government of India besides planning and implementing many innovative state funded schemes like Namathugamam, Comprehensive Rural Infrastructure Development scheme, and Rural Road maintenance scheme. Hence, villagers in Tamil Nadu have relatively better facilities and services in terms of electricity, drinking water, road connectivity, transport, education and health when compared to most other states.

At this juncture it is found that the speed rate of urbanization in Tamil Nadu is increasing, among the major causes identified for the migration. Unemployment and inadequate infrastructure facilities are referred by the development experts. And so the government took further steps to strengthen its endeavour to improve the quality of life in rural areas. And thereby introduced an innovative flagship programme namely THAI. THAI scheme is unique in many respects it takes habitation has the basic unit for planning this will address the issues like disparities in development and skewed distribution of assets. It includes hitherto excluded segment of the societies. Under THAI a massive and comprehensive survey was undertaken involving people and status of basic minimum facilities and infrastructures available in each habitation and the gap to be fulfilled to ensure a decent living environment at each habitation.

On the basis of priority provision of water supply, street lights, roads, burial grounds, and pathways to burial grounds have been emphasized. Considering the number of habitations and average population, fund allotment was earmarked, i.e., minimum grant of Rs. 20 lakhs to maximum Rs. 50 lakhs under four ranges of habitations. Considering the role of local bodies in bringing economic development and social justice, under the scheme major activities of mobilizing public, administration of survey for identification of felt needs, and prioritization and finalization of works with the approval of gram sabha was entrusted to village panchayat. The plan implementation was given to block panchayat because of human resources and technical expertise. Principles of governance like transparency, accountability, participation and inclusiveness have been ensured through effective IEC, application of Tamil Nadu Tender Transparency Act and online monitoring and reporting of all activities. During the period of 2011-12 to 2015-16, the scheme was implemented in all the village panchayats of Tamil Nadu. Considering the above referred innovative nature of the scheme, a study was considered necessary to assess its impact and its effectiveness.

It is found out that the families living in the habitations have developed faith in habitation based grassroots planning as it promised to fulfil their basic minimum needs. Moreover, during the planning process participation of people was encouraged through discourses with elected representatives, union officials and engineers in the gram sabha meetings. It is found out that because of the transparent discourses and transactions villagers understood the rights and entitlements of the marginalized to whom the development rights have been denied so far. Hence, when ordering the priority of works and the locations consensus was arrived at in the gram sabha meetings. Accordingly, habitations where the poor and marginalized are living have been successfully selected for this scheme. It is found out that at many habitations in each village panchayat the promises have been fulfilled. But there are gaps. Demands made by villagers are yet to be fulfilled especially in respect of street lights, and burial ground facilities. People expected that the state government has to continue the scheme to fulfil the promises it made. If the scheme is continued it would be the uncomparable achievement in the history of Tamil Nadu in respect of providing basic infrastructure for the transformation of the rural areas. In this chapter an attempt is made to highlight the major achievements of this scheme in the life of the marginalised and the poor living in the remote villages without such basic facilities to lead a decent dignified human life.

In this respect references were made from the Focus Group Discussion (FGD), Interview with the key stakeholders, Physical Verification on the planning process, implementation, and role of local bodies in all the above processes.

Sendurai Village Panchayat

People responded very positively during the survey and the planning processes. They reported that their major felt needs were attended through this scheme. The conditions of the burial ground have been improved. Further provision of street lights, water supply and road facilities have also been attended to. Accordingly, it was reported that at five habitations all such facilities have been provided. But at four habitations the selected works were proposed to be carried out from the union general fund and the village fund. This change was

made as in course of time the residence of many habitations demanded additional street lights and new street lights than the total number of street lights finalized under THAI. Bringing mutual understanding and acceptance among the people of many habitations was successfully achieved through the lengthy and participatory discussion during the gram sabha meeting.

During the planning process it was finalized to provide fifty street lights but during the gram sabha meeting the participants hailed from remotest habitations and the extension area of the main habitation demanded additional street lights than finalized for them. The ward members emphasized that, "by providing a few more number of tube lights additionally and provision of new street lights at the extension area the concept of provision of minimum street lights at all habitations would be completed. They further reported that the habitations are spread in all directions and the distance between the habitations also a long one besides all of them located at the foothills. In the meantime, the officials informed the participants' provision of new and additional street lights than the decided earlier could be possible if the villagers agreed to forgo some works sanctioned to them. When it was proposed to cancel providing facilities at burial ground at four habitations, the public of concerned habitations strongly objected. The officials enabled all the participants to understand the significance of provision of street lights under the scheme as there was no other large amount available in any other scheme to provide more street lights at one stroke. After a lengthy and serious discussion, a consensus was arrived at. Cancellation of providing facilities at four burial grounds was effected after consultation duly made with higher officials. Now there are 75 street lights provided in ten habitations. The main achievement in this respect is that at Periyurpatti habitation highest numbers of street lights (25) have been provided. The overall expenditure in providing street lights at Sendurai village panchayat is a higher side comparatively to other sample villages. It is because of reaching the remote area, covering the long distance and provision of more new poles. Because of THAI and the participatory discussion with the practical guidance of officials, it was possible to achieve this.

There is a case for merit of participatory habitation based planning and implementation of THAI scheme. At Thirunuthupatti hamlet of Sendurai village panchayat CC road was sanctioned. During the formation of CC road, the beneficiaries around 15 respondents discussed with the engineers that the full utility of CC road could be possible if only a proper drainage system provided along with the CC road. The engineer suggested that if the householders agreed to meet the expenditure of laying PVC pipe line under the CC road drain out of sewage water from houses could be possible. The residents have agreed to do so. It was carried out.

> *"Because of the opportunity available for clarifications and interaction between the officials and ourselves during the planning process, the suggestion given by the engineer was well taken, Muthuvel, one of the residents informed. He further shared that we discussed among ourselves and decided to spend our own money. We purchased the PVC pipe at needed length to get connection from our home to the main drainage line which is laid down under the CC road, for easy disposal of waste water. Further to avoid dropping down of solid wastes inside the drainage we ourselves constructed a filter junction with lid to cover. There is no bad smell, smooth running of water without any stagnation of solid waste. Though the CC road is public road it serves us the front portion of our house, very convenient to sit and relax, place for children's play, enjoyment and during night place for study because street lights also provided under THAI. We feel happy that out life style is improved".*

Ambathurai Village Panchayat

The notice board exhibited at public places and at the habitation where the activities under the scheme were carried out was a remarkable one compared to other schemes. Hence public awareness on the salient features of the scheme has improved and resulted in active participation of public during the planning process and their involvement in the activities is also improved, they added. Ward Members informed that they felt happy for sparing their time during the survey and follow-up discussion for fixing priorities as the government machinery itself come down to habitation level to fulfil their felt needs through the scheme which is readily available with allotted fund.

The villagers of Perumalkoilpatti hamlet reported that after the provision of CC road at full length in some streets, from the previous scheme the households' maintained cleanness and the quality of life has been improved. Whereas in remaining streets where CC roads have not been fully executed or yet to be provided, the waste water is overflown, and the area become very unclean and the health of children was affected during the rainy seasons. At that juncture Ms. Lakshmi, living at North Street informed that, "our street is very narrow; at the west of the main street temple and church are located, the streets are wide compared to east side. During the survey we demanded CC road at full length of our street. I represented on behalf of all households the case very seriously. The issue of stagnation of water, overflow of drainage water, and their impact in sudden break off water borne diseases was given in details by me. The officials have given a patient hearing and we succeeded in getting CC road full length of our street".

> *Now in spite of any heavy rain in our village there is no problem in our street. No stagnation of water, no bad smell from the muddy and sluggish ground, and no spreading of diseases. Our children enjoy spending time on the street than in sitting idle inside our small dwelling unit. Our elders frequently come out from the homes and move freely without the fear of falling down. We live in a new environment of clean and neat.*

Kasavanampatti Village Panchayat

Kasavanampatti is the mother village, where a famous temple is located. It is emerging as a pilgrimage centre attracting hundreds and thousands of people during the festivals. The entrance of the village and the campus of the temple are adjoined one. Hence two street lights provided at the entrance of the temple and a nearby street are very necessary and beneficial to public. Mini tanks provided at appropriate locations benefiting local people as well as pilgrims besides extending pipeline to the needy area due to availability of adequate water at the mini tank.

Many participants welcomed the new effort of habitation-based planning as it provided a new status to the basic infrastructure in their habitations. Because of habitation-based survey and plan of action, the village panchayat administration could project the need of habitations than project village panchayat as a whole. Accordingly, mobilization of fund from many other schemes could be attempted successfully, the vice-president opined.

Vilpatti Village Panchayat

The panchayat president informed that though survey format was administered to find the gap in the basic amenities and infrastructure facilities, other felt needs of the people reported during the survey were also noted down. The Ward Members reported that only in six wards under THAI works have been implemented. The Secretary of the Vilpatti panchayat informed that though it was only six wards but overall at 15 habitations various works have been undertaken under the scheme. The participants admitted that the habitation based approach was comparatively good than focusing the entire village panchayat.

The representatives from the tribal area expressed their satisfaction with regard to provision of street lights and CC roads to their area. The representatives of eleventh ward were happy to share that due to provision of street lights they were able to avail the house service connections from the electricity board. CC road provided in many habitation was very useful, especially to school going children and elder for safe mobility during rainy season. It is found that at the hilly village like Vilpatti, the public expectations are mostly provision of CC road, street lights, revetment, drainage, small bridge, culverts and improvement in burial ground and safe water supply than more number of BT roads.

There are other new demands like construction of health sub centre, SHG building and other public amenities.

Thulayanur Village Panchayat

The participants informed that the survey activity was a good attempt as during the survey, officials/engineer from the union office were available and discussed with public on the guidelines of THAI scheme and the fund allocation to the Thulaiyanur village panchayat. The president and vice-president informed that villagers actively participated in the survey and accompanied with the survey team to the spots. The participants reported that comparatively, the basic facilities in respect of water supply and CC road were improved a lot due to THAI.

The participants from Naavichippatti, Besantnagar and Valaiyanvayal told that the culvert, provided at their area were very much useful and it was their long pending demand. At the entrance road of these habitations there is stream through only public have to cross. Since it has been attended to through this scheme people felt that the THAI scheme is the only scheme attended to the unattended demands of the people.

Earlier the public use to cross over the stream where there is no proper culvert. During the rainy season it was a risky one. By providing a *pucca* culvert under the scheme connectivity to main road is improved and safe mobility of all vehicles is possible now.

In respect of utility and overall impact of the THAI scheme, the participants shared that all the works executed under the scheme were properly done and benefited the public. Especially, the facilities provided at burial ground are very much useful. Earlier, for fetching water they used to go to private farm lands in spite of the farm owners not encouraged to take water from their farm land. The participants further told that the farmers felt unhappy to give water from their well for burial related activities as they considered as a bad omen. Now the issue was over as hand pumps are provided in the burial ground.

The participants representing Cholatthavayal, Chinnakkalluvayal and Andakkudippatti hamlets informed that the Thrashing Floor provided under THAI was very much useful. Earlier the site being soil one and was not suitable for drying. Now many farmers are using the floor, it is told.

At the habitation phased planning the government fixed priority in providing minimum basic needs. But the demands of people may be different one. As people of Malaikudipatti, Santhanaviduthi and Andakkudipatti, expressed that "provision of retaining wall and

bathing ghat was their most felt needs as they don't have issue in getting water. It is our usual practice that women and children taking bath at the pond besides washing their clothes. Earlier we demanded to panchayat administration to provide bathing ghat at the pond. But it was not fulfilled. During the introduction of THAI scheme officials and panchayat presidents visited our villages for the survey works. We informed that to ensure our safety and convenient during bathing and washing at the pond provision of bathing ghat and retaining wall was very much essential. We reported that there were two incidents of falling down of elders and got injury due to muddy soil. So we insisted on our demand. But officials told as that it was not under the scheme. But we struck on our demand. In the meantime, participants from other habitations also endorsed our demands during the gram sabha meeting. Considering our explanation and support extended by residents of other habitations we have a well-constructed bathing ghat and a retaining wall to strengthen the bank of the pond". Thanks to the approach of participatory habitation based planning observed by participants of the FGD.

The participants informed that through survey the status of their village panchayat was clearly known to all. Among the needs demanded by them, many were fulfilled. To do the remaining works they expected fund allocation under THAI second phase.

Mimisal Village Panchayat

The panchayat president informed that as the comprehensive water supply was functioning, water is distributed to the public in ten habitations. But water supply is poor due to low pressure, the participants reported. Further they informed that the pipeline provided under THAI could be utilized to mitigate the issue at some extent as allocation of fund for digging new borewell was available through dovetailing.

Public from Kanmaikudiyeeruppu, informed that "our demand of CC road was a long pending one. It is a small habitation located aloof from Mimisal. Due to non-availability of proper road facility, school going children who used to walk/ride bi-cycle along the bund riverside with much tension as they could meet accidents of falling down. During emergency, patients and pregnant women were lifted over improvised cot for safe transportation. Our relatives, friends and other visitors felt suffering to go over to the habitation. Children missed fellowship with their peers. All these issues were resolved after the formation of CC road, pipeline extension and street lights under the scheme, it is possible because of the inclusive policy ensured through habitation based planning".

One of the Respondents

Further the public from the main village Mimisal, demanded CC road and culvert to overcome the problem of flood water. Under THAI their felt needs were fulfilled and the drainage water/flood water is now properly drained out. Now public safely cross over the outlet channel through the culvert, the president informed. After provision of CC road, the disposal of solid waste is successfully done at Mimisal.

Vagavasal Village Panchayat

The residents of Viswakarma Nagar reported the issue of depletion of groundwater and failure of mini power pump and demanded new mini power pumps. Under THAI two new mini tank facilities have been provided in which only at one bore-well of mini tank the ground water was adequate and the quality was good. It serves the families living in other streets. Generally, residents of one street when going other street for fetching water they could not be treated as equal but in this case because of participatory approach a mutual understanding and sharing of concern of households of other streets was well taken.

In provision of adequate water supply there is an issue of 'taste' and it should also be considered. At Thattampatti hamlet public informed that the taste of water is not good and a new hand pump was demanded. Public suggested during the survey that near the Kailasamuni Temple where the water source is adequate as well as tasty. Accordingly, a hand pump was provided under the scheme. The yields as well as taste of water from the hand pump were good. It is the merit of participatory planning.

The connectivity road provided at AvudayarOorani is not only useful to 25 households as well as to farming community in respect of transporting inputs for the farming activities and marketing the commodity produced. It is possible because of the detailed guidelines issued under the scheme for giving priority and seriousness shown by the officials in exercising ordering among the felt needs demanded. Otherwise some other roads with less utility would have been selected.

Viralur Village Panchayat

The participants shared that they felt happy over the survey work. With much enthusiasm they have participated during the survey work as the officials encouraged our participation and free discussion when giving the basic needs of each habitation.

The beneficiaries have expressed their happiness over the works undertaken at burial ground especially provision of hand pump and street lights. Some of the participants who made demand of new building for PDS during the survey questioned the reason for left out their demand. The Panchayat Secretary explained that PDS building was not possible due to group politics. As proper site was not identified in the time stipulated under implementation, the money earmarked for PDS shop was utilized for other works.

The villagers of Pallarnatham hamlet reported that, "When death occurs in our family we are suffering from grief but also feel more worry and tension over the burial of dead body peacefully. Due to options of road facilities we have to take the dead body and pass through a private land. Even to fetch water we have to get it from the wells located at private farms most of the occasion the farm owners refused and persuaded by village elders and panchayat president. Though we belong to same caste there is no disputes among us. But we feel very bad on losing our self-dignity. The announcement of THAI was boon to us by which we planned to make demand of providing facilities at our burial ground. Our plight was taken into consideration during the gramsabha meeting accordingly facilities are provided. The provision of hand pump is the great relief to our mental agony. The remaining issue of provision of road facilities was seriously discussed and the alternative root suggested by the president was accepted by all of us. A gravel road was provided on the bank of the pond. The road formation was undertaken under the fund earmarked for strengthening the assets created under MGNREGA. The issue of mental torture prevailed over the decades together was removed with one stroke. Thanks to the new initiative of habitation based planning.

Bommaiyarpalayam Village Panchayat

It is noticeable that contestants in the local body election during their campaign have the practice of promising many of their demands to fulfil if they win in the election. The public also make use of this opportunity to list out all their needs and demands that the ward member/panchayat president has to fulfil if they are elected. Under the THAI scheme, the important felt needs were targeted which gave confidence and hope to panchayat president that she/he could be able to fulfil their promises made to the voters. Further, the fund allocation and planning and implementation of work was scheduled within a year under the scheme. Because of these salient features village panchayat presidents felt fortunate irrespective of political parties they belonged to. The panchayat president of Bommaiyarpalayam informed that the allocation of fund under THAI was very much useful to fulfil major promises she made during the local body election.

The participants expressed their happiness that the need of water supply in all habitations were fulfilled to extent of 99 per cent with the allocation of fund from THAI and other schemes. Under the scheme activities like digging of new bore-well, provision of motor pump, laying of pipe line and OHT could not be possible under other schemes. But under this scheme because of allocation of fund under habitation range, the above demanded works of various habitations was possible to fulfil. The fund resources available at village panchayat and union panchayat is not adequate. Hence, the village panchayat gave a warm welcome to the scheme as it fulfils the felt needs of the people.

It is noticed that Bommaiyarpalayam being a coastal village the demand for provision of CC road was high under THAI and have seven CC roads were provided. The mobility of villagers become easy and convenient. By providing CC roads and BT road at the burial ground area under this scheme, the long felt needs of the people has been fulfilled and they are useful to reach the burial ground and connecting with main areas of living. An important development has to be shared here. It is reported that the ownership of site of the burial ground was an issue between the panchayat and a private Trust. Because of the habitation based planning, the site inspection and physical verification was made by the officials for finalizing the felt needs. They were able to help the panchayat administration in dealing the issue successfully and got the legal rights over the site. Now it becomes the panchayat property.

Singanur Village Panchayat

At Singanur village panchayat there are only three hamlets namely Singanur, Singanur Old Colony and Singanur New Colony. It is a multi-caste village panchayat but the population of SC community is considerably larger than other communities.

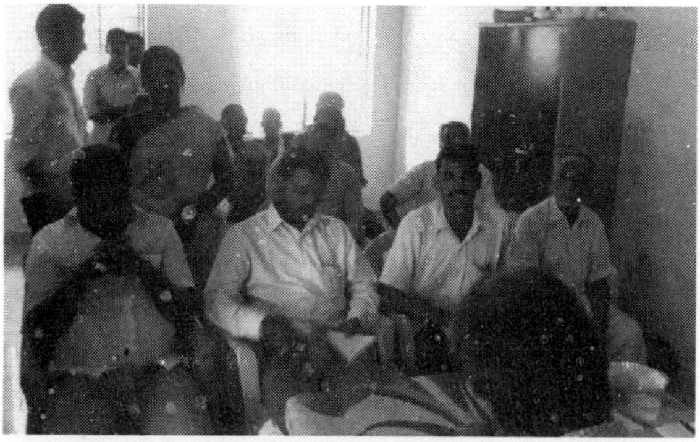

During the FGD, women attended in large number than men. The women federation is very active and involve in all the activities of the village panchayat. The leader of the panchayat level federation and the book keeper of village Poverty Reduction Committee under Puthu Vazhvu Thittam shared many positive information about the scheme.

Earlier at the mother village Singanur, water supply was once in two/three days. Now water is provided daily at Singanur and it is more than adequate to all streets. The street lights provided are very much useful during the late evening, the area is very visible and safe. A long pending demand of villagers namely construction of a waiting shed at the cremation ground and provision of CC road to approach the cremation ground was fulfilled. Earlier the passage was full of thrones and narrow due to encroachment. Now a neat and standard road is available and the villagers take easily the dead bodies to the burial ground, the participants informed.

Residents of Athikulam Street informed that there was no street light since independence as it is located in a long distance even from the nearest transformer. Many households lived without EB connection. The administration of village panchayat gave priority in addressing the issue in the water supply than to street lights due to paucity of fund. "When the scheme was announced and the survey was undertaken, we pointed out the non-fulfilment of our demand and emphasized to give priority. Accordingly, under the scheme five numbers of new poles were arranged to bring electricity connection in our street. It is a new dawn to us. Now there are two street lights and we have electricity connection to our houses. Our children and elders are enjoying the lighting facility. Especially children move out, without any fear go over to meet their friends who are living in nearby streets, play/read with them and enjoy their company. Earlier they missed their peer group".—Er. Kathik, Athikulam Street explained.

In Singanur New Colony about 70 families belong to various communities are living. The new colony is extending towards all directions. There is a hand pump erected by a real estate owner. The motor pump fitted with the hand pump was stolen. Hence, the HP is not functioning. The bore, wells available at some houses are also not so successful. Hence, there is scarcity of water. During the

It is found that at Kamaraj colony there are about 200 families where due to scarcity in supply of water, the residents dug pit and reduced the height of public tap fetched water which was a threat to health and sanitation besides equal distribution. Under the scheme a separate OHT at a capacity of 30000 liters was constructed at that habitation. Hence all the pit taps were removed and proper and equal distribution of water is ensured to all families, the participants informed.

survey they demanded water supply. Accordingly, under the scheme two mini power pumps one at the eastern side and the remaining one at western side of the extension area were provided. Fortunately, both bore-wells are functioning successfully and fulfil their need.

The participants remarked that they felt happy over the survey and the collection the details of needs at each habitation. The priority given under the scheme for providing facilities at burial ground at habitation was not considered earlier. But under the scheme that issues were addressed successfully. They suggested allocating fund under the scheme for doing repair at old colony houses as there was no any scheme for doing repair works.

Thennamadevi Village Panchayat

It is a very small village in Koliyanur panchayat union. The president belongs to SC community, she is very active and successful in getting support from union officials and union councillor. She has good rapport with the SHG members who actively participated in the activities of the village panchayat.

The participants shared their opinion on the planning process and implementation process very openly. They reported that the quality of works is satisfactory and all the works taken in the scheme are very useful. Construction of *'Kariyakottai'* a building at cremation ground is very useful to conduct post-funeral ceremony—they told. Previously the environment was very awkward and during the raining season public was not able to conduct ceremony. Now the ceremony is conducted in a honourable way in a clean environment.

During the FGD, the president informed that though the fund allocated under the scheme was not adequate to meet all demands of the villagers, the baseline survey to find the status and demands of basic needs was very helpful to asses and project our felt needs.

Further, the scope of dovetailing to fill the gap in THAI helped to strengthen the rapport with the all elected representatives.

> *Due to baseline survey and fixing of priority works under THAI for successful implementation, the joint efforts of union councilor, community leaders and village panchayat council, was realized, at Annamalai Nagar, an extension area of Thennamadevi village panchayat. A mini power pump with syntax tank was provided under THAI. The bore well was dug successfully and fortunately the water was very tasty. It was possible because consultation and site inspection was made involving all", the President informed.*

The BT road provided under the scheme is served as an approach road to burial ground, farm area besides connecting other habitations. Because of mobilization of additional fund from the union (with the efforts of union councillor) the BT road provided was extended. Now it fulfilled the old demand of connecting road from Poothamedu habitation to Thennamadevi the main village.

Vellimalai Village Panchayat

The participants mostly women informed that works implemented under scheme were very useful. They shared that deepening of well was very important work. As during the summer there was scarcity of water. Family members used to go a long distance to fetch water from private wells. After deepening, the level of water at wells was increased and there would not be any scarcity of water during the coming summer, the village panchayat president informed. The union chairman who also attended the meeting acknowledged that the fund allocation under THAI for different categories of basic needs was a good effort.

The participants explained that provision of BT road at Thazh-Valapadi habitation lead to Mezh-Valapadi was a beginning through the scheme but by mobilizing fund from Union General Fund, NABARD and RIS, the BT road was further laid at 6.3 km. distance during subsequent years. Now the road connectivity is ensured up to Kannimathivalavu, Mel-Thavanur, Tal-Thavanur habitations. Hence, the drudgery faced in mobility/transporting of goods and commodities by families of these remote habitations was removed thanks to habitation based planning, the participants added.

In respect of construction of cremation shed, the participants remarked that it was useful during rainy season. By earmarking the jurisdiction of burial ground and providing facilities at the earmarked site, the encroachment of the same is prevented, the participants pointed.

The participants hailed from habitations namely Mel-Kendikkal, Thazhtheru, Thazh-Thevanur, Thazh-Kendikkal felt happy in respect of providing CC road which served as a safe passage to children and elders especially during rainy season.

The Union Engineer opined that "the scheme was a successful one in many ways. The allocation of fund to fulfill various basic needs is a good approach. Though it was a minimum allocation, it served better in respect of improving the condition of distribution of water supply to remote habitations, provision of street lights at extension areas and CC road facility to habitations located at high level area. Further as per the guideline dovetailing was successfully mobilized. The famous 'KodaiVizha' enables inter-linkage among various line departments which ensure important needs of villagers and visitors. Mutual understanding and mutual helps have been generated among officials of various line departments in this respect. Especially the union administration by properly roping DRDA for influencing the officials of other line departments and improve the basic needs of the Hilly villages, THAI strengthened that inter-linkages".

4.2. Achievements

Water Supply

In the distribution of water supply quantity per head per day is improved. This resulted into quality in change of personal hygiene, and environmental sanitation. Manual labourers who belong to SC habitation are able to take bath to maintain personal hygiene and keep the home clean and its surrounding. It is visible, especially more appreciable where the CC roads are provided.

Major events like ceremonies conducted at individual family level and commune or neighbourhood level or even at habitation level when organized the panchayat administration is being requested to distribute adequate water at the public tap to the area of concerned beneficiaries. This request is at a considerable extent fulfilled, it is learnt.

Further due to availability of facilities like power pumps, pipeline extension and hand pumps at many habitations, the rush at the public tap of main streets has been reduced a lot. Yet another major impact is ending of quarrel and commotion among various communities in sharing the commons.

In a few habitations misuse of water at the mini power pump structure was found out during the physical verification by research team. Village panchayat administration could not perform the duty of vigilance and supervision. In the context of New Panchayat Raj System, the need of the hour is the strengthening of the user committee like Village Water and Sanitation Committee (VWSC). This is not in place and in action. They are in namesake only.

Because of the involvement of the people in the overall exercise of habitation based planning, there is a great awakening among the people on many issues relating to water governance. Because of this information, empowerment took place among the public, the embarrassment between the government and the public is reduced. This scheme has educated the public about the science of water governance. It is inferred from the FGD. People who participated have adequate knowledge about water related issues and water governance. They speak comprehensively. It is a remarkable one.

Because of the meaningful participation of public in the joint initiative of officials and elected representatives, a new environment is dawn in the annals of local governance system. Here it could be noticed that the officials have played their proactive role to living success to this scheme. It is being shared by the participants of the FGD.

Street Lights

Providing street lights at public places, streets and lanes is one of the assigned duties of the village panchayats. But during the earlier periods there was no challenge as the area of village panchayat was very limited. In course of time there are extension areas within each village panchayat and the villagers expect the urban facilities with such standard in respect of street lights at public places. Hence in fulfilling this basic need, the local bodies have to face challenges and priority is not given to the remote habitations. Because of this delay public could not be able to avail EB connection services to their dwelling units. Realizing their felt needs, the state government brought street lights in the priority list under the scheme.

The utility of street lights could be witnessed at extension areas and at remote habitations of any village panchayat. The most popular scheme namely one light to one hut, provision of housing under IAY, CM Green House etc., add more fuel to the demand of provision of street lights raised by the public. The public of hilly villages appreciated the government decision of provision of street lights under THAI and earmarked funds for it in that respect. In the habitations scattered around and in remote up and downs of hilly villages provision of street lights is a challenging task. The scheme duly addressed the issue successfully. Individual households get EB house service connection because of street lights provided at their street. The fear of children and aged over dangerous animals and snake is over now. Women and elders still have the habit of going out of habitation or at the backyard of their dwelling units for attending natural calls. Now there are street lights or EB connection available at their houses. Hence, they are in safe living.

Provision of solar light at burial ground helps a lot the villagers during power end. When they perform rituals for the dead bodies in the night before the cremation or burial if the electric light goes off, it would be very difficult to continue to process. Since the solar light is provided, without any break or disturbance the rituals can be performed. It happened many times in the past two years. People have realized the worthiness of the light during those periods. These are all small things for others, and for the people in the rural areas these are all big things and major achievements.

Roads

Under roads there are two types. One is the internal road, i.e. CC pavement needed to ensure cleanliness, safety and easy mobility to all especially to children and elderly persons.

The CC road and inter-block pavement provided on the streets/ lanes brings a new environment and a new life to all age groups. To children it is a place for play with their peers; elders play the traditional 'Adupuli Attam' and 'Thayakattam'. Adults especially women have their formal SHG meet under the street light or have informal chat; some take rest or sleep on the camp cot. More or less it is an additional space complimenting and enriching their living conditions.

CC road provided to ensure safe and easy entry into the burial ground and up to the platform meant for funeral helps to reduce the hardship. Elders and physically challenged individuals are facing a hardship to walk on the muddy and earthen roads during the rainy season. CC road ensure safe mobility and safe move of vehicles meant for them.

BT road connecting other habitations, or to the major roads is very useful in many ways. Activities like agriculture, petty trade and enterprises, and all the livelihood of villagers are improved due to the connectivity. Visiting to service institutions becomes easy and in time; services of city buses or mini buses bring a new meaning in their life.

Burial Ground

Burial ground is a part of our familial and social life. A set of minimum facilities (i.e. a 3-meter width CC pavement of the required length up to the entrance, a brick compound wall without a gate covering the entire perimeter, cremation shed with RCC roof and chimney facilities besides platform, CC pathway up to platform, hand pump, lights and pathway to burial ground) are clearly indicated under this scheme. From this projection of activities, the objective and importance of its utility is ensured. The social conflict and tension prevailed in connection of using the burial ground have been eliminated by giving priority to SC habitation.

Buildings

Under buildings among the sample villages threshing floor has been provided in a few villages. Under 'other works' in some sample villages bathing ghat, revetment, culvert and retaining walls have been identified as felt needs, actually during the verification it is found that they are the real felt needs specifically referred by women. By providing the above referred facilities women are taking their bath and washing their clothes easily in a safe and good environment.

It is found that the framework for the scheme has been developed very meaningfully. It emphases not only provision of needs but attention is given to ensure utility. During the physical verification it is observed that all the works/facilities provided are under public utility. None of the facilities provided under the scheme is kept unutilized. This is the merit of participatory grassroots planning.

4.3. Conclusion

The scheme becomes popular, known to many, as the display boards are attractive, and featured the work details with estimated cost. Public expected that for successful identification of the right location of water point, all available scientific technologies along with traditional experience have been applied.

Many expressed happy over the fixing of priorities like street lights, CC roads and provision of facilities at burial grounds. Due to survey, villagers of each habitation/hamlet came to know the status and gap in the infrastructure facilities clearly. Villagers expected to fulfil the demands made by youth like playground facilities and sports equipment and materials. At many villages approach road to burial ground serves as a multipurpose one. Formation of these roads are well done considering the challenges like level of the burial ground site, the condition of clay soil, and the problems of encroachments.

Economically poor families shared that to facilitate their livelihood opportunities provision of common infrastructure at cluster level could be considered under the scheme in future for benefiting SHG women.

The participants shared that the opportunity of dovetailing/ convergence was not known to them earlier. In spite of the delay in filling the gap, they expressed happy over the benefit they availed due to habitation based planning and dovetailing.

The participants of hilly panchayats told that at remote habitations there is a threat from wild animals. Hence priority has to be given to provide more number of street lights, CC roads and pathways to ensure safety instead of allocating a lump sum to provide BT road.

The key stakeholders are officials, elected representatives and the common public. Bringing them together and synergizing of their efforts is a challenging task. But it was achieved successfully through a process. It was the will and commitment of the policy-makers and the state administration.

There are differences in demands of villagers of plain area from that of hilly and coastal area. Hence, adequate attention is needed in fulfilling the basic demands of villagers. THAI at a considerable extent succeeded in this respect. It is found that instead just providing facility like new mini tank, the actual felt needs like additional public taps, extension of pipe line from the mini-tank where the supply of water is enough to feed additional public taps have been provided under the scheme. It is the merit of habitation based planning.

The Research Team noticed during the field visit that at Viralur, the min syntax tank provided under THAI is misused. The villagers used to take bath and wash clothes at the tap itself. The water was drained into a garden raised by a household where banana trees are grown. Fortunately, at the later stage provision of syntax tank is prohibited under THAI by the government. Comparing the situation in the state of Kerala, the water and sanitation committee in that state played its role very effectively in monitoring the distribution of water and preventing the misuse of water. The need of the hour in Tamil Nadu is rejuvenating the functioning of Village Water and Sanitation Committee.

Table 4.1: General Particulars of the Participants of FGD

Sl. No.	*Name of the Village Panchayat*	*No. of Participants*			*Age Group*					*Education*						*Occupation*			
		Male	*Female*	*Total*	*Up to 25*	*26-35*	*36-45*	*46-55*	*56 above*	*Primary*	*Secondary*	*Hr. Sec.*	*College*	*Technical*	*Illiterate*	*Agri.*	*Agri. Labour*	*Business*	*Others*
1	Vilpatti	9	7	16	1	2	8	4	1	3	2	9	2	0	0	8	5	1	2
2	Sendurai	10	8	18	0	5	7	5	1	6	3	7	1	1	0	10	7	0	1
3	Kasavanampatti	11	3	14	2	4	2	3	3	4	2	3	2	1	1	2	3	1	8
4	Ambathurai	16	2	18	0	4	7	5	2	2	5	7	2	2	0	11	3	1	3
5	Viralur	10	5	15	2	3	7	3	0	5	1	8	0	1	0	7	4	4	0
6	Thulaiyanur	7	4	11	0	2	6	2	1	1	3	5	2	0	0	8	0	0	3
7	Mimisal	8	2	10	0	2	5	1	2	1	3	4	0	1	1	3	1	5	1
8	Vagavasal	6	2	8	0	2	2	3	1	2	2	3	1	0	0	7	0	0	1
9	Singanur	10	7	17	1	5	5	3	3	3	1	5	5	3	0	4	2	0	11
10	Bommaiyarpalayam	8	9	17	1	6	10	0	0	0	3	13	1	0	0	7	0	0	10
11	Thennamadevi	2	28	30	3	21	6	0	0	11	4	13	2	0	0	4	6	0	20
12	Vellimalai	17	13	30	0	10	15	5	0	11	3	12	0	0	4	28	0	0	2
	Total	114	90	204	10	66	80	34	14	49	32	89	18	9	6	99	31	12	62

Source: Computed.

5

Major Findings and Conclusion

5.1 Major Findings

- Detailed guidelines for implementation of 'THAI' scheme published by the Department of Rural Development and Panchayat Raj is served as a ready reference for selecting appropriate works (from the choices available) to address the issues in providing minimum basic infrastructure facilities at habitation level.
- The success of 'THAI' scheme is due to its flexibility approach. It does not put conditions in selecting appropriate works. It permits to select and provide appropriate interventions. Hence, works like pipeline extension, additional street lights and street light fitting have been provided.
- Because of the availability of the negative list/prohibited works in the guidelines, a better clarity has been gained in selecting works by the survey team.
- The orientation given to survey teams enabled the team members to understand basic principles in micro level planning exercise. Especially they understand the important principle of deliberation among the various stakeholders resulted in making the special gram sabha meeting fruitful and successful in prioritizing and finalizing the appropriate works.
- HRD process is improved in respect of micro level planning among the all level of officials of the Department of RD&PR due to their orientation and involvement in the innovative 'THAI' scheme. Moreover, they could visualize the mindset of the rural population with regard to the projection of their

need of not only minimum facilities and infrastructure but also their trend in demanding new needs for a decent living environment.

- Because of the IEC and transparency under THAI scheme, public of all habitations got motivation and made claim their stakes in availing the development facilities at their own habitation also.
- In majority of the habitations the concerned ward members actively participated during the survey. They helped in mobilizing the households, SHG members and village elders for participation in the planning process.
- People in general expressed their satisfaction happy over the habitation-based planning.
- Conducting a special gram sabha and sharing of survey details—works selected under THAI considered as a remarkable one as it evoked a sense of stakeholders.
- Real felt needs of the villagers have been taken into consideration under THAI.
- Fund allocation is distributed among many habitations instead of concentrating at a few villages.
- Habitations located in remote area and SC colonies got preferences.
- As the survey team consists of administrative officials, technical officials and elected representatives, the team was able to explain the concept of habitation based planning and fund allocation for essential needs.
- Villagers made demands not outside the priority earmarked under THAI. Hence, their aspiration is known to the policy-makers.
- This helped to have an understanding on the overall demands in each habitation and how the needed resource mobilization and allocation have to be taken by the policy-makers is emphasized.
- Notice board played a key role in popularizing the scheme. People told that it was an attractive and informative one.
- Public considered works under water supply and improvement in the burial grounds are remarkable works.
- Elders especially belong to SC community informed that the provision of approach road and water facility at burial ground, have discriminated social conflicts between caste Hindus and SCs.

- Street lights provided at the extension and colony area and remote habitation in hilly village panchayat helps to move freely during nights without fear.
- Invariably the works implemented are found in good standard. Sufficient attention is given to level up CC roads/ approach roads toward burial ground. So as it become very useful in all seasons.
- Mini power pumps reduced the undue pressure at public taps, especially at SC colonies adequate water supply is ensured. The major problems faced by the women in fetching drinking water have been solved.
- Now they can fetch water to their requirement. They get adequate water to their level of needs.
- They get water wherever they are in house as mini pumps are at their hamlets.
- It has reduced the drudgery for women.
- Since the SC women are fetching water in their hamlets itself, they need not go to main hamlets. Hence, their dignity is protected.
- Now the time spent for water fetching by the number has been reduced to the maximum.
- At high level area CC roads arrest the mud slide and provide safe mobility to elders and children.
- Approach road to burial ground serves as a multipurpose one.
- BT roads under THAI considered as a new opening. Generally any BT road below a distance of one kilometer is not selected under other schemes but because of allotment of 30 per cent out of total fund allocation for road work even a distance of 400 mts. to 650 mts has been considered. WBM-BT road could be taken under THAI. In course of time in many villages these road works get preferences and extended more than one kilometer by dovetailing additional funds. Connectivity is extended to unconnected habitations.
- In respect of implementation of THAI, the survey undertaken was an eye opener, as by reviewing of provision of water to each street/habitation, per head-wise helped them to plan properly. And so water supply works were given priority under THAI.
- So for a comprehensive survey aiming to find the available

facilities and gaps to be fulfilled at each habitation in a village panchayat is not administered in the earlier period.

- A large sum was allotted under many schemes during every tenure of local bodies. Due to lack of scientific micro-level planning and with lack of due attention to priorities, the fund allotted to village panchayats is not adequate or unequally distributed. 'THAI' scheme addressed this issue successfully.

5.2 Overall Impact

- Time spent for fetching drinking water was reduced besides drudgery of walking a long distance during the time of scarcity of water that too during summer. The tension among the families who have gone out for the employment for fetching water from the public taps was ended, as the mini power pump facility assured them supply of water whenever needed.
- It is reported that improvement is found in their personal hygiene, cleanliness at inside and the premises of their houses, washing of clothes become easy and they enjoy wearing of clean dresses. Conflict among the women at water points are ended due to provision of needed water supply in all habitations and more than adequate water is supplied at many habitations.
- Street lights in the extension area, new lanes, remote habitations, premises of school area, entrance of habitations and SC habitations were provided which brought many changes in the attitude, perception of the people about the government.
- School children and elders benefited a lot especially at the hilly panchayat street lights provided helped to notice the presence of wild animals/snakes and ensure safety of the villagers. They are able to walk freely without fear during the night time.
- The earlier condition of muddy and slippery road got a new face—smooth, all weather proof, and motorable and safe walk especially to children and elders. Because of CC road was laid in front of the houses, hence families are motivated to keep neat and clean. During evening family members used to sit and share and many elders are sleeping at night. During

the time of family ceremonies erection of *'Pandal'*—thatched roofing/shamiana become very easy and comfortable.

- BT roads are useful for transportation of all type of vehicles. It connects other hamlets and main roads. Transportation of inputs and agricultural products become easy and quick. Because of availability of BT road, transportation of essential food materials under Public Distribution System (PDS) become easy and quick.
- A package of facilities like compound wall, funeral shed, pathway, and hand pump have been provided. In three village panchayats waiting shed-cum-hall for conducting ceremonies activities related to the day of burial/funeral and its post-period have been provided. It is very convenient during the rainy season as well as peak summer. Earlier these ceremonies were conducted at open ground. Now it is in a respectful and decent manner organised by communities.
- At the site of burial ground encroachments have been removed and boundaries are earmarked. The site becomes very clean and neat. The drudgery of bringing water from individual farmers' well was ended. Many farmers did not give permission to get water from their own well as they considered it as a bad omen. Because of approach road and pathway provided in lifting of dead body become easy and comfortable. Separate burial ground with facilities at SC habitation meant a lot to them.
- They are very much useful to the villagers. Threshing floors are properly used by households and farmers.
- The retaining wall provided at Oorani arrested the soil erosion. Bathing ghat is very useful to women for their safety.
- Because of the above new facilities provided at many habitations, the overall facelift is witnessed in respect of minimum infrastructure facilities. Also it pictures the availability of urban standard in rural areas also.
- All the above impact is possible due to
  - the initiative of micro-level planning—administering of scientific survey, habitation based planning,
  - priority of essential needs and time bound execution of the scheme activities with role clarity to village panchayat and block panchayat,
  - besides constant and effective monitoring and digital

documentation for successful implementation.

- It is reported that the need of water supply in all 12 sample villages fulfilled at about 80 per cent.
- In respect of BT road about 75 per cent is over.
- Street lights are needed only to newly extended areas.
- The majority among the stakeholders expressed their overall satisfaction on the effectiveness of planning. Minimum basic needs in majority of the habitations are fulfilled.
- It is found that they are becoming as informed citizen, play their participatory role besides empowering in representing their further needs to improve Physical Quality of Life Index (PQLI).
- It is to be mentioned here that the deliberative process in the gram sabha meetings paid rich dividends to the panchayats.
- The panchayats played an important role in planning and carrying out this scheme and thereby the panchayat institution is strengthened.

5.3 Suggestions

- It is learnt that in general villagers expected not a price-meal work, but a full-fledged plan for improving the basic facility for fruitful utilization. The research team made enquiry with panchayat presidents regarding the scope of converging fund from other resources. The panchayat presidents informed that the scope for dovetailing is a limited one due to absence of proper conversion exercise among the line departments.
- In respect of improving the infrastructure facilities of burial ground, the total area has to be protected at one stretch under THAI or by dovetailing other resources.
- The solar light provided at the burial ground could be stolen by anti-social elements. Hence providing electrical street light could be considered there.
- In respect of street lights at many village panchayats instead of providing adequate number of new street lights in extension area/remote area, under THAI changing the bulbs in existing EB lamp post as well as new lights at subsequent posts are undertaken. Necessary guideline has to be issued to give priority to extension/remote habitations.

- With regard to addressing issues in water supply, at many villages pipelines are very old. Further due to road improvement, the level of pipelines become low and water supply is disturbed due to low pressure. During the survey though people express their complaint on the water supply, all the related issues like level of ground water, condition of pipeline pressure problem, power of motor pumps, and other technical issues have to be properly looked into before sanctioning new works like mini power pump or hand pumps etc.
- Over a period of time, the lifestyle of rural populace is also changed as the style of urban population. Hence, the issue of liquid/solid waste management is a tough task to deal. Provision of *pucca* drainage in the villages is yet to be given attention under THAI, at very needy area; provision of drainage facility could be permitted.
- Conducting survey under THAI is a right approach. But officials alone could not shoulder the responsibility of administering the survey format. Local educated youths could be selected and oriented to do survey under the supervision by a team of officials exclusively allotted for survey and its follow up like fixing priorities and plan for dovetailing/ convergence to fill the specific gaps. Diverting officials frequently to look after other routine works/activities during the THAI survey other works could be avoided so as the habitation-wise planning becomes a model work.
- In respect of coastal area, distribution of water supply is always a challenging one. The major technical issues come across are saline of water, question of availability of potable water at ground even after digging a thousand feet, rusting of RCC structure (OHT) and adequate supply of voltage of power supply. Hence, development works at coastal area have to be planned involving higher level technologist along with local technical experts.
- In respect of road works, 30 per cent fund is earmarked out of total allocation under THAI. But it is learnt that to provide 2 layer BT road within the 30 per cent allocation could not be possible to complete a long distance road. Though mobilization of fund from other scheme is attempted it takes time to get sanction. Habitation-based planning is the right

step as the villagers actively participated in survey and listed out their most felt needs. They expected adequate fund allocation under THAI to fulfil road works.

- During planning of special scheme like THAI, especially for coastal villages, villagers demanded special works like drainage, culverts, construction of stone bunds to arrest the intrusion of sea water and plantation of trees like Casuarinas at waste land along the coastal area to reduce the speed of cyclone, besides disaster mitigation plan activities like ensuring a *pucca* exit route etc., have to be added under THAI.
- It is reported that by allotting more fund to village panchayat further to complete the balance essential/minimum basic needs in all habitations will facilitate the improvement of the PQLI in all family members in all habitations.
- Burial ground facilities lacked in some habitations have to be fulfilled.
- The further sustainability lives in tuning up of micro planning process and making effective linkages with all concerned institutions where fund for providing basic infrastructure development in rural area is available/earmarked.

5.4 Conclusion

Providing basic infrastructure facilities in the villages for all the segments especially in caste ridden communities in Indian setting is a tough and challenging task. Programme capture is an Indian phenomenon. Indian villages are affected with all kinds of disparities and discriminations. The governance and administrative unit created at the village level through the constitution with a basic objective of deepening of democracy, achieving economic development and social justice has to perform the above. They are also challenging tasks. Against this background, the Government of Tamil Nadu has introduced an important scheme—'THAI' with an objective of providing basic minimum facilities to the neglected areas and habitations of the village panchayats by developing a participatory planning with the active involvement of the stakeholders. This scheme moves from panchayat level to habitation level planning to reach out to the unreached. In this sense, it is innovative and creative from the perspective of social justice. The scheme has been in operation from

2011/12 to 2015/16 with a huge outlay. Every village panchayat has got an amount in range of 20 lakhs to 50 lakhs of rupees depending on the size of the village panchayat in terms of the number of habitations. Here the main question is to what extent the aim and objectives of the scheme have been realized. If yes at what level and what are the bottlenecks the panchayats have experienced in the process of implementing the scheme through the panchayats.

Basically, the scheme has got rich potentials to address the basic issues of the marginalized. But it depends on the way in which it is being executed. To evaluate the impact from the perspectives of the objectives, twelve gram panchayats from there different districts in order to capture the variations through a scientific sampling. Intensive fieldwork has been carried out. In-depth interview has been conducted with different respondents who involved in the planning and implementation process. Focus group discussions have been conducted with the beneficiaries of the scheme. By adopting all those nuances needed data have been collected. From the data collected from the field, analysis has been done. From the analysis following observations have been made.

In order to reach out the unreached, by taking the scheme benefits to the unreached areas the people of the whole panchayats have been convinced through a dialogue process that took place in gram sabha. It is a model for other panchayats. Since officials have involved in the process, the plight of the neglected have been explained and through a deliberative process everyone was convinced that taking these facilities to the remotest place is necessary. This is a unique achievement of the process. Normally any scheme operated through line departments will bypass the panchayats. But in this case, however, the scheme has got difficulty it is, it has implemented through panchayats and it addressed the long pending demands of the *dalits* and other neglected segments of the rural community. When it reached the poor *dalit* women, *dalit* aged men, the joy they enjoyed is unfathomable. To address the social justice issues in the rural areas methodology adopted in this scheme will be of much useful. Both officials and the elected representatives have been oriented and sensitized on the data collection process scientifically and the micro planning exercises. Though the project is innovative in addressing the problems of the neglected hitherto, it emphasizes the importance of the process through the scheme is implemented. The decision making process of the panchayats cannot be bypassed. All decisions have to be taken through gram sabha through a deliberative process. By doing so the panchayat system has been strengthened and people are sensitized on the issues of marginalization and deprivation. This scheme created hope among the hopeless that their voices will be heard and their basic needs will be attended to. Panchayats are trained in participatory decision making process. On the basis issues people are oriented and sensitized. People have been oriented to look at water issues very scientifically. While interacting with the beneficiaries they argued with data and facts on water.

Basically, the scheme put an end to the village feuds on sharing water, burial ground and other common. Generally, village conflicts arose between *dalits* and non-*dalits* on sharing the commons more specifically water and cremation ground. All these causes for the conflicts have been eliminated through providing facilities to the *dalit* areas. From this perspective it addressed the social justice issues. For the planning exercise large scale mobilization had taken place. Large number of *dalits* have participated and evinced interest in the planning process because they believed that they are the biggest beneficiaries in this process.

A comprehensive survey was carried out in the villages which is very useful to look at the conditions of the people in the rural areas and for visioning for the villages. The data collected through the survey will be useful for further planning for availing 14th Finance Commission awards. It helps many ways to comply with the conditions stipulated by the Central Government to avail the Finance Commission's Award. Apart from the above one will find a fine synergy between the officials and the elected representatives in planning and implementing the scheme as both take credit out of the scheme.

Absolutely there is no waste. All the infrastructure created are in perfect use by the stakeholders since the scheme has got flexibilities in taking decisions to use the resources. Further there is provision for dovetailing the schemes, will enable the panchayat to realize the objective of the schemes. Dovetailing of the schemes have helped the panchayats to realize many of the felt needs. But it is not comprehensive as rigidity in line departments has continued in the functioning of the line department. Extensive popularization of the scheme has raised hope among all the segments of the society. People gained knowledge about planning and this will be useful for the planning exercise to be done for availing the schemes meant for rural areas. The scheme has given assurance to the all segments of the community. But it addressed the issues of the marginalized. Since it raised hope among all the segments, realizing the objectives depends on the continuation of the scheme.

In general, it addressed the issues regarding the basic facilities to enable the poor *dalits* to lead a decent dignified life. The equity issue so far unaddressed has been addressed. It made development process more inclusive. It raised hope among the *dalits* that they get their share in all the schemes as they got through this scheme. The works like pathway to burial ground, creating water resources in *dalit* colony, laying roads to faraway colonies, creating facilities in burial ground and crematorium, providing street lights to SC colonies have given the sense that through this scheme social justice issues have been addressed. As a result, participation of SC members in gram sabha has been increased. Many of root causes for caste conflict have been removed from the villages. Drudgery of the *dalit* women and old men are removed. Linkage between gram panchayats and block panchayats has been strengthened through this scheme.

5.5 Constraints

Sustaining the enthusiasm of the people and the officials depends on the continuation of the scheme. Huge hope has been raised among the *dalits*. Next level demands have to be solved. Otherwise the assets created in the SC colonies and other remote areas have to face problem in maintenance through panchayats due to the village social dynamics. In the scheme it is mentioned performance based award would be given to best performed panchayats and districts. In this regard there is no action. It would bring enthusiasm among the panchayats on a competitive basis.

Annexure-I

Case Studies

Case Study-1

At new colony of Singanur village panchayat the electricity supply to street lights was provided directly due to paucity of fund to construct new line for street lights. Under THAI a new line was provided from the transformer by erecting 16 new poles to connect 24 street lights at four streets in the new colony. Because of that arrangement, the functioning of street lights and its repair and maintenance become easy and safe. Earlier more expenditure was occurred for maintenance, also during raining days the EB field staff could not able to attend repair due to direct line supply. Now all these issues were solved thanks to THAI, the participants shared.

Due to functioning of street lights, the practice of open defecation was stopped and the environment at the entrance of village as well as at the front of the Government Higher Secondary School is kept clean, the Panchayat Secretary informed.

A New Dawn

Singanur is a small village panchayat located along the NH7. At the entrance of the village, the Aadi Dravida Higher Secondary School is functioning. The school is located very near to Singanur Old Colony. There is no street light available at the entrance of the Singanur Old Colony. The darkness could not be addressed since the Independence. It is used as a place for open defecation. Now-a-days at the A.D. Higher Secondary School special coaching classes for 10th and 12th standard students. The girls/boys coming from the nearby villages located at the radius of 6/7 km. have to wait for bus at the entrance of the village. They fear over the safety as there is no any street lights at the side of the school/at the beginning of the colony street. Hence, the families use the place for open defecation during the night time.

The village panchayat took efforts to provide street lights but it was a challenging task due to limitation of fund to get connection from the transformer existing at the distance of more than 100 meter. Further at the left side of the school, Athikulam Street is existed. It is an old settlement, mostly hutments, about 20 in number. Since independence there is no street light at that street due to long distance. Hence, EB service to their houses was not provided. Some houses avail electricity from their farm connection unofficially.

Earlier arranging of a new transformer by EB was prevented by the colony people. They feared over the possibility of fire accident which could affect the safety of school children. Hence, the new transformer was arranged at the colony street near the site of the burial ground located away from the school.

The village panchayat tried to provide street lights at Athikulam Street and at the village entrance. So as it could be benefited to school children/passengers at bus shelter and at the site of a pond. But due to paucity of fund and priority was given to address issues in providing water supply, the work for providing street light was delayed.

"The announcement of THAI" was a fortune one to us, the villagers said. As the priority was given to street light under THAI, the administration of village panchayat decided to make use of THAI allocation for street lights. Accordingly, 10 street lights were provided, including at the entrance and at old colony street. At the Athikulam street also two new street lights are provided after extending the EB line up to Athikulam.

The street lights at the village entrance, near the school and at the Athikulam street was possible due to THAI. It brings a dawn, ending the darkness in the life of about 20 families in that habitation. The villagers expressed that "now only they are free from the darkness covered them in spite of independence attained".

There are other developments:

- Open defecation prevented.
- Safety of school children ensured.
- The passenger waiting at the bus shelter feel safe.
- The women using the pond benefited even during night they could use the pond.
- The waiting hall constructed under THAI where ceremonies related to post-funeral being performed is located at the entrance site. There is no light at the building. Now the street lights provided under THAI at the entrance of the village provide lighting facilities to the entire area, benefiting many.

Case Study-2

At Pillaichavadi of Bommaiyarpalayam panchayat, the burial ground site is a portion of land of Annadana Trust, a private one. For the past one hundred years, the villagers used the site for burial. During the implementation of THAI, the issue of ownership was raised by an individual and the negotiation process with him was failed. But the site was under the usage of villagers for long period and so the individual was convinced in course of time. After the completion of provision of approach passage to burial ground under THAI, the individual acknowledged the possession of the site by the villagers and put his signature to ensure official declaration. If the work is not taken under THAI, the issue of ownership stood as a hurdle for the development of the habitation. Now the issue prevailed over a period of one hundred years was tackled, thanks to habitation based planning, the president explained.

Other Impact

In earlier period, the condition of roads was very worst—water stagnated, muddy/dust full due to coastal area. Under THAI scheme many roads are converted into CC road—very useful during all seasons especially during the time of disaster.

The mini power pump provided under THAI helped to reduce the rush at public taps in Kuilampalayam village. Due to difference of level, water supply to streets located at higher level area become possible after provision of mini power pump at Ellaipidari Amman Koil area. About 50 householders have shared that they have been relieved from the day to day tension as now they have adequate water everyday.

A New Trend

The villagers put new demands not the type of basic needs but more than that. They requested to provide library facilities, community-cum-marriage hall, building for panchayat level federation of SHGs, high mass lights at the side of beach, facilities to attract tourists and standby generators and motors during disaster to flush out flood water. It shows that the residents envision 'living in a decent environment', as many basic facilities are fulfilled after habitation based planning approach under THAI.

Case Study-3: Adequate potable water even during summer at hilly habitation

In block of Kalrayanhills, Vellimalai is the largest village panchayat consists of 29 habitations. Melvazhapady is one among the 29 habitations of Vellimalai panchayat having 100 households with a population of 388. During the summer season Melvazhapady faces a severe drought. There is only one open well constructed long years back and it is used to become dry too. That well is located near a stream and the path to reach the well is steeper. It is difficult for the women to carry of the water filled pots.

During this course of time a new open well is sanctioned under IGFF for an estimate amount of Rs. 5.00 lakhs. The well construction has been completed but the yield of the well is not adequate to fulfil the need of householders in the habitation of Melvazhapady. That was the serious issue and so the families made frequent demands to address the issues. During the survey the villagers demanded the same. Hence, under THAI scheme in the year 2011-12 at an estimate amount of Rs.1.00 lakh deepening further of that well was taken and carried out successfully.

As of now the deepening work was completed and the well is gifted with a good supply of water sufficient to all families. It supplies adequate water to all the families of Melvazhapady through already existing Over Head Tank of capacity of 10,000 lit. With the availability of 20 no. of public tap points in the streets, the issue of water scarcity during the summer was ended.

The womenfolk informed that they felt very much over their suffering of going long distance to fetch water from private wells. Also due to non-availability of proper approach path to the private farms, they faced hardship of carrying water pots along the risky routes. They could go over to fetch water during evening only after reaching home and so they worried much over the safety of their children in their absence. All these issues were successfully addressed because of THAI. The women folk expressed that "now we fetch water from public taps easily acceptable at our convenient time, also adequate even during summer. And so we have great relief from agonies".

Case Study-4: From Risky to Safe Living

In Kalrayanhills block, at Vellimalai village panchayat,

Kannumathivalavu is one among the 29 habitations having 20 households with a population of 173. The houses in this habitation are located in a single street at the both sides of the street. It was the street with earthen road previously and also without any street light. The villagers explained that "During the rainy season the street become muddy, slippery and waterlogging. Even sometimes the logged water accumulated and entered in some of the houses. This created an unhealthy situation in this area. Being a hilly area there is more chances for the movements of poisonous insects and snakes around the houses". So the need of the street lights and CC road was demanded by them during the survey.

Under THAI scheme, a CC road has been provided along with 4 street lights. Now the essential needs of this habitation are fulfilled through THAI. The householders told that "by having a safe environment we could live without fear".

It is possible because of flexibility in selecting appropriate works under habitation based planning and priority to essential needs instead of a set of tied-up scheme activities.

Case Study-5: Reaching the Un-reached

In Vellimalai Panchayat from Melvazhapady to Thaldhevanur road is previously an earthen road. This road serves the people of Thazvazhapady, Kannumathivalavu, Melthevanur and Thalthevanur habitations of total population 751.

Due to non-availability of pucca road facility, the school going children studied up to the Middle School located in or nearby villages. But for their High Schooling they have to travel a long distance of 7 km from their village. Hence, a numbers of children discontinued their studies after the middle school. The pregnant women required regular check-ups in PHC. But it is impossible for them to attend the PHC frequently due to bad condition of the road. Even the mobile medical unit and the 108 ambulance services are not able to reach above mentioned habitations because of the bus facilities was available only at Vellimalai.

Hence villagers took the risk of walking through the forest path way to reach the Pottiyam panchayat, which is located at the foot of the hills, to purchase their home needs and other goods. Tapioca is the major agricultural crop in these villages; farmers struggled to transport agriculture inputs and market their products. The total length of the road is 5.50 km. The road is earthen for the entire stretch. During the rainy season, the condition of the earthen road was very dangerous due to the heavy runoff on the road surface. People demanded to form a *pucca* road during the THAI survey.

This road was taken up under THAI-2011-12 to an estimate cost of Rs. 20.00 lakhs and to a length of 1.00 km and improved up to BT standard. In this case THAI scheme is the initiator of this Road project. After laying under THAI scheme, the balance length has been completed under dovetailing RIS and NABARD schemes. Now people are travelling on the new BT road. Flying school buses, ambulance vehicles, medical team visits and mobile Public Distribution Shop accessible to the villagers of these remote habitations.

This is possible because of THAI, which aims to include hitherto excluded segment of the community. Villagers told that "a new transformation is occurred. All students continue their education; health conditions of villagers improved; safe delivery is ensured to pregnant women; ration commodities are accessible to all eligible card holders; accessibility to emergency ambulance service meant a lot to us", they added.

Dindigul District

THAI scheme was introduced from the year 2011/12. At that time of introduction, those village panchayats, which are coming under habitation range of 26 and above and 16 to 25 have been identified under THAI. During the survey under THAI at Sendurai (habitation range 16-25) there were no serious issues in the distribution of water supply as in Sendurai, the rainfall was adequate. But during the time of evaluation study which is initiated only in the year 2015/16, villagers from many hamlets reported that they suffered a lot due to failure of monsoon since 2011/12 consecutively. During the field visit of the Research Team, villagers from many habitations who used to receive more than 40 liters per day per person earlier reported severe scarcity of water. Hence, during the planning process works like augmentation of rainwater, recycling of water practice, economic use of water, supply of water for other than drinking purposes have to be considered under THAI, they suggested.

It is learnt that priorities were given to CC road, burial ground and street lights, no any work under water supply was undertaken, due to depletion of groundwater and failure of many bore-well-dug in earlier period, the President of Ambathurai reported.

The residents of Perumalkoilpatti of Ambathurai Village Panchayat proposed to end the issue of scarcity of water. But could be addressed only by identifying a separate water source for Perumalkoilpatti habitation and a separate pipeline has to be planned, the president informed. Due to need of a large sum that proposal was not taken into consideration under THAI, the President reported. He suggested that in planning provision of basic facilities, especially water supply, the government has to ensure the needed amount under THAI.

It is learnt that the residents of many habitations of Vilpatti Village Panchayat expected that under THAI many no. of CC road would be provided. They told that due to ups and downs, the mobility through the earthen roads was a risky one. Hence, their major demand is provision of CC roads and retaining wall along the major passage to prevent the soil erosion.

Their next demand is street lights and facilities at all burial grounds. The villagers of Vilpatti enforced that common land is hardly available in the hilly villages. Also habitations are scattered. During the Planning for the improvement of all basic needs, special attention has to be exercised for hilly villages, as the situations are different from villages which are located at plain area, it is suggested.

In habitation based planning category of basic needs have been identified and listed out. Fund allocation under important work colony ensured better felt needs for finalizing priorities under THAI. Otherwise different works like new bore well, mini power pump, GLR and pipeline extensions could not be undertaken. There are the specific felt needs of residents of habitations than the overall village panchayat.

Another interesting finding is that instead of providing CC roads in two hamlets at Kasavanampatti sample village panchayat, BT roads were provided improving the existing metal road which serve as the road for connectivity to farm area as well as to nearby habitation. It is possible because of public participation as well as the ability of survey team in micro planning.

Yet another important observation is that at one of the sample village Ambathurai, none of work under water supply is undertaken under THAI. Though water scarcity was reported during the survey in four habitations, due to non-availability of groundwater and failure of many bore-wells dug earlier, the village panchayat administration in consultation with the block officials decided not to take water service work under THAI and so the fund was utilized for other felt needs namely CC road and street lights.

It is also observed that preference is given to habitation where SC population is more where water supply improvement and provision of street lights and CC road were provided under THAI.

Villupuram District

Though there are issues in the provision of water supply, street lights and CC road in many habitations at Vellimalai Village Panchayat, due to habitation based planning, most needed habitations are identified and preference is given to address the above issues. The BT road is provided at a crucial habitation namely Thalvalapadi by which more than five habitation located around and upper level area get connectivity. Further, a drainage and CC road were provided at Vellimalai where the Block Office, Village Panchayat Office and Ration shop are located in the higher level. Hence, the mobility of vehicle especially heavy vehicles could not be possible during the rainy season. Transporting ration commodities is a challenging task. In that circumstances under THAI, a drainage and CC road were provided considering the seriousness of the issue. Such a felt need has been reported and included in the habitation based planning. It is a case for the merit of THAI scheme.

Within the available fund, under THAI, at Singanur Village Panchayat preference is given to water supply, street lights and CC road. Further providing basic amenities at burial ground, the real felt needs of the public were taken into consideration than to spend money for unfelt needs.

During the habitation based planning public of Thennamadevei Village Panchayat reported water supply, street lights, CC road and facilities at the site for burial ground. Except CC road, the other felt needs demanded by the villagers have been fulfilled. It is an example for successful habitation based planning.

Because of habitation based planning at Bommaiyarpalayam Village Panchayat, water supply, street light, and CC road have been provided at the most needy habitations. BT road is serving connectivity to main bazar area. At all habitations many basic facilities are available at burial ground except approach road. Hence, approach road only provided under THAI.

Pudukottai District

Public participation was very good at Thulaianur Village Panchayat, by which many felt needs were identified and priority was given to the real needs other than grouped under THAI scheme.

Balanced view was taken in providing street lights and CC road considering the needs and condition of street lights/habitation respectively in the hamlet villages. Works have been distributed to many habitations than concentrating a few. The BT roads provided under THAI were very much useful as it connects the main road lead to district headquarters. All the above felt needs are fulfilled because of habitation based planning.

Because of the habitational planning at Mimisal, the Coastal Village Panchayat, the available fund under THAI scheme was fruitfully distributed to these habitations where the needs were very essential

At Vagavasal Village Panchayat, in spite of many hamlets demanded many felt needs apart from the work type earmarked under THAI, the villagers were able to identify prioritized needs and successfully finalized the needier works during the planning process. The habitation based planning enriched the view of micro planning among the general public beyond enabling the key stakeholders to sustain the spirit and initiative of micro level planning, it is found.

At Viralur Village Panchayat, attention was given in analyzing the issues and fixing priorities where the available resources under THAI have to be spared to fulfil the felt needs. Further being an affair of one-year duration, THAI scheme has to be completed within the duration of the financial year earmarked for each village panchayat. At the same time to fill the gaps existed after THAI, dovetailing was taken into consideration. Such a wholesome planning is the hall mark of THAI though there is a hardship in ensuring additional resource mobilization to fill the gaps.

Annexure-II

Table 1: Details of the no. of works completed in sample Village Panchayats

Sl. No.	Name of the Village Panchayat	Total No. of Habitation	No. of Habitation Work done	Water						Road		S L		Building			
				NB	MPP	PLE	OHT	HP	GLR & DW	CCR	BT & WBM	Street Light	BG	C&D	TF	RW	BG
1.	Sendurai	24	13	3	4	-	-	-	-	6	-	75	1	-	-	-	-
2.	Ambathurai	11	9	-	-	-	-	-	-	10	3	34	1	-	-	-	-
3.	Kasavanampatti	11	10	-	4	7	-	-	-	-	3	9	1	-	-	-	-
4.	Vilpatti	26	15	-	-	-	-	-	1	7	1	16	1	-	-	-	-
5.	Thulaiyanur	29	19	-	6	-	-	-	-	8	5	18	1	-	2	2	3
6.	Mimisal	10	7	-	-	8	-	-	-	2	3	5	1	1	-	-	-
7.	Vagavasal	16	10	-	5	1	1	1	-	1	3	32	1	-	-	1	-
8.	Viralur	18	12	-	6	-	-	2	-	4	1	20	6	-	-	-	-
9.	Bommaiyarpalayam	4	4	-	2	-	-	-	-	7	1	13	5	3	-	-	-
10.	Singanur	3	3	-	2	-	1	-	-	3	-	10	2	-	-	-	-
11.	Thennamadevi	4	3	-	2	-	-	-	-	-	1	4	3	-	-	-	-
12.	Vellimalai	20	18	-	4	-	-	-	3	8	1	7	1	1	-	-	-
	Total	**176**	**123**	**3**	**35**	**16**	**2**	**3**	**4**	**56**	**22**	**243**	**24**	**5**	**2**	**3**	**3**

Source: Computed.

NB—New Bore well, MPP—Mini Power Pump, PLE—Pipe Line Extension, OHT—Over Head Tank, HP—Hand Pump, GLR&DW—GLR Deepening Well, CCR—Cement Concrete Road, BT&WBM—Block Thar & With Blue Metal Road, SL—Street Light, BG—Burial Ground, C&D—Culvert and Drainage, TF—Threshing Floor, RW—Retaining Wall, BG—Bathing Ghat.

Table 2: Details of the amount spent on each item of works in sample Village Panchayats

Name of the Village Panchayat	Total Amount Allocated	Total Amount Spent	Water						Road		SL		Building			
			NB	MPP	PLE	OHT	HP	GLR & DW	CCR	BT & WBM	Street Light	BG	C&D	T F	R W	BG
	Amount in Lakhs															
1. Sendurai	40.00	39.85	6.99	5.99	0	0	0	0	7.85	0	16.05	2.97	0	0	0	0
2. Ambathurai	40.00	41.25	0	0	0	0	0	0	17.18	9.2	13.3	1.57	0	0	0	0
3. Kasavanampatti	30.00	27.8	0	8.82	3.03	0	0	0	0	11.55	1.06	3.34	0	0	0	0
4. Vilpatti	40.00	42.95	0	0	0	0	0	3.54	12.21	20	3.2	4	0	0	0	0
5. Thulaiyanur	50.00	49.05	0	5.69	0	0	0	0	9.04	15	2.16	2.64	2.5	3.81	2.98	5.23
6. Mimisal	30.00	29.95	0	0	13.21	0	0	0	3	8.99	2.25	1	1.5	0	0	0
7. Vagavasal	50.00	46.34	0	5.44	5.9	3.5	6.97	0	6.56	12.72	1	1.5	0	0	2.75	0
8. Viralur	40.00	39.75	0	6	0	0	1	0	7.05	12.72	2.05	10.93	0	0	0	0
9. Bommaiyarpalayam	40.00	39.42	0	3.5	0	0	0	0	11.38	5	2.86	9.55	7.13	0	0	0
10. Singanur	20.00	20	0	2.49	0	4.25	0	0	6.06	0	1.2	6	0	0	0	0
11. Thennamadevi	20.00	20	0	3.49	0	0	0	0	0	6.07	0.54	9.9	0	0	0	0
12. Vellimalai	50.00	49.38	0	6	0	0	0	4.77	7.99	19.95	5.68	2.99	1	1	0	0
Total		**445.74**	**6.99**	**47.42**	**22.14**	**7.75**	**7.97**	**8.31**	**88.32**	**121.2**	**51.35**	**56.39**	**12.13**	**4.81**	**5.73**	**5.23**

Source: Computed.

NB—New Bore well, MPP—Mini Power Pump, PLE—Pipe Line Extension, OHT—Over Head Tank, HP—Hand Pump, GLR&DW—GLR Deepening Well, CCR—Cement Concrete Road, BT&WBM Road—Block Thar & With Blue Metal, SL—Street Light, BG—Burial Ground, C&D—Culvert and Drainage, TF—Threshing Floor, RW—Retaining Wall, BG—Bathing Ghat.

Table 3: Details of the habitation-wise no. of works completed in Sendurai Village Panchayat

District: DINDIGUL		Block: NATHAM					Panchayat: SENDURAI				No. of Hamlets: 24				
Sl. No.	Name of the Habitation	Water						Road		S L	Building				
		NB	MPP	PLE	OHT	HP	GLR & DW	CCR	BT & WBM	Street Light	BG	C&D	TF	RW	BG
1.	Kakkan Colony	-	-	-	-	-	-	-	-	4	-	-	-	-	-
2.	Kalathupatti	-	1	-	-	-	-	1	-	1	-	-	-	-	-
3.	Karuthanaickenpatti	-	-	-	-	-	-	-	-	8	-	-	-	-	-
4.	Kuppandigoundanpatti	1	-	-	-	-	-	-	-	7	-	-	-	-	-
5.	Mamarathupatti	-	1	-	-	-	-	-	-	6	-	-	-		
6.	Mettupatti	-	-	-	-	-	-	1	-	-	-	-	-	-	-
7.	Nallapitchanpatti	-	-	-	-	-	-	-	-	5	-	-	-	-	-
8.	Pandhipomminaiyakkanur	-	1	-	-	-	-	1	-	-	1	-	-	-	-
9.	Periyurpatti	-	-	-	-	-	-	-	-	25	-	-	-	-	-
10.	Sendurai	1	1	-	-	-	-	1	-	14	-	-	-	-	-
11.	S. Kurumbapatti	-	-	-	-	-	-	1	-	1	-	-	-	-	-
12.	Thirunoothupatti	-	-	-	-	-	-	1	-	4	-	-	-	-	-
13.	Vadakkupudur	1	-	-	-	-	-	-	-	-	-	-	-	-	-
	Total	**3**	**4**	**0**	**0**	**0**	**0**	**6**	**0**	**75**	**1**	**0**	**0**	**0**	**0**

Source: Computed.

NB—New Bore well, MPP—Mini Power Pump, PLE—Pipe Line Extension, OHT—Over Head Tank, HP—Hand Pump, GLR&DW—GLR Deepening Well, CCR—Cement Concrete Road, BT&WBM Road—Block Thar & With Blue Metal, SL—Street Light, BG—Burial Ground, C&D—Culvert and Drainage, TF—Threshing Floor, RW—Retaining Wall, BG—Bathing Ghat.

Table 4: Details of the amount spent on each item of works in Sendurai Village Panchayat

District: DINDIGUL | Block: NATHAM | Panchayat: SENDURAI | No. of Hamlets: 2

Sl. No.	Name of the Habitation	Water						Road		S L	Building				
		NB	MPP	PLE	OHT	HP	GLR & DW	CCR	BT & WBM	Street Light	BG	C&D	TF	RW	BG
		Amount in Lakhs													
1.	Kakkan Colony	0	0	0	0	0	0	0	0	0.20	0	0	0	0	0
2.	Kalathupatti	0	1.50	0	0	0	0	1.00	0	2.65	0	0	0	0	0
3.	Karuthanaickenpatti	0	0	0	0	0	0	0	0	2.25	0	0	0	0	0
4.	Kuppandigoundanpatti	2.00	0	0	0	0	0	0	0	0.35	0	0	0	0	0
5.	Mamarathupatti	0	1.50	0	0	0	0	0	0	2.30	0	0	0	0	0
6.	Mettupatti	0	0	0	0	0	0	1.50	0	0	0	0	0	0	0
7.	Nallapitchanpatti	0	0	0	0	0	0	0	0	0.25	0	0	0	0	0
8.	Pandhipomminaiyakkanur	0	1.49	0	0	0	0	1.50	0	0	2.97	0	0	0	0
9.	Periyurpatti	0	0	0	0	0	0	0	0	2.90	0	0	0	0	0
10.	Sendurai	3.00	1.50	0	0	0	0	2.48	0	3.20	0	0	0	0	0
11.	S. Kurumbapatti	0	0	0	0	0	0	1.00	0	1.75	0	0	0	0	0
12.	Thirunoothupatti	0	0	0	0	0	0	3.70	0	0.20	0	0	0	0	0
13.	Vadakkupudur	2.00	0	0	0	0	0	0	0	0	0	0	0	0	0
	Total	**7.00**	**5.99**	**0**	**0**	**0**	**0**	**11.18**	**0**	**16.05**	**2.97**	**0**	**0**	**0**	**0**

Source: Computed.

NB—New Bore well, MPP—Mini Power Pump, PLE—Pipe Line Extension, OHT—Over Head Tank, HP—Hand Pump, GLR&DW—GLR Deepening Well, CCR—Cement Concrete Road, BT&WBM Road—Block Thar & With Blue Metal, SL—Street Light, BG—Burial Ground, C&D—Culvert and Drainage, TF—Threshing Floor, RW—Retaining Wall, BG—Bathing Ghat.

Table 5: Details of the habitation-wise no. of works completed in Kasavanampatti Village Panchayat

District: DINDIGUL *Panchayat: KASAVANAMPATTI* *Block: REDDIYARCHATIRAM* *No. of Hamlets: 11*

Sl. No.	Name of the Habitation	Water						Road		SL	Building				
		NB	MPP	PLE	OHT	HP	GLR & DW	CCR	BT & WBM Road	Street Light	BG	C&D	TF	RW	BG
1.	Pothinayakkanpatti	-	-	1	-	-	-	-	1	1	-	-	-	-	-
2.	Govindapuram	-	1	-	-	-	-	-	-	-	-	-	-	-	-
3.	Guyavanayakkanpatti	-	1	-	-	-	-	-	-	2	-	-	-	-	-
4.	Karattupatti	-	-	-	-	-	-	-	-	1	-	-	-	-	-
5.	Kittampatti	-	-	1	-	-	-	-	-	-	-	-	-	-	-
6.	Koralampatti	-	1	1	-	-	-	-	1	1	-	-	-	-	-
7.	Kurumbapatti	-	1	-	-	-	-	-	-	-	-	-	-	-	-
8.	Pappankulam	-	-	1	-	-	-	-	-	1	-	-	-	-	-
9.	Kasavanampatti	-	-	2	-	-	-	-	1	3	1	-	-	-	-
10.	Thirumalpatti	-	-	1	-	-	-	-	-	-	-	-	-	-	-
	Total	**0**	**4**	**7**	**0**	**0**	**0**	**0**	**3**	**9**	**1**	**0**	**0**	**0**	**0**

Source: Computed.

NB—New Bore well, MPP—Mini Power Pump, PLE—Pipe Line Extension, OHT—Over Head Tank, HP—Hand Pump, GLR&DW—GLR Deepening Well, CCR—Cement Concrete Road, BT&WBM Road—Block Thar & With Blue Metal, SL—Street Light, BG—Burial Ground, C&D—Culvert and Drainage, TF—Threshing Floor, RW—Retaining Wall, BG—Bathing Ghat.

Table 6: Details of the amount spent on each item of works in Kasavanampatti Village Panchayat

District: DINDIGUL | *Panchayat: KASAVANAMPATTI* | *Block: REDDIYARCHATIRAM* | *No. of Hamlets: 11*

Sl. No.	Name of the Habitation	Water					Road			S L		Building			
		NB	MPP	PLE	OHT	HP	GLR & DW	CCR	BT & WBM Road	Street Light	BG	C&D	TF	RW	BG
		Amount in Lakhs													
1.	Pothinayakkanpatti	0	0	0.30	0	0	0	0	4.55	1.04	0	0	0	0	0
2.	Govindapuram	0	1.50	0	0	0	0	0	0	0	0	0	0	0	0
3.	Guyavanayakkanpatti	0	2.30	0	0	0	0	0	0	2.08	0	0	0	0	0
4.	Karattupatti	0	0	0	0	0	0	0	0	1.04	0	0	0	0	0
5.	Kittampatti	0	0	0.30	0	0	0	0	0	0	0	0	0	0	0
6.	Koralampatti	0	2.30	0.30	0	0	0	0	1.15	1.03	0	0	0	0	0
7.	Kurumbapatti	0	2.72	0	0	0	0	0	0	0	0	0	0	0	0
8.	Pappankulam	0	0	0.40	0	0	0	0	0	1.04	0	0	0	0	0
9.	Kasavanampatti	0	0	1.42	0	0	0	0	5.85	2.03	3.34	0	0	0	0
10.	Thirumalpatti	0	0	3.10	0	0	0	0	0	0	0	0	0	0	0
	Total	**0**	**8.82**	**3.03**	**0**	**0**	**0**	**0**	**11.55**	**1.06**	**3.34**	**0**	**0**	**0**	**0**

Source: Computed.

NB—New Bore well, MPP—Mini Power Pump, PLE—Pipe Line Extension, OHT—Over Head Tank, HP—Hand Pump, GLR&DW—GLR Deepening Well, CCR—Cement Concrete Road, BT&WBM Road—Block Thar & With Blue Metal, SL—Street Light, BG—Burial Ground, C&D—Culvert and Drainage, TF—Threshing Floor, RW—Retaining Wall, BG—Bathing Ghat.

Table 7: Details of the habitation-wise no. of works completed in Ambathurai Village Panchayat

District: DINDIGUL		*Panchayat: AMBATHURAI*						*Block: ATHOOR*					*No. of Hamlets: 13*		
Sl. No.	*Name of the Habitation*	*Water*						*Road*		*SL*	*Building*				
		NB	*MPP*	*PLE*	*OHT*	*HP*	*GLR & DW*	*CCR*	*BT & WBM*	*Street Light*	*BG*	*C&D*	*TF*	*RW*	*BG*
1.	Indirapuram	-	-	-	-	-	-	1	2	2	-	-	-	-	-
2.	Kathirpatti	-	-	-	-	-	-	-	1	-	1	-	-	-	-
3.	Kollapatti	-	-	-	-	-	-	-	-	2	-	-	-	-	-
4.	Muruganpatti	-	-	-	-	-	-	3	-	-	-	-	-	-	-
5.	Perumalkoilpatti	-	-	-	-	-	-	1	-	14	-	-	-	-	-
6.	Rajakaliamman Nagar	-	-	-	-	-	-	3	-	8	-	-	-	-	-
7.	Rengasamy Nagar	-	-	-	-	-	-	2	-	1	-	-	-	-	-
8.	Velampatti	-	-	-	-	-	-	-	-	3	-	-	-	-	-
9.	Padmanaba Nagar	-	-	-	-	-	-	-	-	4	-	-	-	-	-
	Total	**0**	**0**	**0**	**0**	**0**	**0**	**10**	**3**	**34**	**1**	**0**	**0**	**0**	**0**

Source: Computed.

NB—New Bore well, MPP—Mini Power Pump, PLE—Pipe Line Extension, OHT—Over Head Tank, HP—Hand Pump, GLR&DW—GLR Deepening Well, CCR—Cement Concrete Road, BT&WBM Road—Block Thar & With Blue Metal, SL—Street Light, BG—Burial Ground, C&D—Culvert and Drainage, TF—Threshing Floor, RW—Retaining Wall, BG—Bathing Ghat.

Table 8: Details of the amount spent on each item of works in Ambathurai Village Panchayat

District: DINDIGUL | *Panchayat: AMBATHURAI* | *Block: ATHOOR* | *No. of Hamlets: 13*

Sl. No.	Name of the Habitation	Water						Road		SL		Building			
		NB	MPP	PLE	OHT	HP	GLR & DW	CCR	BT & WBM	Street Light	BG	C&D	TF	RW	BG
		Amount in Lakhs													
1.	Indirapuram	0	0	0	0	0	0	1.18	4.24	0.11	0	0	0	0	0
2.	Kathirpatti	0	0	0	0	0	0	0	4.96	0	1.57	0	0	0	0
3.	Kollapatti	0	0	0	0	0	0	0	0	0.19	0	0	0	0	0
4.	Muruganpatti	0	0	0	0	0	0	7.23	0	0	0	0	0	0	0
5.	Perumalkoilpatti	0	0	0	0	0	0	1.10	0	0.11	0	0	0	0	0
6.	Rajakaliamman Nagar	0	0	0	0	0	0	4.94	0	0.29	0	0	0	0	0
7.	Rengasamy Nagar	0	0	0	0	0	0	2.73	0	0.19	0	0	0	0	0
8.	Velampatti	0	0	0	0	0	0	0	0	0.29	0	0	0	0	0
9.	Padmanaba Nagar	0	0	0	0	0	0	0	0	0.15		0	0	0	0
	Total	**0**	**0**	**0**	**0**	**0**	**0**	**17.18**	**9.20**	**1.33**	**1.57**	**0**	**0**	**0**	**0**

Source: Computed.

NB—New Bore well, MPP—Mini Power Pump, PLE—Pipe Line Extension, OHT—Over Head Tank, HP—Hand Pump, GLR&DW—GLR Deepening Well, CCR—Cement Concrete Road, BT&WBM Road—Block Thar & With Blue Metal, SL—Street Light, BG—Burial Ground, C&D—Culvert and Drainage, TF—Threshing Floor, RW—Retaining Wall, BG—Bathing Ghat.

Table 9: Details of the habitation-wise no. of works completed in Vilpatti Village Panchayat

District: DINDIGUL *Panchayat: VILPATTI* *Block: KODIAKKANAL* *No. of Hamlets: 26*

Sl. No.	Name of the Habitation	Water						Road		S L	Building				
		NB	MPP	PLE	OHT	HP	GLR & DW	CCR	BT & WBM	Street Light	BG	C&D	TF	RW	BG
1.	Mattupatti	-	-	1	-	-	-	-	-	2	-	-	-	-	-
2.	Anna Ramasamy Nagar	-	-	-	-	-	-	1	-	2	-	-	-	-	-
3.	Bharathi Annanagar	-	-	-	-	-	-	1	-	2	-	-	-	-	-
4.	Kurunji Nagar	-	-	-	-	-	-	-	-	2	-	-	-	-	-
5.	Pallangi	-	-	-	-	-	-	-	-	2	-	-	-	-	-
6.	Perumpallam	-	-	-	-	-	-	-	-	2	-	-	-	-	-
7.	Pethuparai	-	-	-	-	-	-	-	-	2	-	-	-	-	-
8.	Vellaparai	-	-	-	-	-	-	-	-	2	1	-	-	-	-
9.	V.O.C. Nagar	-	-	-	-	-	-	1	-	-	-	-	-	-	-
10.	Attuvampatti	-	-	-	-	-	-	1	-	-	-	-	-	-	-
11.	Attuvampatti Colony	-	-	-	-	-	-	1	-	-	-	-	-	-	-
12.	Chinnapallam	-	-	-	-	-	-	1	1	-	-	-	-	-	-
13.	Ganeshapuram	-	-	-	-	-	-	1	-	-	-	-	-	-	-
14.	Paraipatti	-	-	-	-	-	-	1	-	-	-	-	-	-	-
15.	Uppuparai Methu	-	-	-	-	-	-	1	-	-	-	-	-	-	-
	Total	**0**	**0**	**1**	**0**	**0**	**0**	**7**	**1**	**16**	**1**	**0**	**0**	**0**	**0**

Source: Computed.

NB—New Bore well, MPP—Mini Power Pump, PLE—Pipe Line Extension, OHT—Over Head Tank, HP—Hand Pump, GLR&DW—GLR Deepening Well, CCR—Cement Concrete Road, BT&WBM Road—Block Thar & With Blue Metal, SL—Street Light, BG—Burial Ground, C&D—Culvert and Drainage, TF—Threshing Floor, RW—Retaining Wall, BG—Bathing Ghat.

Table 10: Details of the amount spent on each item of works in Vilpatti Village Panchayat

District: DINDIGUL		*Panchayat: VILPATTI*						*Block: KODIAKKANAL*							*No. of Hamlets: 26*
Sl. No.	*Name of the Habitation*	*Water*						*Road*		*SL*	*Building*				
		NB	*MPP*	*PLE*	*OHT*	*HP*	*GLR & DW*	*CCR*	*BT & WBM*	*Street Light*	*BG*	*C&D*	*TF*	*RW*	*BG*
		Amount in Lakhs													
1.	Mattupatti	0	0	3.54	0	0	0	0	0	0.40	0	0	0	0	0
2.	Anna Ramasamy Nagar	0	0	0	0	0	0	2.72	0	0.40	0	0	0	0	0
3.	Bharathi Annanagar	0	0	0	0	0	0	3.45	0	0.40	0	0	0	0	0
4.	Kurunji Nagar	0	0	0	0	0	0	0	0	0.40	0	0	0	0	0
5.	Pallangi	0	0	0	0	0	0	0	0	0.40	0	0	0	0	0
6.	Perumpallam	0	0	0	0	0	0	0	0	0.40	0	0	0	0	0
7.	Pethuparai	0	0	0	0	0	0	0	0	0.40	4.00	0	0	0	0
8.	Vellaparai	0	0	0	0	0	0	0	0	0.40	0	0	0	0	0
9.	V.O.C. Nagar	0	0	0	0	0	0	1.00	0	0	0	0	0	0	0
10.	Attuvampatti	C	0	0	0	0	0	1.15	0	0	0	0	0	0	0
11.	Attuvampatti Colony	0	0	0	0	0	0	0.80	0	0	0	0	0	0	0
12.	Chinnapallam	0	0	0	0	0	0	1.15	19.75	0	0	0	0	0	0
13.	Ganeshapuram	0	0	0	0	0	0	1.94	0	0	0	0	0	0	0
14.	Paraipatti	0	0	0	0	0	0	2.15	0	0	0	0	0	0	0
15.	Uppuparai Methu	0	0	0	0	0	0	4.90	0	0	0	0	0	0	0
	Total	**0**	**0**	**3.54**	**0**	**0**	**0**	**19.25**	**19.75**	**3.20**	**4.00**	**0**	**0**	**0**	**0**

Source: Computed.
NB—New Bore well, MPP—Mini Power Pump, PLE—Pipe Line Extension, OHT—Over Head Tank, HP—Hand Pump, GLR&DW—GLR Deepening Well, CCR—Cement Concrete Road, BT&WBM Road—Block Thar & With Blue Metal, SL—Street Light, BG—Burial Ground, C&D—Culvert and Drainage, TF—Threshing Floor, RW—Retaining Wall, BG—Bathing Ghat.

Table 11: Details of the habitation-wise no. of works completed in Thulaiyanur Village Panchayat

District: PUDUKOTTAI		Panchayat: THULAIYANUR						Block: THIRUMAYAM					No. of Hamlets: 29		
Sl. No.	Name of the Habitation	Water						Road		SL		Building			
		NB	MPP	PLE	OHT	HP	GLR & DW	CCR	BT & WBM	Street Light	BG	C&D	TF	RW	BG
1.	Maavur	-	3	-	-	-	-	-	1	-	1	-	-	-	-
2.	Malaikudipatti	-	-	-	-	-	-	-	-	-	-	-	-	-	1
3.	Santhanaviduthi	-	-	-	-	-	-	1	-	-	-	-	-	-	1
4.	Andakkudipatti	-	-	-	-	-	-	-	1	-	-	-	1	-	1
5.	Kulathupatti	-	1	-	-	-	-	-	-	2	-	-	-	1	-
6.	Adukkapatti	-	-	-	-	-	-	1	-	3	-	-	-	1	-
7.	Navichipatti	-	-	-	-	-	-	1	-	-	-	-	-	-	-
8.	Pesant Nagar	-	1	-	-	-	-	-	-	2	-	-	-	-	-
9.	Valayanvayal	-	-	-	-	-	-	-	-	3	-	-	-	-	-
10.	M. Pudhu Kudieruppu	-	-	-	-	-	-	-	-	2		-	-	-	-
11.	Ammapatti	-		-	-	-	-	-	1	3	-	-	-	-	-
12.	Kollakattupatti	-	-	-	-	-	-	-	1	2	-	-	-	-	-
13.	Puduparali	-	-	-	-	-	-	1	-	1	-	-	-	-	-
14.	Mettupatti	-	-	-	-	-	-	1	-	-	-	-	-	-	-
15.	Melaviduthi	-	-	-	-	-	-	1	-	-	-	-	-	-	-
16.	Chinnakalluvayal	-	-	-	-	-	-	1	-	-	-	-	1	-	-
17.	Moongithapatti	-	-	-	-	-	-	1	-	-	-	-	-	-	-
18.	Cholathavayal	-	-	-	-	-	-	-	1	-	-	-	-	-	-
19.	Thulayanur	-	1	-	-	-	-	-		-	-	-	-	-	-
	Total	**0**	**6**	**0**	**0**	**0**	**0**	**8**	**5**	**18**	**1**	**0**	**2**	**2**	**3**

Source: Computed.

NB—New Bore well, MPP—Mini Power Pump, PLE—Pipe Line Extension, OHT—Over Head Tank, HP—Hand Pump, GLR&DW—GLR Deepening Well, CCR—Cement Concrete Road, BT&WBM Road—Block Thar & With Blue Metal, SL—Street Light, BG—Burial Ground, C&D—Culvert and Drainage, TF—Threshing Floor, RW—Retaining Wall, BG—Bathing Ghat.

Table 12: Details of the amount spent on each item of works in Thulaiyanur Village Panchayat

District: PUDUKOTTAI		Panchayat: THULAIYANUR						Block: THIRUMAYAM					No. of Hamlets: 29		
Sl. No.	Name of the Habitation	Water						Road		SL			Building		
		NB	MPP	PLE	OHT	HP	GLR & DW	CCR	BT & WBM	Street Light	BG	C&D	TF	RW	BG
		Amount in Lakhs													
1.	Maavur	0	1.70	0	0	0	0	0	3.96	0	2.64	0	0	0	0
2.	Malaikudipatti	0	0	0	0	0	0	0	0	0	0	0	0	0	1.99
3.	Santhanaviduthi	0	0	0	0	0	0	0.80	0	0	0	0	0	0	1.99
4.	Andakkudipatti	0	0	0	0	0	0	0	3.20	0	0	0	1.31	0	1.24
5.	Kulathupatti	0	1.00	0	0	0	0	0	0	0.24	0	0	0	1.99	1.99
6.	Adukkapatti	0	0	0	0	0	0	1.60	0	0.36	0	0	0	0.99	0
7.	Navichipatti	0	0	0	0	0	0	1.00	0	0	0	0.75	0	0	0
8.	Pesant Nagar	0	1.00	0	0	0	0	0	0	0.24	0	0.75	0	0	0
9.	Valayanvayal	0	0	0	0	0	0	0	0	0.36	0	1.00	0	0	0
10.	M. Pudhu Kudieruppu	0	0	0	0	0	0	0	0	0.24	0	0	0	0	0
11.	Ammapatti	0	0	0	0	0	0	0	4.32	0.36	0	0	0	0	0
12.	Kollakattupatti	0	0	0	0	0	0	0	1.21	0.24	0	0	0	0	0
13.	Puduparali	0	0	0	0	0	0	1.44	0	0.12	0	0	0	0	0
14.	Mettupatti	0	0	0	0	0	0	1.60	0	0	0	0	0	0	0
15.	Melaviduthi	0	0	0	0	0	0	0.72	0	0	0	0	0	0	0
16.	Chinnakalluvayal	0	0	0	0	0	0	1.00	0	0	0	0	1.21	0	0
17.	Moongithapatti	0	0	0	0	0	0	0.88	0	0	0	0	-	0	0
18.	Cholathavayal	0	0	0	0	0	0	0	2.31	0	0	0	1.30	0	0
19.	Thulayanur	0	2.00	0	0	0	0	0	0	0	0	0	-	0	0
	Total	**0**	**5.70**	**0**	**0**	**0**	**0**	**9.04**	**15.00**	**2.16**	**2.64**	**2.50**	**3.82**	**2.98**	**5.23**

Source: Computed.

NB—New Bore well, MPP—Mini Power Pump, PLE—Pipe Line Extension, OHT—Over Head Tank, HP—Hand Pump, GLR&DW—GLR Deepening Well, CCR—Cement Concrete Road, BT&WBM Road—Block Thar & With Blue Metal, SL—Street Light, BG—Burial Ground, C&D—Culvert and Drainage, TF—Threshing Floor, RW—Retaining Wall, BG—Bathing Ghat.

Table 13: Details of the habitation-wise no. of works completed in Mimisal Village Panchayat

District: PUDUKOTTAI *Panchayat: MIMISAL* *Block: AVUDAYARKOIL* *No. of Hamlets: 10*

Sl. No.	Name of the Habitation	Water						Road		SL	Building				
		NB	MPP	PLE	OHT	HP	GLR & DW	CCR	BT & WBM	Street Light	BG	C&D	TF	RW	BG
1.	Alathur	-	-	3	-	-	-	-	1	3	1	-	-	-	-
2.	Sathirampattinam	-	-	1	-	-	-	1	-	-	-	1	-	-	-
3.	Thappankkottai	-	-	-	-	-	-	-	-	1	-	-	-	-	-
4.	Kanmaykkarai Kudieruppu	-	-	1	-	-	-	-	1	1	-	-	-	-	-
5.	Mimisal	-	-	2	-	-	-	1	-	-	-	-	-	-	-
6.	Mimisal Kudieryppu	-	-	-	-	-	-	-	1	-	-	-	-	-	-
7.	Va. Vu.Si. Nagar	-	-	1	-	-	-	-	-	-	-	-	-	-	-
	Total	**-**	**-**	**8**	**-**	**-**	**-**	**2**	**3**	**5**	**1**	**1**	**-**	**-**	**-**

Source: Computed.

NB—New Bore well, MPP—Mini Power Pump, PLE—Pipe Line Extension, OHT—Over Head Tank, HP—Hand Pump, GLR&DW—GLR Deepening Well, CCR—Cement Concrete Road, BT&WBM Road—Block Thar & With Blue Metal, SL—Street Light, BG—Burial Ground, C&D—Culvert and Drainage, TF—Threshing Floor, RW—Retaining Wall, BG—Bathing Ghat.

Table 14: Details of the amount spent on each item of works in Mimisal Village Panchayat

District: PUDUKOTTAI		Panchayat: MIMISAL						Block: AVUDAYARKOIL				No. of Hamlets: 10			
Sl. No.	Name of the Habitation	Water						Road		SL		Building			
		NB	MPP	PLE	OHT	HP	GLR & DW	CCR	BT & WBM	Street Light	BG	C&D	TF	RW	BG
1.	Alathur	0	0	1.50	0	0	0	0	3.00	1.35	1.00	0	0	0	0
2.	Sathirampattinam	0	0	0.28	0	0	0	2.10	0	0	0	1.49	0	0	0
3.	Thappankkottai	0	0	0	0	0	0	0	0	0.22	0	0	0	0	0
4.	Kanmaykkarai Kudieruppu	0	0	1.19	0	0	0	0	2.99	0.67	0	0	0	0	0
5.	Mimisal	0	0	9.79	0	0	0	0.90	0	0	0	0	0	0	0
6.	Mimisal Kudieryppu	0	0	0	0	0	0	0	3.00	0	0	0	0	0	0
7.	Va. Vu.Si. Nagar	0	0	0.44	0	0	0	0	0	0	0	0	0	0	0
	Total	**0**	**0**	**13.20**	**0**	**0**	**0**	**3.00**	**8.99**	**2.24**	**1.00**	**1.49**	**0**	**0**	**0**

Source: Computed.

NB—New Bore well, MPP—Mini Power Pump, PLE—Pipe Line Extension, OHT—Over Head Tank, HP—Hand Pump, GLR&DW—GLR Deepening Well, CCR—Cement Concrete Road, BT&WBM Road—Block Thar & With Blue Metal, SL—Street Light, BG—Burial Ground, C&D—Culvert and Drainage, TF—Threshing Floor, RW—Retaining Wall, BG—Bathing Ghat.

Table 15: Details of the habitation-wise no. of works completed in Vagavasal Village Panchayat

District: PUDUKOTTAI	*Panchayat: VAGAVASAL*							*Block: PUDUKOTTAI*							*No. of Hamlets: 10*
Sl. No.	*Name of the Habitation*	*Water*						*Road*		*S L*	*Building*				
		NB	*MPP*	*PLE*	*OHT*	*HP*	*GLR & DW*	*CCR*	*BT & WBM*	*Street Light*	*BG*	*C&D*	*TF*	*RW*	*BG*
1.	Janakipatti	-	-	-	-	-	-	-	-	-	1	-	-	-	-
2.	Rajapatty	-	1	-	-	-	-	1	-	20	-	-	-	1	-
3.	Kandravayal	-	-	-	-	-	-	-	-	1	-	-	-	-	-
4.	Sri Kanthiranthanyagi Amman Nagar	-	1	-	-	-	-	-	-	7	-	-	-	-	-
5.	Vagavasal	-	-	-	1	-	-	-	-	4	-	-	-	-	-
6.	Kedayapatty	-	-	-	-	-	-	-	1	-	-	-	-	-	-
7.	Edayapatti	-	1	1	-	-	-	-	1	-	-	-	-	-	-
8.	Ayyavayal	-	-	-	-	-	-	-	1	-	-	-	-	-	-
9.	Thattampatty	-	-	-	-	1	-	-	-	-	-	-	-	-	-
10.	Viswakarma Nagar	-	2	-	-	-	-	-	-	-	-	-	-	-	-
	Total	**-**	**5**	**1**	**1**	**1**	**-**	**1**	**3**	**32**	**1**	**-**	**-**	**1**	**-**

Source: Computed.

NB—New Bore well, MPP—Mini Power Pump, PLE—Pipe Line Extension, OHT—Over Head Tank, HP—Hand Pump, GLR&DW—GLR Deepening Well, CCR—Cement Concrete Road, BT&WBM Road—Block Thar & With Blue Metal, SL—Street Light, BG—Burial Ground, C&D—Culvert and Drainage, TF—Threshing Floor, RW—Retaining Wall, BG—Bathing Ghat.

Table 16: Details of the amount spent on each item of works in Vagavasal Village Panchayat

District: PUDUKOTTAI | *Panchayat: VAGAVASAL* | *Block: PUDUKOTTAI* | *No. of Hamlets:10*

Sl. No.	*Name of the Habitation*	*Water*						*Road*		*S L*		*Building*			
		NB	*MPP*	*PLE*	*OHT*	*HP*	*GLR & DW*	*CCR*	*BT & WBM*	*Street Light*	*BG*	*C&D*	*TF*	*RW*	*BG*
1.	Janakipatti	0	0	0	0	0	0	0	0	0	1.50	0	0	0	0
2.	Rajapatty	0	1.10	0	0	0	0	2.49	0	0.20	0	0	0	2.75	0
3.	Kandravayal	0	0	0	0	0	0	0	0	0.10	0	0	0	0	0
4.	Sri Kanthiranthanayagi Amman Nagar	0	1.10	0	0	0	0	0	0	0.30	0	0	0	0	0
5.	Vagavasal	0	0	0	0.35	0	0	0	0	0.70	0	0	0	0	0
6.	Kedayapatty	0	0	0	0	0	0	0	7.28	0	0	0	0	0	0
7.	Edayapatti	0	1.08	0.59	0	0	0	0	6.38	0	0	0	0	0	0
8.	Ayyavayal	0	0	0	0	0	0	0	1.09	0	0	0	0	0	0
9.	Thattampatty	0	0	0	0	0.70	0	0	0	0	0	0	0	0	0
10.	Viswakarma Nagar	0	2.16	0	0	0	0	0	0	0	0	0	0	0	0
	Total	**0**	**5.44**	**0.59**	**0.35**	**0.70**	**0**	**2.49**	**14.75**	**1.30**	**1.50**	**0**	**0**	**2.75**	**0**

Source: Computed.

NB—New Bore well, MPP—Mini Power Pump, PLE—Pipe Line Extension, OHT—Over Head Tank, HP—Hand Pump, GLR&DW—GLR Deepening Well, CCR—Cement Concrete Road, BT&WBM Road—Block Thar & With Blue Metal, SL—Street Light, BG—Burial Ground, C&D—Culvert and Drainage, TF—Threshing Floor, RW—Retaining Wall, BG—Bathing Ghat.

Table 17: Details of the habitation-wise no. of works completed in Viralur Village Panchayat

District: DINDIGUL		*Panchayat: VIRALUR*						*Block: VIRALIMALAI*				*No. of Hamlets:12*			
Sl. No.	*Name of the Habitation*	*Water*						*Road*		*Street Lights*	*Building*				
		NB	*MPP*	*PLE*	*OHT*	*HP*	*GLR & DW*	*CCR*	*BT & WBM*	*Street Light*	*B G*	*C&D*	*T F*	*R W*	*B G*
1.	Kaaniyaalampatti	-	1	-	-	-	-	-	-	-	1	-	-	-	-
2.	Viralur	-	1	-	-	-	-	1	-	-	1	-	-	-	-
3.	Pallarnatham	-	1	-	-	-	-	-	-	3	1	-	-	-	-
4.	Purasankaalpatti	-	-	-	-	-	-	-	-	-	1	-	-	-	-
5.	Pillampatti	-	-	-	-	-	-	-	-	-	1	-	-	-	-
6.	Sankampatti	-	-	-	-	-	-	-	-	-	1	-	-	-	-
7.	Kotikaalpatti	-	2	-	-	1	-	1	-	8	-	-	-	-	-
8.	Nathakadu	-	-	-	-	-	-	1	-	-	-	-	-	-	-
9.	Vadakkipatti	-	-	-	-	-	-	-	1	-	-	-	-	-	-
10.	Ponnikulathupatti	-	-	-	-	1	-	-	-	-	-	-	-	-	-
11.	Kumaradinatham	-	1	-	-	-	-	-	-	-	-	-	-	-	-
12.	Iramakkavundanpatti	-	-	-	-	-	-	1	-	9	-	-	-	-	-
	Total	**-**	**6**	**-**	**-**	**2**	**-**	**4**	**1**	**20**	**6**	**-**	**-**	**-**	**-**

Source: Computed.

NB—New Bore well, MPP—Mini Power Pump, PLE—Pipe Line Extension, OHT—Over Head Tank, HP—Hand Pump, GLR&DW—GLR Deepening Well, CCR—Cement Concrete Road, BT&WBM Road—Block Thar & With Blue Metal, SL—Street Light, BG—Burial Ground, C&D—Culvert and Drainage, TF—Threshing Floor, RW—Retaining Wall, BG—Bathing Ghat.

Table 18: Details on the habitation-wise no. of works completed in Bommaiyarpalayam Village Panchayat

District: VILLUPURAM		*Panchayat: Bommaiyarpalayam*						*Block: VANUR*				*No. of Hamlets:*			
Sl. No.	*Name of the Habitation*	*Water*						*Road*		*SL*	*Building*				
		NB	*MPP*	*PLE*	*OHT*	*HP*	*GLR & DW*	*CCR*	*BT & WBM*	*Street Light*	*BG*	*C&D*	*TF*	*RW*	*BG*
1.	Kuilampalayam	-	1	-	-	-	-	1	1	2	-	-	-	-	-
2.	Pillaichavadi Colony	-	1	-	-	-	-	1	-	-	-	-	-	-	-
3.	Bommaiyarpalayam	-	-	-	-	-	-	3	-	11	-	3	-	-	-
4.	Pillaichavadi Village	-	-	-	-	-	-	2	-	-	-	-	-	-	-
	Total	**-**	**2**	**-**	**-**	**-**	**-**	**7**	**1**	**13**	**-**	**3**	**-**	**-**	**-**

Source: Computed.

Table 19: Details of the habitation-wise no. of works completed in Singanur Village Panchayat

District: VILLUPURAM		*Panchayat: SINGANUR*						*Block: MARAKKANAM*				*No. of Hamlets:*			
Sl. No.	*Name of the Habitation*	*Water*						*Road*		*SL*	*Building*				
		NB	*MPP*	*PLE*	*OHT*	*HP*	*GLR & DW*	*CCR*	*BT & WBM*	*Street Light*	*BG*	*C&D*	*TF*	*RW*	*BG*
1.	Singanur	-	2	-	1	-	-	1	-	-	1	-	-	-	-
2.	Singanur Old Colony	-	-	-	-	-	-	1	-	4	1	-	-	-	-
3.	Singanur New Colony	-	-	-	-	-	-	1	-	6	-	-	-	-	-
	Total	**-**	**2**	**-**	**1**	**-**	**-**	**3**	**-**	**10**	**2**	**-**	**-**	**-**	**-**

Source: Computed.

Table 20: Details of amount spent on each type of work in Singanur Village Panchayat

District: VILLUPURAM		*Panchayat: SINGANUR*						*Block: MARAKKANAM*				*No. of Hamlets:*			
Sl. No.	*Name of the Habitation*	*Water*						*Road*		*SL*	*Building*				
		NB	*MPP*	*PLE*	*OHT*	*HP*	*GLR & DW*	*CCR*	*BT & WBM*	*Street Light*	*BG*	*C&D*	*TF*	*RW*	*BG*
1.	Singanur	–	2.49	-	4.25	-	-	2.10	-	-	3.00	-	-	-	-
2.	Singanur Old Colony	–	-	-	-	-	-	1.60	-	0.48	3.00	-	-	-	-
3.	Singanur New Colony	–	-	-	-	-	-	2.36	-	0.72	-	-	-	-	-
	Total	0	2.49	0	4.25	0	0	6.06	0	1.20	6.00	0	0	0	0

Source: Panchayat Union Office.

NB—New Bore well, MPP—Mini Power Pump, PLE—Pipe Line Extension, OHT—Over Head Tank, HP—Hand Pump, GLR&DW—GLR Deepening Well, CCR—Cement Concrete Road, BT&WBM Road—Block Thar & With Blue Metal, SL—Street Light, BG—Burial Ground, C&D—Culvert and Drainage, TF—Threshing Floor, RW—Retaining Wall, BG—Bathing Ghat.

Table 21: Details of the habitation-wise no. of works completed in Thennamadevi Village Panchayat

District: VILLUPURAM | Panchayat: THENNAMADEVI | Block: MARAKKANAM | No. of Hamlets:

Sl. No.	Name of the Habitation	Water						Road		SL	Building				
		NB	MPP	PLE	OHT	HP	GLR & DW	CCR	BT & WBM	Street Light	BG	C&D	TF	RW	BG
1.	Thennamadevi	-	-	-	-	-	-	-	1	-	1	-	-	-	-
2.	Poothamedu	-	2	-	-	-	-	-	-	4	1	-	-	-	-
3.	Thennamadevi Colony	-	-	-	-	-	-	-	-	-	1	-	-	-	-
	Total	-	**2**	-	-	-	-	-	**1**	**4**	**3**	-	-	-	-

Source: Computed.

NB—New Bore well, MPP—Mini Power Pump, PLE—Pipe Line Extension, OHT—Over Head Tank, HP—Hand Pump, GLR&DW—GLR Deepening Well, CCR—Cement Concrete Road, BT&WBM Road—Block Thar & With Blue Metal, SL—Street Light, BG—Burial Ground, C&D—Culvert and Drainage, TF—Threshing Floor, RW—Retaining Wall, BG—Bathing Ghat.

Table 22: Details on amount spent on each type of works in Thennamadevi Village Panchayat

District: VILLUPURAM		*Panchayat: THENNAMADEVI*						*Block: MARAKKANAM*				*No. of Hamlets:*			
Sl. No.	*Name of the Habitation*	*Water*						*Road*		*SL*	*Building*				
		NB	*MPP*	*PLE*	*OHT*	*HP*	*GLR & DW*	*CCR*	*BT & WBM*	*Street Light*	*BG*	*C&D*	*TF*	*RW*	*BG*
1.	Thennamadevi	-	-	-	-	-	-	-	6.07	-	3.30	-	-	-	-
2.	Poothamedu	-	3.49	-	-	-	-	-	-	0.54	3.30	-	-	-	-
3.	Thennamadevi Colony	-	-	-	-	-	-	-	-	-	3.30	-	-	-	-
	Total	**0**	**3.49**	**0**	**0**	**0**	**0**	**0**	**6.07**	**0.54**	**9.90**	**0**	**0**	**0**	**0**

Source: Computed.

NB—New Bore well, MPP—Mini Power Pump, PLE—Pipe Line Extension, OHT—Over Head Tank, HP—Hand Pump, GLR&DW—GLR Deepening Well, CCR—Cement Concrete Road, BT&WBM Road—Block Thar & With Blue Metal, SL—Street Light, BG—Burial Ground, C&D—Culvert and Drainage, TF—Threshing Floor, RW—Retaining Wall, BG—Bathing Ghat.

Table 23: Details of the habitation-wise no. of works completed in Vellimalai Village Panchayat

District: VILLUPURAM		Panchayat: VELLIMALAI						Block: KALVARAYAN HILLS						No. of Hamlets:10	
Sl. No.	Name of the Habitation	Water						Road		SL	Building				
		NB	MPP	PLE	OHT	HP	GLR & DW	CCR	BT & WBM	Street Light	BG	C&D	TF	RW	BG
1.	Gangappadi	-	-	-	-	-	-	1	-	-	-	-	-	-	-
2.	Kannumathivalavu	-	-	-	-	-	-	1	-	1	-	-	-	-	-
3.	Konakkadu	-	-	-	-	-	-	-	-	1	-	-	-	-	-
4.	Kottaputhur	-	1	-	-	-	1	-	-	-	-	-	-	-	-
5.	Mealmolipattu	-	-	-	-	-	1	-	-	-	-	-	-	-	-
6.	Mealvenniur	-	-	-	-	-	-	1	-	-	-	-	-	-	-
7.	Vellimalai	-	-	-	-	-	-	-	-	2	1	1	1	-	-
8.	Mealkendikkal	-	1	-	-	-	-	1	-	-	-	-	-	-	-
9.	Mealvazapadi	-	-	-	-	-	1	-	-	-	-	-	-	-	-
10.	Mealathevanur	-	-	-	-	-	-	-	-	1	-	-	-	-	-
11.	Nadumathur	-	-	-	-	-	-	1	-	-	-	-	-	-	-
12.	Thazmathur	-	-	-	-	-	-	1	-	-	-	-	-	-	-
13.	Thazsathanur	-	1	-	-	-	-	-	-	-	-	-	-	-	-
14.	Thazthevanur	-	-	-	-	-	-	1	-	1	-	-	-	-	-
15.	Thazvazappadi	-	-	-	-	-	-	-	1	-	-	--	-	-	-
16.	Uthukadu	-	-	-	-	-	-	-	-	1	-	-	-	-	-
17.	Thoranangkatttivalavu	-	1	-	-	-	-	-	-	-	-	-	-	-	-
18.	Thazhkendikkal	-	-	-	-	-	-	1	-	-	-	-	-	-	-
	Total	**-**	**4**	**-**	**-**	**-**	**3**	**8**	**1**	**7**	**1**	**1**	**1**	**-**	**-**

Source: Computed.

NB—New Bore well, MPP—Mini Power Pump, PLE—Pipe Line Extension, OHT—Over Head Tank, HP—Hand Pump, GLR&DW—GLR Deepening Well, CCR—Cement Concrete Road, BT&WBM Road—Block Thar & With Blue Metal, SL—Street Light, BG—Burial Ground, C&D—Culvert and Drainage, TF—Threshing Floor, RW—Retaining Wall, BG—Bathing Ghat.

Table 24: Details of amount spent on each type of work in Vellimalai Village Panchayat

District: VILLUPURAM		Panchayat: VELLIMALAI						Block: KALVARAYAN HILLS				No. of Hamlets:			
Sl. No.	Name of the Habitation	Water						Road		SL	Building				
		NB	MPP	PLE	OHT	HP	GLR & DW	CCR	BT & WBM	Street Light	BG	C&D	TF	RW	BG
1.	Gangappadi	-	-	-	-	-	-	1.00	-	-	-	-	-	-	-
2.	Kannumathivalavu	-	-	-	-	-	-	1.00	-	0.16	-	-	-	-	-
3.	Konakkadu	-	1.50	-	-	-	-	-	-	1.15	-	-	-	-	-
4.	Kottaputhur	-	-	-	-	-	1.00	-	-	-	-	-	-	-	-
5.	Mealmolipattu	-	-	-	-	-	2.78	-	-	-	-	-	-	-	-
6.	Mealvenniur	-	-	-	-	-	-	1.00	-	-	-	-	-	-	-
7.	Vellimalai	-	-	-	-	-	-	-	-	4.91	2.99	1.49	1.00	-	-
8.	Mealkendikkal	-	1.50	-	-	-	-	1.00	-	-	-	-	-	-	-
9.	Mealvazapadi	-	-	-	-	-	1.00	-	-	-	-	-	-	-	-
10.	Mealathevanur	-	-	-	-	-	-	1.00	-	-	-	-	-	-	-
11.	Nadumathur	-	-	-	-	-	-	-	-	0.15	-	-	-	-	-
12.	Thazmathur	-	-	-	-	-	-	-	-	-	-	-	-	-	-
13.	Thazsathanur	-	1.50	-	-	-	-	1.00	-	-	-	-	-	-	-
14.	Thazthevanur	-	-	-	-	-	-	1.00	1.99	0.15	-	-	-	-	-
15.	Thazvazappadi	-	-	-	-	-	-	-	-	-	-	-	-	-	
16.	Uthukadu	-	-	-	-	-	-	-	-	0.15	-	-	-	-	-
17.	Thoranangkatttivalavu	-	1.50	-	-	-	-	-	-	-	-	-	-	-	-
18.	Thazkendikkal	-	-	-	-	-	-	1.00	1.99	-	-	-	-	-	-
	Total	**0**	**6.00**	**0**	**0**	**0**	**4.78**	**8.00**	**1.99**	**5.67**	**2.99**	**1.49**	**1.00**	**0**	**0**

Source: Panchayat Union Office.

NB—New Bore well, MPP—Mini Power Pump, PLE—Pipe Line Extension, OHT—Over Head Tank, HP—Hand Pump, GLR&DW—GLR Deepening Well, CCR—Cement Concrete Road, BT&WBM Road—Block Thar & With Blue Metal, SL—Street Light, BG—Burial Ground, C&D—Culvert and Drainage, TF—Threshing Floor, RW—Retaining Wall, BG—Bathing Ghat.

Table 25: District-wise details of Expenditure Percentage in Water Supply

Sl. No.	Name of the District	Water supply							
		Overall Expenditure in THAI	New Borewell	Mini Power Pump	Pipe Line	OHT	Hand Pump	GLR/ Deepening Well	Total Expenditure
		Rupees in Lakhs							
1.	Dindigul	**151.85**	6.99 (4.60)	14.81 (9.75)	3.03 (1.99)	0 (0)	0 (0)	3.54 (2.33)	***28.37 (18.68)***
2.	Pudukottai	**165.09**	0 (0)	17.13 (10.38)	19.11 (11.57)	3.5 (0.2)	7.97 (4.83)	0 (0)	***47.71 (28.90)***
3.	Villupuram	**128.8**	2.3 (0.18)	13.18 (10.23)	0 (0)	4.25 (3.30)	0 (0)	4.77 (3.70)	***24.5 (1.90)***
		445.74	**9.29**	**45.12**	**22.14**	**7.75**	**7.97**	**8.31**	**100.58**

Source: Computed.

* Parentheses indicate the percentage.

Table 26: District-wise details of Expenditure Percentage in Road Works

Sl. No.	Name of the District	Road Works			
		Overall Expenditure in THAI	CC Road	BT & WBM Road	Total Expenditure
		Rupees in Lakhs			
1.	Dindigul	**151.85**	37.24 (24.52)	40.75 (26.83)	***77.99*** ***(51.36)***
2.	Pudukottai	**165.09**	25.65 (15.54)	49.43 (29.94)	***75.08*** ***(45.48)***
3.	Villupuram	**128.8**	25.43 (19.74)	31.02 (2.41)	***56.45*** ***(43.83)***
	Total	**445.74**	**88.32**	**121.20**	**209.52**

Source: Computed.
* Parentheses indicate the percentage.

Table 27: District-wise details of Expenditure Percentage in Street light

Sl. No.	*Name of the District*	*Street Light Works*		
		Overall Expenditure in THAI	*Street Light*	*Total Expenditure*
		Rupees in Lakhs		
1.	Dindigul	**151.85**	33.61 (22.13)	33.61 (22.13)
2.	Pudukottai	**165.09**	7.46 (4.52)	7.46 (4.52)
3.	Villupuram	**128.8**	10.28 (7.98)	10.28 (7.98)
	Total	**445.74**	**51.35**	**51.35**

Source: Computed.

* Parentheses indicate the percentage.

Table 28: District-wise details of Expenditure Percentage in Building Works

Sl. No.	Name of the District	Building works						
		Overall Expenditure in THAI	*Burial Ground*	*Culvert and Drainage*	*Threshing Floor*	*Retaining Wall*	*Bathing Ghats*	*Total Expenditure*
		Rupees in Lakhs						
1.	Dindigul	**151.85**	11.88 (7.82)	0 (0)	0 (0)	0 (0)	0 (0)	***11.88 (7.82)***
2.	Pudukottai	**165.09**	16.07 (9.7)	4.00 (2.42)	3.81 (2.31)	5.73 (3.47)	5.23 (3.17)	***34.84 (21.10)***
3.	Villupuram	**128.8**	28.44 (22.08)	8.13 (6.31)	1.00 (0.77)	0 (0)	0 (0)	***37.57 (29.17)***
	Total	**445.74**	**56.39**	**12.13**	**5.81**	**5.73**	**5.23**	**114.29**

Source: Computed.

* Parentheses indicate the percentage.

Table 29: Details of expenditure and Percentage in Water supply in sample village panchayats

Sl. No.	Name of the Village Panchayat	Water Supply												
		Total Amount Spent	New Borewell	Per-centage	Mini Power Pump	Per-centage	Pipe Line	Per-centage	OHT	Per-centage	Hand Pump	Per-centage	GLR/ Deepening Well	Per-centage
		Rs. Lakhs	Rs. Lakhs		Rs. Lakhs		Rs. Lakhs		Rs. Lakhs		Rs. Lakhs		Rs. Lakhs	
1.	Sendurai	39.85	6.99	***17.54***	5.99	***15.03***	0	***0***	0	***0***	0	***0***	0	***0***
2.	Ambathurai	41.25	0	***0***	0	***0***	0	***0***	0	***0***	0	***0***	0	***0***
3.	Kasavanampatti	27.8	0	***0***	8.82	***31.73***	3.03	***10.90***	0	***0***	0	***0***	0	***0***
4.	Vilpatti	42.95	0	***0***	0	***0***	0	***0***	0	***0***	0	***0***	3.54	***8.24***
5.	Thulaiyanur	49.05	0	***0***	5.69	***11.60***	0	***0***	0	***0***	0	***0***	0	***0***
6.	Mimisal	29.95	0	***0***	0	***0***	13.21	***44.11***	0	***0***	0	***0***	0	***0***
7.	Vagavasal	46.34	0	***0***	5.44	***11.74***	5.9	***1.27***	3.50	***7.55***	6.97	***15.04***	0	***0***
8.	Viralur	39.75	0	***0***	6	***15.09***	0	***0***	0	***0***	1	***2.51***	0	***0***
9.	Bommaiyarpalayam	39.42	2.3	***5.83***	1.2	***3.04***	0	***0***	0	***0***	0	***0***	0	***0***
10.	Singanur	20	0	***0***	2.49	***12.45***	0	***0***	4.25	***21.25***	0	***0***	0	***0***
11.	Thennamadevi	20	0	***0***	3.49	***17.45***	0	***0***	0	***0***	0	***0***	0	***0***
12.	Vellimalai	49.38	0	***0***	6	***12.15***	0	***0***	0	***0***	0	***0***	4.77	***9.66***
	Total	**445.74**	**9.29**		**45.12**		**22.14**		**7.75**		**7.97**		**8.31**	

Source: Computed.

Table 30: Details of expenditure and Percentage in Road works in sample village panchayats

Sl. No.	*Name of the Village Panchayat*	*Road Works*				
		Total Amount Spent	*CC Road*	*Percentage*	*BT & WBM Road*	*Percentage*
		Rs. Lakhs	*Rs. Lakhs*		*Rs. Lakhs*	
1.	Sendurai	39.85	7.85	***19.70***	0	***0***
2.	Ambathurai	41.25	17.18	***41.65***	9.2	***22.30***
3.	Kasavanampatti	27.80	0	***0***	11.55	***41.55***
4.	Vilpatti	42.95	12.21	***28.43***	20	***46.56***
5.	Thulaiyanur	49.05	9.04	***18.43***	15	***30.58***
6.	Mimisal	29.95	3	***10.01***	8.99	***30.01***
7.	Vagavasal	46.34	6.56	***14.16***	12.72	***27.45***
8.	Viralur	39.75	7.05	***17.73***	12.72	***32.00***
9.	Bommaiyarpalayam	39.42	11.38	***28.87***	5	***12.68***
10.	Singanur	20	6.06	***30.30***	0	***0***
11.	Thennamadevi	20	0	***0***	6.07	***30.35***
12.	Vellimalai	49.38	7.99	***16.18***	19.95	***40.40***
	Total	**445.74**	**88.32**		**121.2**	

Source: Computed.

Table 31: Details of expenditure and Percentage in Building works in sample village panchayats

Sl. No.	*Name of the Village Panchayat*	*Building Works*										
		Total Amount Spent	*Burial Ground*	*Per-centage*	*Culvert and Drainage*	*Per-centage*	*Threshing Floor*	*Per-centage*	*Retaining Wall*	*Per-centage*	*Bathing Ghats*	*Per-centage*
		Rs. Lakhs	*Rs. Lakhs*		*Rs. Lakhs*		*Rs. Lakhs*		*Rs. Lakhs*		*Rs. Lakhs*	
1.	Sendurai	39.85	2.97	***7.45***	0	***0***	0	***0***	0	***0***	0	***0***
2.	Ambathurai	41.25	1.57	***3.81***	0	***0***	0	***0***	0	***0***	0	***0***
3.	Kasavanampatti	27.8	3.34	***12.01***	0	***0***	0	***0***	0	***0***	0	***0***
4.	Vilpatti	42.95	4	***9.31***	0	***0***	0	***0***	0	***0***	0	***0***
5.	Thulaiyanur	49.05	2.64	***5.38***	2.5	***5.07***	3.81	***7.75***	2.98	***6.08***	5.23	***10.66***
6.	Mimisal	29.95	1	***3.34***	1.5	***5.01***	0	***0***	0	***0***	0	***0***
7.	Vagavasal	46.34	1.5	***3.24***	0	***0***	0	***0***	2.75	***5.93***	0	***0***
8.	Viralur	39.75	10.93	***27.50***	0	***0***	0	***0***	0	***0***	0	***0***
9.	Bommaiyarpalayam	39.42	9.55	***24.23***	7.13	***18.09***	0	***0***	0	***0***	0	***0***
10.	Singanur	20	6	***30.00***	0	***0***	0	***0***	0	***0***	0	***0***
11.	Thennamadevi	20	9.9	***49.50***	0	***0***	0	***0***	0	***0***	0	***0***
12.	Vellimalai	49.38	2.99	***6.05***	1	***2.02***	1	***2.02***	0	***0***	0	***0***
	Total	**445.74**	**56.39**		**12.13**		**4.81**		**5.73**		**5.23**	

Source: Computed.

Table 32: Details of expenditure and Percentage in street lights in sample village panchayats

Sl. No.	Name of the Village Panchayat	Street Lights		
		Total Amount Spent	Street Light	Percentage
		Rs. Lakhs	Rs. Lakhs	
1.	Sendurai	39.85	16.05	***40.28***
2.	Ambathurai	41.25	13.30	***32.24***
3.	Kasavanampatti	27.80	1.06	***3.81***
4.	Vilpatti	42.95	3.2	***7.45***
5.	Thulaiyanur	49.05	2.16	***4.40***
6.	Mimisal	29.95	2.25	***7.51***
7.	Vagavasal	46.34	1	***2.15***
8.	Viralur	39.75	2.05	***5.16***
9.	Bommaiyarpalayam	39.42	2.86	***7.25***
10.	Singanur	20	1.20	***6.00***
11.	Thennamadevi	20	0.54	***2.7***
12.	Vellimalai	49.38	5.68	***11.50***
	Total	**445.74**	**51.35**	

Source: Computed.

Table 33: Details of Percentage in Water supply in sample village panchayats

Sl. No.	*Name of the Village Panchayat*	*Water Supply*						*Total %*
		New Borewell	*Mini Power Pump*	*Pipe Line*	*OHT*	*Hand Pump*	*GLR/ Deepening Well*	
1.	Sendurai	17.54	15.03	0	0	0	0	**32.57**
2.	Ambathurai	0	0	0	0	0	0	**0**
3.	Kasavanampatti	0	31.73	10.90	0	0	0	**42.63**
4.	Vilpatti	0	0	0	0	0	8.24	**8.24**
5.	Thulaiyanur	0	11.60	0	0	0	0	**11.60**
6.	Mimisal	0	0	44.11	0	0	0	**44.11**
7.	Vagavasal	0	11.74	1.27	7.55	15.04	0	**35.60**
8.	Viralur	0	15.09	0	0	2.51	0	**17.60**
9.	Bommaiyarpalayam	5.83	3.04	0	0	0	0	**8.87**
10.	Singanur	0	12.45	0	21.25	0	0	**33.70**
11.	Thennamadevi	0	17.45	0	0	0	0	**17.45**
12.	Vellimalai	0	12.15	0	0	0	9.66	**21.81**

Source: Computed.

Table 34: Details of Percentage in Road in sample village panchayats

Sl. No.	Name of the Village Panchayat	Road		Total %
		CC Road	BT & WBM Road	
1.	Sendurai	19.70	0	**19.70**
2.	Ambathurai	41.65	22.30	**63.95**
3.	Kasavanampatti	0	41.55	**41.55**
4.	Vilpatti	28.43	46.56	**74.99**
5.	Thulaiyanur	18.43	30.58	**49.01**
6.	Mimisal	10.01	30.01	**40.02**
7.	Vagavasal	14.16	27.45	**41.61**
8.	Viralur	17.73	32	**49.73**
9.	Bommaiyarpalayam	28.87	12.68	**41.55**
10.	Singanur	30.30	0	**30.30**
11.	Thennamadevi	0	30.35	**30.35**
12.	Vellimalai	16.18	40.40	**56.58**

Source: Computed.

Table 35: Details of Percentage in street lights in sample village panchayats

Sl. No.	*Name of the Village Panchayat*	*Street Lights*	
		Street Light	*Total %*
1.	Sendurai	40.28	**40.28**
2.	Ambathurai	32.24	**32.24**
3.	Kasavanampatti	3.81	**3.81**
4.	Vilpatti	7.45	**7.45**
5.	Thulaiyanur	4.40	**4.40**
6.	Mimisal	7.51	**7.51**
7.	Vagavasal	2.15	**2.15**
8.	Viralur	5.16	**5.16**
9.	Bommaiyarpalayam	7.25	**7.25**
10.	Singanur	6.00	**6.00**
11.	Thennamadevi	2.70	**2.70**
12.	Vellimalai	11.50	**11.50**

Source: Computed.

Table 36: Details of Percentage in building works in sample village panchayats

Sl. No.	*Name of the Village Panchayat*	*Burial Ground*	*Culvert and Drainage*	*Threshing Floor*	*Retaining Wall*	*Bathing Ghats*	*Total %*
1.	Sendurai	7.45	0	0	0	0	**7.45**
2.	Ambathurai	3.81	0	0	0	0	**3.81**
3.	Kasavanampatti	12.01	0	0	0	0	**12.01**
4.	Vilpatti	9.31	0	0	0	0	**9.31**
5.	Thulaiyanur	5.38	5.07	7.75	6.08	10.66	**34.94**
6.	Mimisal	3.34	5.01	0	0	0	**8.35**
7.	Vagavasal	3.24	0	0	5.93	0	**9.17**
8.	Viralur	27.50	0	0	0	0	**27.50**
9.	Bommaiyarpalayam	24.23	18.09	0	0	0	**42.32**
10.	Singanur	30	0	0	0	0	**30**
11.	Thennamadevi	49.50	0	0	0	0	**49.50**
12.	Vellimalai	6.05	2.02	2.02	0	0	**10.09**

Source: Computed.

Table 37: Details of total no. of habitation based THAI Scheme Implementation

Sl. No.	*Name of the Village Panchayat*	*Total No. of Habitation*	*No. of Habitation THAI Implementation*
1.	Sendurai	24	13
2.	Ambathurai	11	9
3.	Kasavanampatti	11	10
4.	Villpatti	26	15
5.	Thulaiyanur	29	19
6.	Mimisal	10	7
7.	Vagavasal	16	10
8.	Viralur	18	12
9.	Bommaiyarpalayam	4	4
10.	Singanur	3	3
11.	Thennamadevi	4	3
12.	Vellimalai	20	18
	Total	**176**	**123**

Index

Ambathurai Village Panchayat, 7, 87
- improvement through THAI, 9
- status of burial/funeral ground, 12
- status of government building, 12
- status of roads and culvert, 11
- status of street lights, 9
- status of streets and lanes, 12
- status of water supply, 9

Annaithu Grama Anna Marumalarchi Thittam (AGAMT), 1

Bommaiyarpalayam Village Panchayat, 68, 106
- status of buildings, 72
- status of burial/funeral faculties, 72
- status of other facility, 73
- status of roads, 71
- status of school buildings, 73
- status of small ponds/tanks, 73
- status of street lights, 70
- status of water supply, 68

Dindigul district, 7
DRDA, 98

Functioning with rationality, 99

Gram Panchayats, 2

Habitation, 3
Habitation based planning, 116

Kasavanampatti Village Panchayat, 32, 89
- status of burial ground, 35
- status of road works, 34
- status of street light, 32
- status of water supply, 32

Key stakeholders, joint effort of, 93

Local bodies, role of, 113

Mimisal Village Panchayat, 53, 103
- status of burial ground facility, 57
- status of road, 53
- status of street lights, 56
- status of water supply, 53

New Panchayat Raj System,, 84

Planning and implementation process,
- district-wise analysis, 107

Dindigul District, 107
Pudukottai District, 109
Villupuram District , 111
flexibility than uniformity, 110
strength of collective responsibilities, 110
Planning and implementation process, 84
Present study (the),
chapterization, 7
conclusion, 166
constraints, 169
introduction, 1-83
major findings and conclusion, 159-169
major findings, 159
methodology, 5
objectives of, 5
rationale for, 4
sampling, 5
suggestions, 164
tools constructed for, 6
Pudukottai district, 36, 119

Sample villages, process analysis, 85
Sendurai Village Panchayat, 14, 85
status of water supply, 14
road works, 15
status of burial/funeral ground and facilities, 19
process analysis, 85
reaching the unreached, 86
status of street lights, 14, 18
Singanur Village Panchayat, 58, 105
peoples' sentiment respected, 105
status of buildings belonging to government/local bodies, 62
status of burial/funeral ground, 62
status of road works, 60
status of street light, 60
status of water supply, 58
State Planning Commission, 4
Street light facility ensured, 98

Tamil Nadu Village Habitations Improvement (THAI), 1, 115
achievements, 153
buildings, 156
burial Ground, 156
roads, 155
street lights, 154
water supply, 153
benefits acquired by the people, 116-132
case studies, 170
integrated analysis, 133
Ambathurai Village Panchayat, 138
Bommaiyarpalayam Village Panchayat, 147
Kasavanampatti Village Panchayat, 140
Mimisal Village Panchayat, 144
Sendurai Village Panchayat, 135
Singanur Village Panchayat, 148
Thennamadevi Village Panchayat, 151
Thulayanur Village Panchayat, 142
Vagavasal Village Panchayat, 145
Vellimalai Village Panchayat, 152
Vilpatti Village Panchayat, 141
Viralur Village Panchayat, 146
overall Impact, 162
salient features of, 2

Village Water and Sanitation Committee (VWSC), 154

Tamil Nadu, 1, 84
Thennamadevi Village Panchayat, 62, 106
  other activities, 68
  status of burial/funeral ground, 66
  status of government buildings, 67
  status of road works, 64
  status of small ponds, 67
  status of street light, 64
  status of water facility, 62
Thulayanur Village Panchayat, 36, 120
  status of burial/funeral ground, 40
  status of road facility, 38
  status of street lights, 36
  status of water supply, 36
  strength of deliberative democracy, 102
TWAD, 68

Vagavasal Village Panchayat, 41
  new demand made, 96
  participatory management, 95
  planning and implementation process in, 95
  status of burial ground, 44
  status of roads, 44
  status of street lights, 43
  status of water supply, 41
Vellimalai Village Panchayat, 73, 104
  attending felt needs than sending fund, 104
  status of buildings, 79
  status of burial ground, 82
  status of drainage, 79
  status of roads, 79
  status of street lights, 76
  status of water supply, 73
Village Panchayat(s), 3
  details of the sample, 7
  population details of sample, 8
Villpatti Village Panchayat, 23, 92
  building facilities, 29
  status of burial/funeral ground, 29
  status of road facilities, 27
  status of street light, 26
  status of water supply, 23
Villupuram district, 58, 104, 111
Viralur Village Panchayat, 44, 99
  balance maintained in fixing priority, 101
  burial grounds, 50
  information empowerment of villagers, 101
  status of road work, 50
  status of street lights, 49
  status of water supply, 44
  success of consultative process, 100